Glyndebourne Recorded

Glyndebourne Recorded

SIXTY YEARS OF RECORDINGS 1934-1994

Paul Campion and Rosy Runciman

 Julia MacRae Books

LONDON SYDNEY AUCKLAND JOHANNESBURG

First published 1994
1 3 5 7 9 10 8 6 4 2
© 1994 Paul Campion and Glyndebourne Productions Limited
Paul Campion and Glyndebourne Productions Limited have asserted
their right under the Copyright, Designs and Patents Act, 1988
to be identified as the authors of this work

First published in the United Kingdom in 1994 by
Julia MacRae
Random House, 20 Vauxhall Bridge Road, London SW1V 2SA

Random House Australia (Pty) Limited
20 Alfred Street, Milsons Point, Sydney,
New South Wales 2061, Australia

Random House New Zealand Limited
18 Poland Road, Glenfield
Auckland 10, New Zealand

Random House South Africa (Pty) Limited
PO Box 337, Bergvlei, South Africa

Random House UK Limited Reg. No. 954009

A CIP catalogue record for this book
is available from the British Library

ISBN 1 85681 069 0

Typeset by Textype Typesetters, Cambridge
Printed in Great Britain by Clays Ltd, St. Ives Plc

Contents

Illustrations

Foreword I

EMI Music's association with Glyndebourne spans 60 years and started at the instigation of Fred Gaisberg with the first recording (in June 1934 and June 1935) of *Le nozze di Figaro* conducted by Fritz Busch. This was a pioneering event because it was the earliest 'complete' recording of a Mozart opera and arguably one of the finest sets of *Figaro* ever recorded. It was quickly followed by the Busch recordings of *Così fan tutte* (1935) and *Don Giovanni* (1936) reissued over the years and both now available on CD.

Fifty years later, with another great Mozartian, Bernard Haitink, EMI recorded the three da Ponte operas once again, matching the great Mozart singers of the Thirties who included Willi Domgraf-Fassbaender, Heddle Nash, Ina Souez, John Brownlee, Roy Henderson, Luise Helletsgruber and Irene Eisinger with those of the Eighties, for example, Claudio Desderi, Carol Vaness, Thomas Allen, Felicity Lott, Maria Ewing, Lillian Watson and Richard Van Allan.

In the post war period between these recordings, one of the most notable of the projects undertaken by Glyndebourne and EMI was Vittorio Gui's celebrated series of recordings of Rossini which, produced by David Bicknell, feature great artists such as Alda Noni, Sesto Bruscantini, Juan Oncina, Marina de Gabarain and Victoria de los Angeles.

By definition, this book covers the past, but mention should also be made of the future. While the new theatre was under construction, the latest collaboration between EMI and Glyndebourne has been the recording, from the Glyndebourne concert performances at the Royal Festival Hall, of Lehár's *Die lustige Witwe* conducted by Franz Welser-Möst. 1993 also saw the release on TV and video of Trevor Nunn's *Porgy and Bess* based on the award winning recording of the 1986/87 Glyndebourne production conducted by Simon Rattle, featuring powerful performances from Willard White, Cynthia Haymon and an outstanding cast.

Over the years I and my predecessors have enjoyed a warm relationship with Sir George Christie and our friends at Glyndebourne. It is wonderfully refreshing to work with an organisation whose whole *raison d'être* is a love of opera, and it is surely this, communicated by the musicians and singers, which give Glyndebourne's performances and recordings the spontaneity, creative integrity and sheer joy which form the heart of any special opera experience. EMI has been privileged to have recorded at least some of these performances and thereby to see them preserved for the enjoyment of future generations.

In conclusion, I would like to pay a special tribute to Paul Campion and Rosy Runciman whose enthusiasm and knowledge is reflected in the pages that follow. All of us in EMI are looking forward to continuing our recording relationship with the new house and to adding future recordings to Glyndebourne's already distinguished discography.

Richard Lyttelton
President, EMI Classics

Foreword II

This book will be a treasure trove for opera enthusiasts, Glyndebourne enthusiasts, and record and CD buffs.

As we move into a fourth generation of Mozart recordings from Glyndebourne (Busch, Gui, Haitink and, soon, Rattle with the Orchestra of the Age of Enlightenment), it will be interesting to look for the quality that has consistently characterised Glyndebourne's Mozart over some sixty years.

Many companies have been involved in recordings of Glyndebourne productions, or recordings related to Glyndebourne, including Argo, CBS, Decca, Erato, Philips and Unicorn-Kanchana. But there is one company which has shown interest in Glyndebourne from the beginning, and has recognised the qualities and aspirations that belong to Glyndebourne, including, of course, the encouragement of younger singers at the start of their (sometimes very important) careers rather than the necessary procurement of already established stars. That company is EMI whose labels over the years have included in this country HMV, Columbia and Classics for Pleasure and in America RCA Victor, Angel and their subsidiaries.

Glyndebourne relishes its continuing association with EMI, and thanks them for the help they have given in respect of this volume.

With our new theatre promising a more grateful acoustic, we look forward to a future at least as rich in recording prospects as our past.

Anthony Whitworth-Jones
General Director
Glyndebourne

Introduction and Acknowledgements

The story of the founding and success of the Glyndebourne Festival is well known, and has been described in books, articles, radio and television broadcasts over the last sixty years. One part of Glyndebourne's history that has never been fully documented is its legacy of recordings, which date back to the first season in 1934. It is this aspect of the Festival's heritage that has been researched and published to celebrate Glyndebourne's Diamond Jubilee.

Over one hundred and thirty recordings are included in this survey. Most are of complete operas or opera highlights, but several are of operettas, choral, orchestral and instrumental works. Some are BBC broadcasts, preserved in public archives in London, but never issued commercially, and a few are unauthorised recordings probably taken from radio transmissions. Authorised video recordings, taken from television broadcasts, currently form the fastest growing area of 'Glyndebourne Recorded' and are fully listed. Between them these all serve as an enduring tribute to the people who, over the years, have contributed to the Festival's success, whether artists, musicians, technicians or administrators. The recordings also acknowledge the vision of many members of the recording industry, whose enterprise and skill ensured that these performances were preserved for future generations.

The book is divided into two main parts, each of which covers a different aspect of the story. The first section of Part One is concerned with the commercial audio recordings. Most of these are operatic and are of works which have been performed at Glyndebourne itself, at the Edinburgh Festival, at the Royal Festival Hall or in the West End of London. Also included are a number of recordings that were not made under the Glyndebourne banner but which, either because of the work or the singer, have a special association with the house. We have discovered details of several Glyndebourne recordings which were planned but never took place, and these, too, are discussed in this section of the book. In a number of cases recordings are grouped together in a chapter because of a common theme, rather than chronologically. For example, the three Rossini recordings conducted by Vittorio Gui are found in Chapter 5, although eight years separate the first from the last; and in Chapter 8 five operas are discussed in which Raymond Leppard played a prominent part over a period of nineteen years.

The first part continues with details of commercial recordings of works never performed at Glyndebourne, but in which either the chorus or orchestra participated. Most familiar among these will be the series of Gilbert and Sullivan operettas conducted by Sir Malcolm Sargent. The orchestral recordings made in the 1950s by the Glyndebourne Festival Orchestra (in reality the Royal Philharmonic), conducted by Vittorio Gui, are also included.

Part Two is concerned with television recording at Glyndebourne. An essay enlarges on its fascinating history and illustrates how that history has influenced public attitude to opera. All the television transmissions released on commercial video since 1984 are fully documented. In six instances, namely *L'heure espagnole*, *L'enfant et les sortilèges*, *La clemenza di Tito*, *The Queen of Spades*, *Glyndebourne – A Celebration of 50 Years* and *The Glyndebourne Gala*, videos are listed without an issue number. In each of these cases the video has already been released in the US and is due for release in the UK.

Glyndebourne has a limited association with laserdiscs. These were first launched in the UK in 1984 when the catalogue included three Glyndebourne operas, *La Cenerentola*, *Idomeneo* and *Intermezzo*. Details of these original releases may be found at the bottom of the video entries. In 1993 the video of *Porgy and Bess* was also released on the new format laserdisc. For some time Glyndebourne productions distributed on laserdisc in Japan and America have been highly successful and a warm reception is now expected in Britain.

Video distributors have a tendency to change as regularly as the seasons. In order to avoid confusing the overseas reader by giving information which may already be out of date, the name of the company holding worldwide distribution rights has been given below each video entry. This company should be contacted for current information about obtaining Glyndebourne videos in your country. The addresses are:

NVC Arts International, The Forum, 74/80 Camden Street, London NW1 0JL or Apt. 22-E, 350 West 50th Street, New York, NY 10019

Primetime, Seymour Mews House, Seymour Mews, Wigmore Street, London W1H 9PE

RM Associates, 46 Great Marlborough Street, London W1V 1DB

Appendix A is is a listing of broadcast Glyndebourne performances that have survived in public archives, all of which may be heard in London after giving due notice. Reference numbers are given for each item in order to facilitate quick identification. To hear BBC and National Sound Archive material application should be made to:

The Listening Service, NSA, 29 Exhibition Road, London SW7 2AS
Telephone: 071-412 7418

and for recordings held by Music Performance Research Centre to:

MPRC, Barbican Music Library, Barbican Centre, London EC2Y 8DS
Telephone: 071-638 0672

We are keenly aware that many other private recordings of Glyndebourne performances survive in collections in all parts of the world. These have not been included in the book, as to do so would only frustrate the reader who might wish to hear them without having the opportunity to do so.

In Appendix B all the Glyndebourne television transmissions not commercially released on video are listed. Sadly, but understandably, many of the early transmissions went out live and were never recorded for posterity. Appendix C gives details of the only commercial film about Glyndebourne – *On Such A Night*, made by Rank in 1955. Lastly we list a number of unauthorised sound recordings that have been released over the years on LP and CD. Throughout Part Two entries are listed in chronological order of recording rather than issue or transmission dates.

Where possible we have given the following details about every commercial recording, both audio and video, that is listed:

a. Title, composer, librettist and language of the performance.
b. Full cast details, conductor, orchestra, leader, continuo players, chorus and chorus master.
c. Recording dates, venues, recording producers and engineers.
d. For 78s, the matrix and take numbers and contents of each side, with the take number originally selected for issue underlined. The straight and automatic coupling sequences are also indicated.
e. The first television transmission date of each video.
f. The original issue number, format, date and principal re-issue details in the UK and, for audio recordings, in the USA (and in one case, France).
    Information about the authors and contents of sleeve and booklet notes is also given.
g. The timings of compact discs and videos.
h. The names of sponsors.
i. For video recordings, the copyright holders and distributors.

After 1956 all Glyndebourne's commercial audio recordings were made in stereo. Recordings which were made in mono only (from 1934 to 1956) are so indicated next to the session dates. Until the 1970s most stereo issues were also available in mono form, and details are given of both versions where appropriate.

Rosy Runciman, the Archivist at Glyndebourne since 1987, has been preparing the background information for this book for five years. She has made a special study of the broadcasts and video releases and wrote the essay in Part Two. In 1992 Rosy was joined by Paul Campion, who has since researched the commercial audio recordings and has written the text of the first part. Every attempt has been made to check the facts in the text thoroughly. The authors alone accept responsibility for errors and would be glad to learn of any corrections or additions that readers are able to make.

Acknowledgements

This book would not have been possible without the help of many people. First and foremost we would like to thank EMI for their generous grant. They, in particular Richard Lyttelton, President of EMI Classics, came to our rescue at a critical moment and without their support the whole project would have foundered. There are many others at EMI to whom we owe a great debt: Ruth Edge, the Archivist, and her staff, Marius Carboni, Manager of Press and Promotion for the Classical Division, and his staff, Charles Rodier, Richard Abram, Ken Jagger, Ken Townsend, Kate Byrne, Polly Miller, Simon Woods, David Murray and Clare Notley of Classics for Pleasure.

At Glyndebourne we have received unfailing support and encouragement from George Christie, Anthony Whitworth-Jones, Mark Beddy and Helen O'Neill. Helen and her assistant Joanna Townsend have been especially helpful in reading the text and correcting our errors. The Music Librarian, Sarah Plummer, has searched out appropriate scores and videos and answered numerous enquiries. Moran Caplat, former General Administrator, has assisted with many archival queries. We are grateful to them all.

We thank everyone who has allowed us to use quotations, particularly *Gramophone*, whose reviews have been used extensively.

Of the many other people and organisations who have assisted us in providing and checking information, our thanks go to Tim Day, Curator of Western Art Music, at the National Sound Archive. He has been involved in the project from its earliest days and since then has answered a constant stream of enquiries with endless patience.

We would also like to thank the staff of the Library and Listening Service at the National Sound Archive; Keith Hardwick, Stuart Eltham and David Martin, formerly with EMI, John Parry of Decca, Michael Letchford of Warner Classics, Phil Leask of Pearl Records, Paula Morris of Philips Classics UK, Nigel Brandt of Kanchana Records, Jon Tolansky of the MPRC, Sally Hine of the BBC Sound Archives, Veronica Benjamin, Manager of the BBC Videotape Enquiry Service, John Vernon, producer of many of the Glyndebourne/BBC tv transmissions, Derek Lewis, formerly BBC Record Librarian, the late Brian Gould, Michael Gray, Walter Woyda and Donna Seeney at Pickwick Video. We are grateful to all the other people, too numerous to mention, who have given us information and helpful advice.

Finally our thanks go to our publisher, Julia MacRae, for her constant faith in a specialist project in times of recession.

Paul Campion and Rosy Runciman
October 1993

Part One

The Audio Recordings

[1]   Early Mozart Recordings, 1934–1936

1934–5

LE NOZZE DI FIGARO

Music by Wolfgang Amadeus Mozart

Libretto by Lorenzo da Ponte after Beaumarchais

Sung in Italian

Figaro	Willi Domgraf-Fassbaender (baritone, German)
Susanna	Audrey Mildmay (soprano, English)
Don Basilio	Heddle Nash (tenor, English)
Marcellina	Constance Willis (contralto, English)
Cherubino	Luise Helletsgruber (soprano, Austrian)
Count Almaviva	Roy Henderson (baritone, Scottish)
Countess Almaviva	Aulikki Rautawaara (soprano, Finnish)
Bartolo	Norman Allin (bass, English) (1934)
	Italo Tajo (bass, Italian) (1935)
Antonio	Fergus Dunlop (bass, English)
Barbarina	Winifred Radford (soprano, English)
Don Curzio	Morgan Jones (tenor, Welsh)

Glyndebourne Festival Chorus	
Glyndebourne Festival Orchestra	Leader George Stratton
Conductor	Fritz Busch
Recorded	Glyndebourne theatre
	6.6.1934, 24 and 28.6.1935
Mono recording	
Recording Producer	David Bicknell
Balance Engineers	Edward Fowler and Arthur Clarke

MOZART OPERA SOCIETY VOLUME ONE

MATRIX/TAKE	DATE	STRAIGHT NOS/ AUTO NOS		SCORE NUMBER AND MUSICAL ITEM	SINGERS
2BR 318–_1_–1A	6.6.34	DB 2474 DB 7836	7	Act 1 Cosa sento	AM RH HN
2BR 319–1–_1A_	6.6.34	DB 2474 DB 7836	13 14	Act 2 Susanna, or via Aprite, presto	AM AR RH
2BR 320–_1_–1A	6.6.34	DB 2475 DB 7837	15	Finale Act 2 Esci omai	AM AR RH
2BR 321–1–1A _2_–2A	6.6.34	DB 2475 DB 7838		Finale Act 2 Susanna, son morta	AM AR RH WDF
2BR 322–_1_–1A	6.6.34	DB 2476 DB 7839		Finale Act 2 Conoscete, signor	AM AR RH WDF FD
2BR 323–_1_–1A	6.6.34	DB 2476 DB 7840		Finale Act 2 Nè in volto	AM AR RH WDF FD
2BR 324–_1A_ _2_–2A	6.6.34	DB 2477 DB 7841		Finale Act 2 Voi signor, che giusto	AM AR CW RH HN WDF NA
2BR 330–1–_1A_	6.6.34	DB 2477 DB 7841	18	Act 3 Riconosci in quest' amplesso	AM CW RH MJ NA WDF
2BR 326–_1_–1A	6.6.34	DB 2478 DB 7840	28	Finale Act 4 Pian pianin	AM AR LH RH WDF
2BR 327–_1_–1A	6.6.34	DB 2478 DB 7839		Finale Act 4 Oltre la dote	AM AR RH WDF
2BR 328–1–1A _2_–2A	6.6.34	DB 2479 DB 7838		Finale Act 4 Pace, pace, mio dolce	AM AR LH CW WR RH HN MJ FD NA WDF
2BR 329–_1_–1A	6.6.34	DB 2479 DB 7837		Finale Act 4 Contessa perdona	AM AR LH CW WR RH HN MJ RD NA WDF
2BR 331–1	6.6.34	Not issued			Damaged before production Title unknown

MOZART OPERA SOCIETY VOLUME TWO

MATRIX/TAKE	DATE	STRAIGHT NOS/ AUTO NOS	SCORE NUMBER AND MUSICAL ITEM		SINGERS
Act 1					
2ER 86–*1*–2	28.6.35	DBS 2583 DBS 7926		Overture	Orchestra
2ER 45–1–2	24.6.35	DB 2584 DB 7927	1	Cinque, dieci	AM WDF
2ER 46–1–2	24.6.35	DB 2584 DB 7928	2	Se a caso madama	AM WDF
2ER 41–*1*–2	24.6.35	DB 2585 DB 7929	3	Se vuol ballare	WDF
2ER 96–1–2	28.6.35	DB 2585 DB 7930	4	La vendetta	IT
2ER 99–*1*–2	28.6.35	DB 2586 DB 7931	5	Via resti servita	AM CW
2ER 47–1–2	24.6.35	DB 2586 DB 7931	6	Non so più	LH
2ER 40–1–2	24.6.35	DB 2587 DB 7930	9	Non più andrai	WDF
Act 2					
2ER 93–1–2	28.6.35	DB 2587 DB 7929	10	Porgi amor	AR
2ER 94–1–2	28.6.35	DB 2588 DB 7928	11	Voi che sapete	LH
2ER 95–*1*–2	28.6.35	DB 2588 DB 7927	12	Venite inginocchiatevi	AM

MOZART OPERA SOCIETY VOLUME THREE

MATRIX/TAKE	DATE	STRAIGHT NOS/ AUTO NOS	SCORE NUMBER AND MUSICAL ITEM		SINGERS
Act 3					
2ER 90–_1_–2	28.6.35	DB 2589 DB 7932	16	Crudel! Perchè	AM RH
2ER 89–_1_–2	28.6.35	DB 2589 DB 7933	17	Hai già vinta- Vedrò, mentr'io	RH
2ER 97–_1_–2	28.6.35	DB 2590 DB 7934	19	E Susanna- Dove sono (Pt 1)	AR
2ER 98–1–_2_	28.6.35	DB 2590 DB 7935		Dove sono (Pt 2)	AR
2BR 325–1–_1_A 2–_2A_	6.6.34	DB 2591 DB 7936	20 21	Sull'aria Ricevete, o padroncina	AM AR Chorus
2ER 43–_1_–2	24.6.35	DB 2591 DB 7936	22	Finale Act 3 Ecco la marcia	AM AR RH WDF Chorus
2ER 44–_1_–2	24.6.35	DB 2592 DB 7935		Fandango- E, già solita	RH WDF Chorus
Act 4					
2ER 42–_1_–2	24.6.35	DB 2592 DB 7934	26	Tutto è disposto Aprite un po'	WDF
2ER 91–1–_2_	28.6.35	DB 2593 DB 7933	27	Giunse alfin- Deh vieni (Pt 1)	AM
2ER 92–_1_–2	28.6.35	DB 2593 DB 7932		Deh vieni (Pt 2)	AM

Original issue
Mozart Opera Society under the auspices of HMV.
A separate illustrated booklet accompanies each volume containing notes for that volume compiled by Walter Legge.

Volume 1

DB 2474–9	(6 12" 78s Straight Coupling)	6.1935
DB 7836–41	(6 12" 78s Automatic Coupling)	6.1935

Volume 2

DBS 2583 and DB 2584–8	(6 12" 78s Straight Coupling)	12.1935
DBS 7926 and DB 7927–31	(6 12" 78s Automatic Coupling)	12.1935

Volume 3

DB 2589–93	(5 12" 78s Straight Coupling)	12.1935
DB 7932–6	(5 12" 78s Automatic Coupling)	12.1935

| M   14042–7 | (USA) (6 12" 78s) |
| DM 16899–904 | (USA) (6 12" 78s) |

| M   14054–9 | (USA) (6 12" 78s) |
| DM 16905–10 | (USA) (6 12" 78s) |

| M   14066–70 | (USA) (5 12" 78s) |
| DM 16911–5 | (USA) (5 12" 78s) |

Re–issues

CFP 117–8	(2 12" LPs)	10.1970
Victor LCT 6001	(USA) (2 12" LPs)	
Victor WCT 54	(USA) (Set of 7" 45s)	
Victor LVT 2000	(USA) (2 12" LPs)	
Seraphim 1C–6128	(USA) (3 12" LPs)	
Turnabout TV 4114–6	(USA) (3 12" LPs)	
Turnabout THS 65081–3	(USA) (3 12" LPs)	

| Pearl GEMM CDS 9375 | (2 CDs – 62'45"/56'27") | 1989 |

The accompanying seven page booklet includes historical notes and a synopsis by Charles Haynes. The notes include brief recollections of the recording by Roy Henderson.

AS 1007/08   (USA) (2CDs)

The Gramophone Company

15th March 1934
Alfred Nightingale Esq
c/o J. Christie Esq
Glyndebourne
Sussex

Dear Mr Nightingale,

I am making arrangements to motor down to Glyndebourne with Mr Palmer, Mr Streeton and also our technical man Mr Dart, on Monday, arriving there at about 3 o/c. We should like to look over the theatre and test the acoustics.

Would you mind if Mr Cesar Saerchinger, correspondent to many American papers and especially *Musical Courier*, also came down on Monday? I have asked him to take the 1.10 train as there is no room in our motor. He will arrive at Glyndebourne station at 2.20; perhaps you could have a car there to meet him and bring him along.

If this visit is not convenient please wire me.

Looking forward to seeing you, I remain,

Yours sincerely,
F.W. Gaisberg

This letter is the earliest surviving evidence that Fred Gaisberg, International

Artistes' Manager of The Gramophone Company, was considering making records at John Christie's new opera house at Glyndebourne, nestling in the downs ten miles north of Brighton in Sussex. Alfred Nightingale was Christie's General Manager and undertook many of the arrangements in the early days, when the owner himself was occupied with other aspects of his new venture.

Obviously impressed by the acoustics of the theatre, Gaisberg and Rex Palmer, his assistant in the Artistes' Department, returned to Glyndebourne ten weeks later to see a performance of *Le nozze di Figaro* during the first week of the Festival, which opened on 28 May 1934. Gaisberg was anxious not to commit himself to the expense of recording before he had actually heard the singers and orchestra under the German conductor Fritz Busch, whom Christie had invited to take charge of all the performances. He went so far as to arrange to record parts of a live performance at the end of May, to ascertain whether the music in the theatre would reproduce well on 78 rpm discs – the only medium then generally available for sound reproduction. Two sets of these live test recordings were pressed; one was kept at The Gramophone Company's headquarters and the other sent to Busch at Glyndebourne so that a careful assessment of their quality could be made. In the intervening sixty years The Gramophone Company's set has been lost, but one side of that sent to Busch has been re-discovered at Glyndebourne. It is of Willi Domgraf-Fassbaender singing at the end of the first act, concluding with *Non più andrai*. The record reproduces well and at the aria's conclusion the audience applauds enthusiastically. The good quality of these tests was sufficient to convince Gaisberg that recording in the theatre would be a practical proposition, and, more importantly, an artistic success. Contractual arrangements were hurriedly finalised, and on 6 June the first commercial recordings of Glyndebourne Festival Opera were made. A new era in the history of operatic recording had begun.

The inspiration for Christie's ambitious plans to present opera at Glyndebourne was his wife, the soprano Audrey Mildmay. Their aim was to find excellent singers from both Britain and overseas, and to offer sufficient rehearsal time – a luxury then virtually unknown – in order to give performances of the highest artistic standard. At first the public was reluctant to believe that a journey to Sussex, some fifty miles from London, would offer the opportunity to see productions of such high quality; having once seen operas which were not only well sung but also, unusually well acted, and having enjoyed the beauty of the downland setting, they were captivated. By 1939 the Festival had grown from a twelve performance season of two operas to a thirty-eight performance season of five operas. Audrey Mildmay herself took part in productions of three different operas during those six seasons – *Le nozze di Figaro*, *Don Giovanni* and *Don Pasquale*. Her singing teacher, Jani Strasser, with whom she had studied in Vienna, was invited to become Head of Music Staff, a post he held until 1972. Throughout that period he was very influential in maintaining Glyndebourne's musical standards in the opera house itself and on the Glyndebourne recordings.

Carl Ebert, whose career as a producer and opera manager in Germany had been cut short in 1933 by his refusal to work with the Nazis, was invited to direct the first production at Glyndebourne, and was responsible for all the productions in the pre-war seasons. He returned to Glyndebourne in 1947 and continued to work there until his retirement in 1963. Whilst on record the work of Fritz Busch, the singers and the orchestral players continues to be enjoyed, Ebert's productions cannot be heard; so it is easy to underestimate his contribution to the success of Glyndebourne's recorded legacy. Thanks to the imagination of Mildmay, Christie, Busch, Ebert, Strasser and Rudolf Bing, the Glyndebourne Festival set standards of production and musical excellence that were, and still are, unrivalled.

Until Gaisberg planned the first session of *Le nozze di Figaro* in June 1934, no attempt had ever been made to record a Mozart opera. Operas by Verdi, Puccini and Leoncavallo had been made for the gramophone, mainly in Italy, but apart from some individual arias and duets Mozart had been largely ignored. Initially Gaisberg did not plan to be too ambitious. He and Christie agreed that at this first session only excerpts of *Le nozze di Figaro* would be recorded. If these proved successful, the remainder of the opera, and perhaps others as well, might be made during a future season at Glyndebourne.

The plan for 6 June was to record fourteen 12" sides, including the finales of the second and fourth acts. HMV's mobile recording unit, in the form of a large van equipped with two turntables, was driven down to Glyndebourne and parked outside the theatre. With Fritz Busch and the orchestra in the pit, the members of the cast took their places in front of the microphone and sang the chosen excerpts more or less in the sequence in which they appear in the opera. This procedure continued, with a pause between takes, sufficient only to allow the engineers in the van time to place fresh waxes on the turntables. Every item was recorded simultaneously on two turntables; this ensured that if one wax of a take became damaged at any stage, a spare would always be available and the performance would not be entirely wasted. The waxes recorded on the second turntable were marked in the customary way with the matrix number, but with the additional suffix 'A', so that the two could be clearly differentiated. Four of the takes that day had to be repeated – it is not known why; these waxes were given the suffix '2', and 'A' where appropriate. After a total of eighteen separate takes that morning, the session was complete, and the van, containing thirty-four recorded waxes, returned to Hayes where the processing could begin.

Gaisberg delegated another of his assistants, J D (David) Bicknell to take charge of the session at Glyndebourne. It was the first of many Glyndebourne recordings that he organised for HMV during the next twenty-nine years, the last being *L'incoronazione di Poppea* in 1963. In due course Bicknell succeeded Gaisberg as Head of the International Artistes' Department, and revealed a similar flair for perceptive negotiation and imaginative record planning.

By 14 June 1934 a set of test pressings had been prepared and was sent to Busch with Gaisberg's glowing comments: 'All the records made of *Figaro* have been heard and are completely successful. They are the finest set of concerted records from any opera I have yet heard and they are a grand tribute to Glyndebourne and to yourself.'

That was not quite true. One of the recorded sides, the last of the series, matrix 2BR 331-1, had been damaged in processing. Unlike the others, it was unique copy – no 'A' version had been made; perhaps there were no further blank waxes available in the van at the end of the session. The title of this damaged side is not noted in EMI's archives.

Christie hoped that at least one of the earlier live performance test recordings would be included in the published set. On 22 December 1934 he wrote to Gaisberg:

> I notice that you are not including Fassbaender's aria at the end of Act 1 recorded during the performance, nor the 'Letter Duet' in Act 3. It seems that Act 1 and Act 3 are so slightly represented. Is it possible in this next season that you may add to the representation of these two Acts?

Gaisberg was not prepared to compromise by mixing the two versions and reassured Christie that: 'There will be a chance to make up the missing numbers from Act 3 and *Non più andrai*, which is precisely what happened in 1935. The 'Letter Duet' was recorded at the commercial session on 6 June, but, with no suitable piece to back it on the 78 record, it was not included in the first album to be issued.

Audrey Mildmay sang Susanna and Willi Domgraf-Fassbaender, Figaro. The Count was the Scottish baritone Roy Henderson, who had the distinction of making one of the first classical recordings (Delius's *Sea Drift*) for the Decca Record Company when it was founded in 1929. The Countess was the soprano Aulikki Rautawaara, a member of the well-known Finnish family of singers; and the Austrian Luise Helletsgruber, who had sung Zdenka in the world première of Strauss's *Arabella* in Dresden the previous year, was Cherubino. Three English singers, Heddle Nash, Norman Allin and Constance Willis, sang Don Basilio, Bartolo and Marcellina respectively.

The orchestra which played at Glyndebourne from 1934 until 1939, and thus appears on all three pre-war Mozart recordings, was known as Glyndebourne Festival Orchestra. It was, in fact, the London Symphony, led by George Stratton. After the Second World War several different orchestras played for Glyndebourne productions, most notably the Royal Philharmonic and the London

Philharmonic, but the LSO never again took part in the Festival.

In May 1935 the commercial production of the first six discs of *Le nozze di Figaro* was at last under way, almost a year after they had been recorded; they were to be sold together in an album, as Volume One of *The Mozart Society* recordings. The *Society* series was inaugurated by Walter Legge, at the time editor of HMV's house magazine *The Voice*. Legge conceived the idea of a record subscription society to which customers would pay *before* the recordings were made. He thus ensured in advance that sufficient funds were available to cover all production expenses. In 1931 *The Hugo Wolf Society* was the first to be formed, when Elena Gerhardt recorded six double sided 78s. During the next seven years several other singers also made records of Wolf's *Lieder* and by 1938 a series of six *Hugo Wolf Society* albums had been issued. Other composers represented in the *Society* series included Beethoven, Haydn and Sibelius. The recordings were made by the EMI group of companies which included Columbia and Parlophone, in addition to the Gramophone Company (generally known as His Master's Voice). They all remained in the British catalogue until 1955, when many classical 78s were deleted with the advent of 45s and LPs. *The Mozart Society* recordings eventually ran to twelve volumes containing four operas – three of which were made at Glyndebourne.

As Glyndebourne's second season commenced in May 1935, Fred Gaisberg made plans with John Christie and his staff for the completion of the recording of *Le nozze di Figaro*, and prepared a schedule to record *Così fan tutte* almost in its entirety. One of HMV's engineers, Arthur Clarke, visited Glyndebourne on 13 June to see the theatre and to meet the musicians whom he would be recording later in the month under Bicknell's guidance. One problem arose with the casting of *Figaro*; Norman Allin, who sang Bartolo the previous year, was not appearing at Glyndebourne and would be unable to record his solo *La vendetta*. Ronald Stear sang the role on stage in 1935, but was considered unsuitable for the recording. The twenty year old Italian Italo Tajo, a member of the chorus, was selected to replace him, and sang the aria at the session on 28 June. Undoubtedly Tajo's subsequent international career benefited from this early recorded appearance as Bartolo at Glyndebourne.

The arrangements for recording were more complex than the single morning session in 1934. On 24 June, eight sides of *Le nozze di Figaro* were made (two takes of each, but without the use of a double turntable), including all of Domgraf-Fassbaender's remaining music. *Figaro* was then temporarily abandoned while *Così fan tutte* was recorded on the mornings of 25, 26 and 27 June, after which, on 28 June, twelve further sides of *Figaro* were made.

To say that *Le nozze di Figaro* was *completed* would be misleading. Gaisberg and Bicknell did not intend to record it as performed at Glyndebourne, but in an abbreviated form, almost entirely without *recitativo secco*. This decision was a commercial one – the fewer records in each album, the more Gaisberg hoped would sell. Several cuts were made in the stage performances, including Barbarina's and Marcellina's arias in Act 4; these, together with the first act chorus *Giovani lieti* were not recorded. Another omission was Don Basilio's aria. Heddle Nash sang it at Glyndebourne and Bicknell planned to include it, but after recording two takes of twelve sides on 28 June, there was simply insufficient time for it at the end of the session. However regrettable the cuts may be, they enabled the opera to be issued on seventeen 78s, compared with the twenty needed for *Così fan tutte* and twenty-three for *Don Giovanni*, in 1936. One record of Volume Two of *Figaro* contains only one side of music – the overture; its coupling was presumably intended to have been Basilio's ill-fated aria. The eleven bars of piano-accompanied *recitativo secco* which survive on *Figaro* were recorded at the 1934 session, and provide the link between the 'Letter Duet' *(Sull'aria)* and the chorus *Ricevete o padroncina* in Act 3.

The *Mozart Society* issued *Le nozze di Figaro* in two versions, straight coupling and automatic coupling. The advantage of the latter was that on automatic gramophones the sides played in succession without the need to turn the record every time, which gave a greater impression of continuous performance. One precaution that was taken when pressing the discs for the automatic version of Volume One was to make the first two sides both *straight* couplings. This ensured that the end of the second act finale would be the last side played before the turn-over, and prevented an unnecessarily long break at a critical point in the plot.

On the labels of the original 78s the singers were not identified; only one name, Fritz Busch, appeared, together with the opera, the title of the item and the legend *Glyndebourne Festival*. However, the singers' names and detailed notes about the music were provided by Walter Legge in the series of booklets which he wrote, one for each volume issued.

In Britain this original *Le nozze di Figaro* has been re-issued twice. Its first re-appearance was on two Classics for Pleasure LPs in 1970, and in 1991 it was released on two CDs by Pearl. The earlier of the two is in remarkably good sound, with the surface noise reduced to an agreeably low level; on Pearl the original surfaces have not been filtered and remain too prominent for any great pleasure to be had from the set. In the United States the opera was issued on 78s, and has since been available on the Victor label (both as 33rpm and 45rpm records), on Seraphim, Turnabout and as a two CD set.

Neville Cardus in *The Manchester Guardian*, 12 July 1935:

... The performances are almost flawless; the freshness of the voices is equalled by the precision of rhythm, balance of parts, and – best of all – the suggestion of a living participation in the music's unending flow of melody. And the orchestra is recorded proportionately and sensitively.

Most of the singers are English: Audrey Mildmay, Constance Willis, Roy Henderson, Norman Allin, and Heddle Nash, for example. It is no exaggeration to say that their work is as fine and as felicitous as anything done by the foreign artists. The album is proof of the lesson taught years ago by Sir Thomas Beecham – that, given scope and coaching, English singers will give opera after the manner born.

Alec Robertson in *The Gramophone*, December 1970, (reviewing the CFP re-issue):

Fritz Busch's interpretation is a model of style, except for a regrettable absence of *appoggiaturas* and for the use of the piano instead of the harpsichord. For some reason, chords ending *secco* recitatives have been left in before some of the numbers, as for instance the Count's accompanied recitative leading to the aria *Vedro mentr'io sospiro* in Act 3 (no 17). I particularly enjoyed Willi Domgraf-Fassbaender's down-to-earth Figaro, Audrey Mildmay's enchanting Susanna and Roy Henderson's aristocratic Count; but everyone is admirably cast. There are four recordings of *Figaro* in the catalogue, but for perfection of ensemble – and that counts for much – I would suggest that this one is the best of all.

1935

COSÌ FAN TUTTE

Music by Wolfgang Amadeus Mozart

Libretto by Lorenzo da Ponte

Sung in Italian

Ferrando	Heddle Nash (tenor, English)
Guglielmo	Willi Domgraf-Fassbaender (baritone, German)
Don Alfonso	John Brownlee (baritone, Australian)
Fiordiligi	Ina Souez (soprano, English)
Dorabella	Luise Helletsgruber (soprano, Austrian)
Despina	Irene Eisinger (soprano, Austrian)

Glyndebourne Festival Chorus	
Glyndebourne Festival Orchestra	Leader George Stratton
Conductor	Fritz Busch
Recorded	Glyndebourne theatre 25–28.6.1935

Mono recording

Recording Producer	David Bicknell
Balance Engineer	Arthur Clarke

MOZART OPERA SOCIETY VOLUME FOUR

MATRIX/TAKE	DATE	STRAIGHT NOS/ AUTO NOS		SCORE NUMBER AND MUSICAL ITEM	SINGERS
Act 1					
2ER 87–1–*2A*	28.6.35	DB 2653 DB 7977		Overture	Orchestra
2ER 48–1–*2*	25.6.35	DB 2653 DB 7978	*1*	La mia Dorabella E la fede (Pt 1)	HN WDF JB
2ER 49–*1*–2	25.6.35	DB 2654 DB 7979	*2* *3*	E la fede (Pt 2) Scioccherie di poeti Una bella serenata	HN WDF JB
2ER 50–1–*2*	25.6.35	DB 2654 DB 7980	*4*	Ah guarda, sorella	IS LH
2ER 51–*1*–2	25.6.35	DB 2655 DB 7981	*5*	Se questo mio core Vorrei dir	IS LH JB
2ER 52–1–*2*	25.6.35	DB 2655 DB 7982	*6*	Sento, o Dio	IS LH HN WDF JB
2ER 53–*1*–2	25.6.35	DB 2656 DB 7983	*8*	Bella vita militar	Chorus
2ER 54–*1*–2	25.6.35	DB 2656 DB 7983	*9*	Non v'è più tempo Di scrivermi	IS LH HN WDF JB
2ER 55–*1*–2	25.6.35	DB 2657 DB 7982	*10*	Soave sia il vento	IS LH JB
2ER 56–*1*–2	25.6.35	DB 2657 DB 7981	*11*	Che vita-Ah, scostati Smanie implacabili	IS LH IE
2ER 57–*1*–2	25.6.35	DB 2658 DB 7980	*12*	In uomini, in soldati	IE JB
2ER 58–*1*–2	25.6.35	DB 2658 DB 7979	*13*	Alla bella Despinetta	IS LH IE HN WDF JB
2ER 59–*1*–2	25.6.35	DB 2659 DB 7978		Che sussurro	IS LH IE HN WDF JB
2ER 60–*1*–2	26.6.35	DB 2659 DB 7977	*14*	Come scoglio	IS

MOZART OPERA SOCIETY VOLUME FIVE

MATRIX/TAKE	DATE	STRAIGHT NOS/ AUTO NOS		SCORE NUMBER AND MUSICAL ITEM	SINGERS
Act 1					
2ER 61–1–2	26.6.35	DB 2660	15	Non siate ritrosi	IS LH HN
		DB 7984	16	E voi ridete?	WDF JB
2ER 67–1–2	26.6.35	DB 2660	17	Un' aura amoroso	HN
		DB 7985			
2ER 62–1–2	26.6.35	DB 2661	18	Ah, che tutto	IS LH HN
		DB 7986			WDF JB
2ER 63–1–2	26.6.35	DB 2661		Il tragico	IS LH IE
		DB 7987			HN WDF JB
2ER 64–1–2	26.6.35	DB 2662		Più domestiche	IS LH IE
		DB 7988			HN WDF JB
2ER 65–1–2	26.6.35	DB 2662		Dove son?	IS LH IE
		DB 7989			HN WDF JB
2ER 66–1–2	26.6.35	DB 2663		Dammi un bacio	IS LH IE
		DB 7990			HN WDF JB
Act 2					
2ER 68–1–2	26.6.35	DB 2663		Andate là	IS LH IE
		DB 7990	19	Una donna	
2ER 69–1–2	26.6.35	DB 2664		Sorella, cosa dici?	IS LH
		DB 7989	20	Prenderò quel brunettino	
2ER 71–1–2	26.6.35	DB 2664	21	Secondate! Aurette amiche	HN WDF
		DB 7988			Chorus
2ER 70–1–2	26.6.35	DB 2665		Cos'è tal	IS LH IE
		DB 7987	22	La mano a me date	HM WDF JB IE
2ER 72–1–2	26.6.35	DB 2665		Oh che bella giornata	IS LH HN
		DB 7986			WDF
2ER 73–1–2	27.6.35	DB 2666	23	Il core vi dono	LH WDF
		DB 7985			
2ER 74–1–2	27.6.35	DB 2666		Barbara! Perchè fuggi?	IS HN
		DB 7984			

MOZART OPERA SOCIETY VOLUME SIX

MATRIX/TAKE	DATE	STRAIGHT NOS/ AUTO NOS		SCORE NUMBER AND MUSICAL ITEM	SINGERS
2ER 75–1–2	27.6.35	DB 2667 DB 7991	25	Per pietà (pt 1)	IS
2ER 76–1–2	27.6.35	DB 2667 DB 7992		Per pietà (Pt 2)	IS
2ER 77–1–2	27.6.35	DB 2668 DB 7993		Amico, abbiamo	HN WDF
2ER 78–1–2	27.6.35	DB 2668 DB 7994	26	Donne mie	HN WDF JB
2ER 88–1–2	28.6.35	DB 2669 DB 7995	29	Ora vedo Fra gli amplessi	IS LH IE IS HN
2ER 85–1–2	27.6.35	DB 2669 DB 7996		Volgi a me	IS HN WDF JB
2ER 79–1–2	27.6.35	DB 2670 DB 7996	30 31	Tutti accusan Fate presto	IE HN WDF JB IS LH IE HN WDF JB Chorus
2ER 80–1–2	27.6.35	DB 2670 DB 7995		Benedetti i doppi	IS LH HN WDF Chorus
2ER 81–1–2	27.6.35	DB 2671 DB 7994		Miei Signori	IS LH IE HN WDF JB Chorus
2ER 82–1–2	27.6.35	DB 2671 DB 7993		Mille barbari	IS LH IE HN WDF JB
2ER 83–1–2	27.6.35	DB 2672 DB 7992		Giusto ciel	IS LH IE HN WDF JB
2ER 84–1–2	27.6.35	DB 2672 DB 7991		V'ingannai, ma fu	IS LH IE HN WDF JB

Original issue
Mozart Opera Society under the auspices of HMV.
A booklet accompanies each volume, containing notes and musical illustrations by Walter Legge.

Volume 4

DB 2563–59	(7 12" 78s Straight Coupling)	3.1936
DB 7977–83	(7 12" 78s Automatic Coupling)	3.1936

Volume 5

DB 2660–6	(7 12" 78s Straight Coupling)	3.1936
DB 7984–90	(7 12" 78s Automatic Coupling)	3.1936

Volume 6

DB 2667–72	(6 12" 78s Straight Coupling)	3.1936
DB 7991–6	(6 12" 78s Automatic Coupling)	3.1936

M 13711–7	(USA) (7 12" 78s)
DM 13718–24	(USA) (7 12" 78s)

M 13725–31	(USA) (7 12" 78s)
DM 13732–8	(USA) (7 12" 78s)

M 13739–44	(USA) (6 12" 78s)
DM 13745–50	(USA) (6 12" 78s)

Re–issues

Conifer 2 C 15143216–8	(3 12" LPs)	1983
Seraphim 1C–6127	(USA) (3 12" LPs)	
Victor LCT 6104	(USA) (3 12" LPs)	
Victor WCT 6104	(USA) (Set of 7" 45s)	
Turnabout TV 4120–22	(USA) (3 12" LPs)	
Turnabout THS 65126–8	(USA) (3 LPs)	

Pearl GEMM CDS 9406	(3CDs – 34'42"/47'50"/70–'04")	12.1990

The fourteen page booklet contains brief biographies of the singers, details of the origins of the opera and a synopsis by Charles Haynes.

EMI CHS7 63864–2	(2 CDs – 77'09"/76'19")	5.1991

The accompanying sixty-six page booklet includes the libretto in Italian; a synopsis in German, French and English; and a background article in French by André Tubeuf and in English and German by John Steane.

CDHB 63864	(USA) (2CDs)

Excerpts

Heddle Nash – EMI Golden Voice Series
Un'aura amorosa

EMI HQM 1089	(1 12" LP)	9.1967

The Art of Ina Souez
Ei parte – Senti – Per pietà – Temerari – Come scoglio

Orion ORS–7293	(USA) (1 12" LP)

The cast of *Così fan tutte* included three singers who had not appeared on the set of *Le nozze di Figaro*; Ina Souez, Irene Eisinger and John Brownlee. At 10am on 25 June 1935, the six soloists began a concentrated period of work, during which they recorded a total of twenty-four waxes, two takes of each side. The following day they completed the first act and began the second by recording twenty-six waxes; on the final morning allocated to *Così*, twenty-six more were made; a further four overlapped into the session for *Le nozze di Figaro* on 28 June. It was a remarkable achievement. In just four days, an almost complete opera had been recorded, with no need for more than one spare wax of each take. This was only possible because of the excellent circumstances in which the recording was made. After a period of intensive rehearsal, (the conductor, singers and orchestra had worked together for a month) they were evidently relaxed and familiar with their 'studio' – ideal conditions for the project. Whether the soloists considered their fees ideal is a matter for conjecture. Fred Gaisberg stipulated the week before the recording that he could not 'agree to more than £70 each' for their participation in the recording – by the standards of the day no mean amount.

The cuts made in *Così fan tutte* were not as brutal as those inflicted on some later Glyndebourne recordings. They were made in some recitatives, in the second act *Volgi a me*, and the finale. Four numbers were omitted from the performance entirely; the duet *Al fato dan legge*, Ferrando's *Ah, lo veggio* and *Tradito, schernito* and Dorabella's *È amore un ladroncello* – customary excisions at the time and still observed in some performances even today.

By September, Fred Gaisberg was becoming impatient and awaited a response to a telegram he had sent to Fritz Busch. A complete set of the recordings made at Glyndebourne in June had been sent to Busch, but he had not yet selected his preferred takes. EMI needed to know which waxes to prepare for manufacture, and, as their issue was planned for November (the second and third volumes of *Figaro*) and December (all three volumes of *Così*), no time could be lost. Busch's wife Greta wrote to Gaisberg on 7 September. Busch was very busy and in Buenos Aires: 'You and the other gentleman at HMV [Bicknell?] would better choose a selection.' She added that in *Così* the singers were too loud and 'oversounding' the orchestral part 'because the orchestra was wrongly placed.' Whether this was her husband's considered opinion or her own is not made clear. If it was a problem, it was too late to rectify it. Gaisberg wrote again to Busch on 1 January 1936, telling him that the cardboard albums for the records were still not ready; release was re-scheduled for March, in which month the opera was indeed issued complete. Although it missed the 1935 Christmas trade, it was distributed well in time to promote the 1936 series of performances.

New English Weekly, 21 May 1936:

The notable thing about this performance is the quite admirable brio, and gusto with which the whole thing is done, and the remarkable way in which the company, none of whom are Italians, enter into the spirit and manner of the light Italian comedy opera or *opera buffa*. It is Mozart at his very best, sparkling like champagne, witty *verveaux* and with a delicious lightness of touch and a supreme deftness. The best singing of the whole is done by Ina Souez as Fiordiligi, Luise Helletsgruber as her sister Dorabella, Heddle Nash as Ferrando, one of the lovers of the two ladies, and Irene Eisinger as the impudent, pert maidservant, Despina, a performance this last that is quite a delight. From John Brownlee as Don Alfonso, and Willi Domgraf-Fassbaender as Guglielmo, some good work came but too stomachic, in the contemporary manner . . . The work is directed with admirable finesse and spirit by Fritz Busch, who as a conductor of Mozart would appear, from this one performance, at least, to bear some comparison even with Beecham.

Edward Greenfield in *Records and Recording*, November 1962, (reviewing an Electrola re-issue):

Busch's well-known dislike of *appoggiaturas* brings to the music a clipped quality that deprives it of much of its seductive grace. His tempi, too, do not always convince. Despina's first aria seems oddly fast, the molto allegro of the sextet in the same act, *Alla bella Despinetta*, lacks excitement, while the sisters' second act duet *Prenderò quel brunettino*, is a little charmless at Busch's fastish pace. In the main, however, his conducting is notable for its spirit and affection. The least pleasing aspect lies in Busch's use of a piano continuo, a stylistic aberration which constantly jars the ear. Not all the singing reaches the same level of artistic distinction as John Brownlee's Alfonso. This is a masterly performance. Brownlee's ripe characterisation brings out the cynical sophisticated nature of the elderly philosopher to perfection. His subtle vocal inflections and acute sense of timing are impeccable and he always displays a complete command of the meaning of the words.

1936

DON GIOVANNI

Music by Wolfgang Amadeus Mozart

Libretto by Lorenzo da Ponte

Sung in Italian

Don Giovanni	John Brownlee (baritone, Australian)
Donna Anna	Ina Souez (soprano, English)
Donna Elvira	Luise Helletsgruber (soprano, Austrian)
Leporello	Salvatore Baccaloni (bass, Italian)
Don Ottavio	Koloman von Pataky (tenor, Hungarian)
Commendatore	David Franklin (bass, English)
Zerlina	Audrey Mildmay (soprano, English)
Masetto	Roy Henderson (baritone, Scottish)

Glyndebourne Festival Chorus	
Glyndebourne Festival Orchestra	Leader George Stratton
Conductor	Fritz Busch
Recorded	Glyndebourne theatre 29–30.6, 1–2 and 5.7.1936
Mono recording	
Recording Producer	David Bicknell
Balance Engineers	Edward Fowler and Arthur Clarke

MOZART OPERA SOCIETY VOLUME SEVEN

MATRIX/TAKE	DATE	STRAIGHT NOS/ AUTO NOS	SCORE NUMBER AND MUSICAL ITEM	SINGERS
Act 1				
2ER 130–1–2	29.6.36	DB 2961 DB 8146	Overture (Pt 1)	Orchestra
2ER 137–1–2	30.6.36	DB 2961 DB 8147 1	Overture (Pt 2) Notte e giorno	Orchestra SB
2ER 138–1–2	30.6.36	DB 2962 DB 8148	Non sperar	IS JB SB DF
2ER 131–1–2	29.6.36	DB 2962 DB 8149 2	Ah, del padre Ma quel mai	IS KP
2ER 132–1–2	29.6.36	DB 2963 DB 8150	Fuggi, crudele	IS KP
2ER 147–1–2	1.7.36	DB 2963 DB 8151 3	Orsù, spicciati Ah! Chi mi dice	JB SB LH
2ER 170–1–2	5.7.36	DB 2964 DB 8152 4	Don Giovanni! Madamina (Pt 1)	JB LH SB SB
2ER 171–1–2	5.7.36	DB 2964 DB 8153	Madamina (Pt 2)	SB
2ER 139–1–2 –3	30.6.36 5.7.36	DB 2965 5 DB 8153	Giovinette Manco male	AM RH Chorus AM JB RH SB
2ER 133–1–2	29.6.36	DB 2965 6 DB 8152	Ho capito Alfin siam	RH AM JB RH
2ER 134–1–2	29.6.36	DB 2966 7 DB 8151	Là ci darem	JB AM
2ER 135–1–2	29.6.36	DB 2966 DB 8150 8	Fermati Ah! Fuggi	LH AM JB LH IS KP JB
2ER 136–1–2	29.6.36	DB 2967 9 DB 8149	Non ti fidar	LH IS KP JB
2ER 142–1–2	30.6.36	DB 2967 DB 8148 10	Povera sventurata Don Ottavio	JB IS KP
2ER 143–1–2	30.6.36	DB 2968 DB 8147	Or sai chi l'onore Come mai	IS KP KP
2ER 144–1–2	30.6.36	DB 2968 11 DB 8146	Dalla sua pace	KP

MOZART OPERA SOCIETY VOLUME EIGHT

MATRIX/TAKE	DATE	STRAIGHT NOS/ AUTO NOS		SCORE NUMBER AND MUSICAL ITEM	SINGERS
Act 1					
2ER 148–1–2	1.7.36	DB 2969		Io deggio	JB SB
		DB 8154	12	Finch'han dal vino	JB
2ER 149–1–2	1.7.36	DB 2969		Masetto, senti	RH AM
		DB 8155	13	Batti, batti (Pt 1)	AM
2ER 150–1–2	1.7.36	DB 2970		Batti (Pt 2)	AM
		DB 8156		Guarda un po'	AM JB RH
			14	Presto, presto	Chorus
2ER 151–1–2	1.7.36	DB 2970		Tra quest'arbori	LH KP IS
		DB 8157			AM RH JB
2ER 152–1–2	1.7.36				
–3	5.7.36	DB 2971		Signor, guardate	LH KP IS
		DB 8158			JB SB
2ER 153–1–2	1.7.36	DB 2971		Riposate, vezzose	LH KP IS
		DB 8159			JB SB RH
					AM
2ER 154–1–2	1.7.36	DB 2972		Ricominciate il	LH KP IS
		DB 8160		suono	JB SB RH
					AM
2ER 155–1–2	1.7.36	DB 2972		Ecco il birbo	LH KP IS
		DB 8160			JB SB IS
					AM
Act 2					
2ER 166–1–2	5.7.36	DB 2973	15	Eh via, buffone	JB SB
		DB 8159			
2ER 167–1–2	5.7.36	DB 2973	16	Ah, taci ingiusto	LH JB
		DB 8158		(Pt 1)	SB
2ER 168–1–2	5.7.36	DB 2974		Ah, taci (Pt 2)	LH JB
		DB 8157			SB
2ER 165–1–2	5.7.36	DB 2974	17	Deh vieni –	JB
		DB 8156		V'è gente	JB RH
2ER 162–1–2	2.7.36	DB 2975	18	Metà di voi–	JB
		DB 8155		Zitto, lascia	AM JB RH
2ER 169–1–2	5.7.36	DB 2975	19	Vedrai carino	AM
		DB 8154			

MOZART OPERA SOCIETY VOLUME NINE

MATRIX/TAKE	DATE	STRAIGHT NOS/ AUTO NOS		SCORE NUMBER AND MUSICAL ITEM	SINGERS
2ER 156–1–2	2.7.36	DB 2976 DB 8161	 20	Di molte faci Sola, sola	LH RH LH IS SB RH AM KP
2ER 157–1–2	2.7.36	DB 2976 DB 8162		Perdon, perdono Sola, sola	LH KP IS SB RH AM
2ER 158–1–2	2.7.36	DB 2977 DB 8163	 21	Dunque quello Ah, pietà	LH AM KP RH LH AM KP SB RH
2ER 159–1–2	2.7.36	DB 2977 DB 8164	22	Il mio tesoro	KP
2ER 172–1–2	5.7.36	DB 2978 DB 8165	23	In quali eccessi	LH
2ER 173–1–2	5.7.36	DB 2978 DB 8166		Mi tradì	LH
2ER 140–1–2	30.6.36	DB 2979 DB 8167		Ah, ah questa è buona	JB SB DF
2ER 141–1–2	30.6.36	DB 2979 DB 8168	24	O statua	JB SB DF
2ER 160–1–2	2.7.36	DB 2980 DB 8168	 25	Calmatevi, idol mio Crudele? Non mi dir (Pt 1)	IS KP
2ER 161–1–2	2.7.36	DB 2980 DB 8167		Non mi dir (Pt 2)	IS
2ER 174–1–2	5.7.36	DB 2981 DB 8166	26	Già la mensa	JB SB
2ER 175–1–2	5.7.36	DB 2981 DB 8165		Questa poi la conosco	LH JB SB
2ER 145–1–2	30.6.36	DB 2982 DB 8164		Ah, signor	JB SB DF
2ER 146–1–2	30.6.36	DB 2982 DB 8163		Tu m'invitasti	JB SB DF
2ER 163–1–2	2.7.36	DB 2983 DB 8162		Ah, dov'è il perfido?	LH IS KP SB RH AM
2ER 164–1–2	2.7.36	DB 2983 DB 8161		Io men vado	LH IS KP SB RH AM

Original issue
Mozart Opera Society under the auspices of HMV.
Each of the three volumes includes an individual accompanying booklet with annotations and translations in Italian and English. In addition there are background essays on the history of *Don Giovanni* by Walter Legge and H V Little.

Volume 7		
DB 2961–8	(8 12" 78s Straight Coupling)	3.1937
DB 8146–53	(8 12" 78s Automatic Coupling)	3.1937

Volume 8		
DB 2969–75	(7 12" 78s Straight Coupling)	3.1937
DB 8154–60	(7 12" 78s Automatic Coupling)	3.1937

Volume 9		
DB 2976–83	(8 12" 78s Straight Coupling)	5.1937
DB 8161–8	(8 12" 78s Automatic Coupling)	5.1937

M 14747–54	(USA) (8 12" 78s)
DM 16426–33	(USA) (8 12" 78s)

M 14763–9	(USA) (7 12" 78s)
DM 16434–40	(USA) (7 12" 78s)

M 14777–84	(USA) (8 12" 78s)
DM 16441–48	(USA) (8 12" 78s)

Re–issues
HMV ALP 1199–1201   (3 12" LPs)   12.1954
A separate line-by-line libretto was available at additional cost.

Victor LCT 6102	(USA) (3 12" LPs)
Victor WCT 59	(USA) (Set of 7" 45s)
Turnabout TV 4117–9	(USA) (3 12" LPs)
Turnabout THS 65084/6	(USA) (3 12" LPs)

EMI CHS7 61030–2   (3CDs – 65'22"/68'32"/37'52")   12.1988
The accompanying two-hundred page booklet includes the libretto in German, Italian, French and English, and a background essay *Glyndebourne's first 'Don Giovanni'* by William Mann.

AS 1004–6   (USA) (3 CDs)

Pearl GEMM CDS 9369   (3 CDs – TPT 168'53")   1991
The eleven page booklet includes reminiscences by Roy Henderson, brief biographies of the cast, a short essay *Don Giovanni – A Comic Opera?* and a synopsis by Charles Haynes.

Excerpts
The Art of Ina Souez
Crudele – Ah non mio bene   – Non mi dir – Don Ottavio – Or sai
Orion ORS–7293   (USA) (1 12" LP)

Rudolf Bing was appointed General Manager of Glyndebourne in 1936, and it was he who corresponded with Gaisberg about arrangements for the forthcoming recording of *Don Giovanni*, which was being produced at Glyndebourne for the first time the following May. The cast was to include John Brownlee, the Italian *buffo* bass Salvatore Baccaloni, (singing at Glyndebourne for the first time), Helletsgruber, Souez, Henderson and Mildmay. As Don Ottavio, Busch had selected Koloman von Pataky, a Hungarian tenor, making what proved to be his only Glyndebourne appearance. Having already obtained two successful opera recordings, Fred Gaisberg was keen to maintain the momentum; Christie, Busch and Bing were no less interested in continuing the series. Apart from providing a modest income from royalties, the two *Mozart Society* issues had served to advertise Glyndebourne's high standards to a wide public, and a third opera recording would obviously be to the benefit of both parties. Gaisberg prepared a schedule for sessions in late June and early July, and submitted it to Bing, who foresaw one difficulty – that the BBC had already arranged to broadcast *Die Zauberflöte* on 30 June; he felt it would be inconvenient to record on the same day. Despite Bing's misgiving, both the broadcast and the recording took place, to the apparent detriment of neither. This was not the only difficulty that Gaisberg encountered with *Don Giovanni*. On 3 June he wrote with some alarm that he expected problems recording in the theatre. It had been enlarged since the first Festival in 1934, with a resultant change in its acoustic properties. The restaurant was suggested as a possible alternative. Fortunately, perhaps, Don Giovanni did not have to attend his banquet in Glyndebourne's dining hall, and the theatre was, after all, used for the five sessions.

Don Giovanni was the longest of the three Mozart recordings made at Glyndebourne in the 1930s. Forty-six sides each required two takes, and two of the sides required three. It seems probable that the first two takes of matrices 2ER 139 and 2ER 152 were recorded on 30 June and 1 July respectively; certainly the third of each were recorded on 5 July, and these were the two which were published in each case. The sequence of recording was not as logical as that scheduled for *Così fan tutte* the previous year. Even the two sides of the overture were recorded on different days. Fourteen takes were made on the first day of recording, twenty on the second (including all those for which David Franklin, the Commendatore, was required), eighteen on the third, eighteen more on the fourth and, on the final day, twenty-four, a much slower rate of progress than that previously achieved.

On 1 October a sample set of records was sent to John and Audrey Christie, who found the labelling confusing. Full cast details were listed on each record label together with the title of the opera and the aria – a good deal of information to print on a small area. Correspondence on the subject continued until May 1937, when in a letter to Gaisberg, Christie wrote:

The numbering of the records has again ignored the corrections which I suggested to you on your proof. My corrections enabled one to see where one was in the opera in respect of scenes and also to see at once which opera a record was made from. At present the chasing of these details by inspection of the record label is quite infuriatingly difficult.

Another problem also troubled the Christies; the choice of takes of two of Zerlina's arias. Busch had initially made his selection but it displeased Christie. He wrote to Gaisberg:

My wife maintains quite definitely that some of her worst records have been used. For instance, record No 9 in Act 1 of *Don Giovanni*. The record was made, I think, three times. The one chosen shows her quite often to be flat. The alternative records, I believe, did not do so.

A conciliatory response to Audrey Mildmay was in order:

I have been investigating the suggestion made in Mr Christie's letter of May 6th, that the masters of *Don Giovanni* which you had selected, were changed by us in the albums placed on the market.
I find that we have used the master which you selected, with only one exception and that is *Vedrai carino*, where we are supplying 2ER 169-2, whilst you chose the -1.
When our Committee heard these records they had received a written report from Dr Fritz Busch, in which he marked the title as follows:
2ER 169-1 not bad
2ER 169-2 *much* better – good

After a meeting on 20 June, agreement about the selection of takes was reached:

Dear Mrs Christie,
             This confirms our interview yesterday on the alternative recordings. Altogether we heard three records and in two cases we will alter the previous masters, as follows:
2ER 149-1 *Batti Batti* – original master
2ER 149-2   "   "   – new master

2ER 169-2 *Vedrai carino* – original master
2ER 169-1   "   "   – new master
You will note that in the case of *Vedrai carino*, although Fritz Busch had formerly selected 2ER 169-2, we are now changing this over to your selection, 2ER 169-1.

So the early sets were released with the 'wrong' takes of these two sides, and copies of them have found their way into numerous collections.

Very little music was cut from this *Don Giovanni*. The principal loss was a duet for Leporello and Zerlina, (composed by Mozart in 1788, the year after the opera's première), which is customarily omitted from modern performances, together with two recitatives, and seven bars from the finale.

These three *Mozart Society* volumes were released in 1937 to great critical acclaim. In 1954 the opera was re-issued in Britain on three LPs and in 1988 on three EMI CDs. It has also appeared on three Pearl CDs, although the sound quality is markedly inferior. In the United States it appeared on Victor 78s, and later on several different LP and 45 rpm issues, including Victor and Turnabout. A selection of excerpts featured on an Orion LP entitled *The Art of Ina Souez*, a tribute to the American-born soprano who sang Donna Anna.

The Musical Times, April 1937:

The Donna Elvira is Luise Helletsgruber, one of the finest artists in the Glyndebourne Company. Everything that she does is vivid. Her Cherubino, her Dorabella and her Donna Elvira live as separate characters in her singing alone . . . The trouble with this artist is that in the first place she is a mezzo-soprano, and in the second, her method puts a touch of labour into her voice-production. The other unsolved problem is Don Ottavio . . . but Koloman von Pataky emphasises his weakness by singing in a sentimental manner with a sentimental technique . . . Baccaloni's vigour and quickness of tongue rise above buffoonery, and Roy Henderson is much too good a singer to leave Masetto without a character. As Don Giovanni, John Brownlee comes off even better on the records than he does in the theatre. He has assurance and ease of style that is both engaging and masterly . . . Of Ina Souez as Donna Anna and Audrey Mildmay as Zerlina there is no need to write; they are both good Mozartians. So is the whole company in everything that it has to do as a team of singers.

David Cairns in *The Sunday Times*, 11 June 1989, (reviewing EMI's CD re-issue):

Brownlee remains in many respects an ideal Don Giovanni. The timbre of his voice may lack honey, and his Italian is a little suspect, but he sings with superb authority. Incisive in rhythm, his virile baritone suggests both the ruthlessness and the touch of madness that basses rarely, if ever, convey. Ina Souez's fiery Donna Anna is one of the best on record, Koloman von Pataky is a fine Don Ottavio, and Luise Helletsgruber, though a trifle undisciplined in her singing, makes a lovely and touching Donna Elvira. If the cast contains others who are less good – Roy

Henderson's strangely mincing Masetto, David Franklin's wooden Commendatore, Audrey Mildmay's lively but rather perkily sung Zerlina – that is true of most recordings in an imperfect world. Some of Busch's tempos now seem on the slow side, but his grasp of structure and his feeling for dramatic colour still command admiration.

The next recording proposed by Fred Gaisberg was *Die Zauberflöte*, which was performed in 1937 with Aulikki Rautawaara as Pamina, the Danish tenor Thorkild Noval as Tamino and Roy Henderson as Papageno (according to some critics, his finest role at Glyndebourne). In early June the music staff prepared a list of timings of the numbers, and a recording schedule was drawn up. Quite suddenly, Gaisberg changed his mind and informed Busch that the plans were cancelled. He hoped instead to record a Mozart Piano Concerto at the opera house, with Rudolf Serkin as soloist, but this too, came to nothing. It was not until November that Christie realised why Gaisberg acted as he had. A new version of *Die Zauberflöte* had just been recorded in Berlin under Sir Thomas Beecham, produced by Walter Legge, and was to be issued as the fourth and final opera in the *Mozart Society* series. Christie was furious and wrote at once to Alfred Clark, Chairman of HMV, complaining of the company's actions. After three extremely successful opera recordings at Glyndebourne, Christie insisted that he should have been consulted about the change of plan. It was, of course, too late to do anything constructive about it, and by December he was sufficiently reconciled to the situation to ask Gaisberg to send him a set of the Berlin performance. By an ironic coincidence, Sir Thomas Beecham again came between Glyndebourne and a recording of *Die Zauberflöte* twenty-three years later. He was booked to conduct and record the opera at the house in 1960, but was taken ill before the season began. That project, too, was cancelled, and Glyndebourne has yet to make its first recording of the opera.

One further Glyndebourne recording was mooted before the outbreak of the second world war. Verdi's *Macbeth* was given its first professional English staging at Glyndebourne in 1938, with the American Francesco Valentino in the title role. The Yugoslav soprano Vera Schwarz sang Lady Macbeth, but was replaced by Margherita Grandi when the opera was presented again in 1939. Christie believed that his excellent 1939 cast, which also included Constance Willis and David Lloyd, should make the first commercial recording of the opera. On 17 March 1939 Rudolf Bing wrote to Rex Palmer at HMV on Christie's behalf:

> I just wonder whether you have ever thought of making records of our production of *Macbeth* by Verdi. I personally should think this opera would be very well suited to recording because of its many arias, chorus finales and so forth. The cast is not large and in consequence would not be

very expensive. Please let me know if you think this suggestion might be of interest to HMV, because if so we would have to make arrangements very far ahead.

Neither Bing nor Christie was deterred by the unenthusiastic reply:

> . . . Your production of this work was of course an amazing artistic success, but we feel it does not lend itself to records in the same way as Mozart . . .

On 12 April Bing wrote again to Palmer, emphasising Christie's enthusiasm and asking HMV to reconsider their decision; Gaisberg agreed to meet Christie to discuss the artistic merits and financial implications of the project. Gaisberg's suggestion was that, as the opera was being performed at Glyndebourne in any case, there would be no need of rehearsals, but simply one session at which twelve or fourteen sides, comprising several of the best scenes, could be recorded. Christie was expected to cover all expenses incurred and in return would receive a higher than usual royalty payment. On 4 July Palmer confirmed HMV's offer:

> About *Macbeth*, I confirm that we will increase our offer to 15% of the retail price. If you wish we would make an advance of £100 on this account which will reduce your initial outlay on artists' fees. We should propose to make six or seven double sided records and the opera is so well rehearsed this could probably be done in one session . . . I attach a list of sixteen record sides from which the choice could be made.
>
> | 1 | The Prelude |
> |---|---|
> | 2 & 3 | The entrance of Lady Macbeth |
> | 4 & 5 | Duet for Lady Macbeth and Macbeth |
> | 6 | Finale of Act 1 |
> | 7 | *La luce langue* |
> | 8, 9, & 10 | Finale Act 2 |
> | 11 | Finale Act 3 |
> | 12 | Chorus of Scots refugees |
> | 13 & 14 | 'Sleepwalking scene' |
> | 15 | Macbeth's scene |
> | 16 | Finale Act 4 |

Christie was not prepared to accept these terms and Bing wrote to Palmer:

> Much as he would like our performance of *Macbeth* to be recorded, he cannot spend still more money on this opera than he has done already by putting it on. While he is quite prepared to accept a lower percentage on the retail price as that offered by you, Mr Christie feels that the expense of the recording should be borne by you.

That concluded the matter and the performances went unrecorded by HMV. But in Sir George Christie's collection at Glyndebourne is a set of records from a live performance of *Macbeth*, probably made during the 1939 Festival. They were privately recorded, possibly from the broadcast of the opera on the BBC on 7 July 1939, and consist of several of the arias and scenes that Rex Palmer had proposed:

1 Lady Macbeth's entrance aria and cabaletta
2 Duet for Macbeth and Lady Macbeth
3 Finale of Act 1
4 *La luce langue*
5 Finale of Act 2
6 'Sleepwalking scene.'

Were they Christie's final attempt to preserve at least part of the performance on record for his own pleasure? After the second world war two further attempts were made to record Glyndebourne's production of *Macbeth*, but they were also doomed to failure.

Eight days after Bing's final letter to HMV, the season came to an end. The next Glyndebourne Festival did not take place for seven years; the first opera to be performed there in 1946 was composed by Benjamin Britten, a young man of whom, in 1939, John Christie had probably not heard.

New Statesman, 15 July 1939:

It is a tragedy that this production [*Macbeth*] is likely to be dropped from the Glyndebourne repertory without the recording of a single note; for it is particularly strong just where so many Glyndebourne productions have been weak – namely, in the quality of the solo singing. This year the company possesses, in Margherita Grandi, a Lady Macbeth of genius, the greatest dramatic soprano of the Italian school heard in this country since the war. It is difficult to believe that a complete recording of the great 'Sleepwalking Scene' by this superb singer would not justify itself commercially, and I beg The Gramophone Company, while there is still time, to consider making one.

[2]   *The Beggar's Opera*, 1940

1940

THE BEGGAR'S OPERA

A Ballad Opera

Music by John Pepusch

Revised version by Frederic Austin

Words by John Gay

Sung in English

Excerpts

Peachum	Roy Henderson (baritone, Scottish)
Mrs Peachum	Constance Willis (contralto, English)
Polly Peachum	Audrey Mildmay (soprano, English)
Macheath	Michael Redgrave (baritone, English)
Lucy Lockit	Linda Gray (contralto, English)
Lockit	Joseph Farrington (bass, English)
Jenny Diver	Ruby Gilchrist (soprano, English)
Filch	Bruce Flegg (tenor, English)
Diana Trapes	Alys Brough (soprano, English)

Chorus   Chorus Master George Austin
Orchestra of fifteen instrumentalists

Conductors   Michael Mudie and Frederic Austin+

Recorded   Studio No 1, Abbey Road
                                         11, 12 and 15.4.1940
Mono recording

Recording Producer   Unknown
Balance Engineer   Arthur Clarke

MATRIX/TAKE	DATE	STRAIGHT NOS/ AUTO NOS		MUSICAL ITEM	SINGERS
2EA8552–*1*–2	12.4.40	C	3159	+Overture (Pepusch)	Orchestra
		C	7537	Through all the employments	RH
				'Tis woman that seduces	BF

MATRIX/TAKE	DATE	STRAIGHT NOS/ AUTO NOS		MUSICAL ITEM	SINGERS
2EA8553–*1*–2	12.4.40	C	3159	If any wench	CW
		C	7538	Our Polly is a sad slut	CW
				Can love be controlled	AM
				O Polly, you might	CW RH AM
2EA8554–*1*–2	12.4.40	C	3160	A fox may steal	RH
		C	7539	O ponder well	AM
				The turtle thus	AM
2EA8555–1–*2*	15.4.40	C	3160	My heart was so free	MR
		C	7540	Were I laid on Greenland's coast	MR AM
				O what pain it is	MR AM
2EA8556–1–*2*	11.4.40	C	3161	Fill every glass	BF Chorus
		C	7541	Let us take the road	BF Chorus
				If the heart of a man	MR
2EA8557–1–*2*	11.4.40	C	3161	Youth's the season	MR Chorus
		C	7542	Before the barn door	RG Chorus
				How cruel	LG
2EA8558–1–*2*	12.4.40	C	3162	When you censure	RH JF
		C	7542	Is then his fate	LG
				How happy I could be	MR
				I'm bubbled	AM LG
2EA8559–1–*2*	15.4.40	C	3162	Cease your funning	AM
		C	7541	Why, how now Madam	AM LG
				No power on earth	AM LG RH JF
2EA8560–1–2	11.4.40				
–*3*	12.4.40	C	3163	+Interlude (Austin)	Orchestra
		C	7540	When young at the bar	LG
				I'm like a skiff	LG
2EA8561–1–*2*	11.4.40	C	3163	Thus gamesters united	JF
		C	7539	The modes of the court	BF MR Chorus
				In the days of my youth	AB RH JF
				A curse attends	AM LG
2EA8562–*1*–2	12.4.40	C	3164	Come sweet lass	LG
–3	15.4.40	C	7538	Hither, dear husband	AM LG
				Which way shall I turn	MR RH JF
				The charge is prepared	MR
2EA8563–*1*	11.4.40	C	3164	Dance of the prisoners	Orchestra
		C	7537	Would I might be hanged	AM LG MR
				Finale: Thus I stand	Company & Chorus

+ These two items conducted by Frederic Austin

MATRIX/TAKE	DATE	STRAIGHT NOS/ AUTO NOS	MUSICAL ITEM	SINGERS
2EA8581–1–2	15.4.40	NOT ISSUED	Cease your funning	AM
			Why, how now Madam	LG AM
			No power on earth	AM LG RH JF
2EA8579–1–2	15.4.40	C 3166*	Virgins are like the fair flower	AM
–3	30.4.40			
			Can love be controlled	AM
			I'm like a ship	AM
2EA8580–1–2	15.4.40	C 3166*	Thus when the swallow	AM
			Cease your funning	AM

Original issue
HMV Album Series 340

C 3159–64	(6 12" 78s Straight Coupling)	5.1940
C 7537–42	(6 12" 78s Automatic Coupling)	5.1940

The accompanying booklet contains historical notes and a synopsis by Frederic Austin.

M 17948–53	(USA) (6 12" 78s)
DM 17960–5	(USA) (6 12" 78s)

Re-issue

Pearl GEMM CD 9917	(1 CD – 50'25" [*Beggar's Opera*] Total CD 74'25")	1991

This issue also contains a twenty-four minute medley from *Lionel and Clarissa*. The synopsis and historical notes included are by Charles Haynes, with an extract from a memoir provided by Roy Henderson.

* Original Issue

C 3166	(1 12" 78)	6.1940

The 1939 season at Glyndebourne closed in mid-July with a performance of *Così fan tutte*. It was to be the last staging of an opera there for seven years. Even had it been possible to assemble casts and an orchestra, wartime restrictions would have made it impracticable for opera lovers to travel to Sussex for a performance. By September, the house and parts of the theatre were being used as accommodation for a hundred evacuee children.

In October 1939 Bing had the idea of presenting a new production which could tour to larger British towns and cities, and might also sustain a run of several months in the West End of London. The work chosen was *The Beggar's Opera*, the ballad opera by Pepusch with a text prepared by John Gay in the 1720s. Two hundred years later, in 1920, a London production had been presented at the Lyric Theatre, Hammersmith, in a version by Frederic Austin. It played there for over 1,400 performances. Bing now invited Austin to assist with the Glyndebourne production, directed by John Gielgud, which came to the Haymarket Theatre in March 1940 after a six week provincial tour. A further tour was planned to follow the West End run, but it was cancelled when, after twelve weeks in London, the production closed: the war situation was becoming more serious and Michael Redgrave, who was the main attraction, had to leave the cast to fulfil other commitments. *The Beggar's Opera* was Glyndebourne's only production of the war years. Despite its short run, it was a triumph of Bing's organisational abilities. Three months after the idea was first mooted, the work was prepared, cast, rehearsed and had started its provincial tour.

As early as November 1939 Walter Legge, Artistic Director of The Gramophone Company, approached Bing with an offer to record *The Beggar's Opera* for HMV. His initial proposal was to issue four 78s, comprising just a small proportion of the music, and he hoped to hold the sessions in early March so that the album could be in the shops by Easter. He suggested 8 March as a suitable day for recording, but both on tour and in London the production was dogged by illness and misfortune. Audrey Mildmay caught German measles, Frederic Austin suffered an accident, several members of the chorus fell ill, Constance Willis lost her voice and, most seriously, Michael Redgrave took an extended period of sick leave.

Redgrave returned to the cast just three days before recording began at Abbey Road studios; without him, of course, it would not have taken place at all. For five years he had been establishing himself on stage and in films as a handsome, debonair romantic actor and he proved to be a competent singer in the role of Macheath. John Christie suggested that the contralto Mary Jarred could replace Constance Willis if she was still indisposed, but fortunately Willis recovered in time to take part. The recording sessions finally took place on 11, 12 and 15 April and were conducted by Michael Mudie, who also took charge of most of the London stage performances. Frederic Austin conducted some performances in the theatre and, it seems, two orchestral passages on the records as well. EMI's recording sheets show that both the Overture and the Interlude were conducted by Austin, whilst Mudie took over for the remainder of the music on those sides; however, the record labels do not credit Austin as conductor. John Christie was present at the sessions and was upset by what he felt was Austin's lack of assertiveness with the cast and orchestra. The discipline, he commented, did not come up to the standard required by Glyndebourne – 'It has shown that Glyndebourne at the moment is on thin ice.'

Twelve sides were recorded, (a 50% increase on Legge's original suggestion), which were available in a special album, but they still represented only fifty minutes' worth – about two thirds – of the music from the score of the *The Beggar's Opera*. In addition, Audrey Mildmay made one further record of songs which was not included in the album; confusingly, some of these songs also featured on records in the main set. At Legge's request one side of this solo disc was dubbed on 30 April from sections of the two original takes which had been recorded on 15 April. The issued matrix 2EA 8579-3 was created using the first two songs from the second take and the last song from the first take. Mildmay's test pressings are still at Glyndebourne.

One further matrix number, 2EA 8581, was used during the sessions, (but never issued), consisting of material already recorded. Why it was given a completely different number, and was not simply numbered matrix 2EA 8559 takes 3 and 4 is not clear.

Eight soloists took part in the recording together with fifteen instrumentalists and a small mixed chorus (which recorded only on 11 April). Apart from Redgrave and the Glyndebourne stalwarts Mildmay, Willis and Henderson, Linda Gray and Ruby Gilchrist sang in smaller roles. Gray was formerly a member of the D'Oyly Carte Company and had sung the leading contralto parts in the Gilbert and Sullivan operas after the sudden and tragic death of Bertha Lewis in 1931.

Ruby Gilchrist was the stage name of Mrs Donald Albery, whose husband was for many years a theatre owner and impressario in London, after whom the Albery Theatre was named. The other singers were recruited from the large number who auditioned. Theatrical work was difficult to come by at the beginning of the war and Bing was inundated by letters from both experienced and inexperienced hopefuls alike when news of the production was announced.

The album of six discs was issued in May 1940, three weeks after the recording sessions, and Audrey Mildmay's solo record was released in June; they were on the popular HMV plum label series. Previous Glyndebourne recordings had all been on the cherry label – more expensive and reserved for 'classical' music. The complete recording has never been re-issued by EMI although five numbers were included in Glyndebourne's *Fiftieth Anniversary Album* in 1984. A CD version of the six record set was released by Pearl in 1991, whose insert notes erroneously give the month of recording as January 1940, and indicate the wrong total playing time for *The Beggar's Opera* excerpts. It should be 50'25", not 60'25".

This CD also includes a medley from Charles Dibdin's *Lionel and Clarissa*, from 1925, featuring such singers as Olive Groves and Nigel Playfair; this was not, of course, a Glyndebourne production, but some interest lies in the fact that it was one of the earliest electrical recordings made in the UK. The warning on the CD insert notes that 'inevitably early recordings bear some surface noise' is justified. EMI's transfer of the excerpts for the Fiftieth Anniversary set are impeccably noisy-free, but Pearl's later transfers are not, which sadly detracts from the pleasure they afford.

The issue of *The Beggar's Opera* was greeted with mixed opinions:

The Observer, 26 May 1940:

The beauty of Miss Mildmay's phrasing and articulation is enhanced when one can listen without the uneasiness produced by her conception of Polly as a young woman filled with reverence for Purcell. On the other hand, Michael Redgrave's singing sounds feeble without his actor's skill to bolster it up. More obviously than on the stage, he robs Macheath of character by giving every song the same endearing softness of expression.

Alec Robertson in *The Gramophone*, June 1940:

I have always thought Roy Henderson to excel in music of serious cast, and though he is too good an artist to fail in anything he undertakes, there is hardly a leer in his Peachum, who sounds far from being a thorough-paced double dealing old gentleman. Constance Willis has a good voice . . . and is an experienced artist, but she too is miscast as the bawdy Mrs Peachum . . . her lack of incisive diction and the thin coating of vulgarity painted over an obvious refinement make her a very unconvincing exponent in this rich part . . . and so we come to Macheath and Polly. I had heard adverse criticism of Michael Redgrave but was very agreeably surprised by his performance. He has a voice of pleasant quality, well controlled and his diction puts all the other artists – even Mr Henderson – in the shade. Miss Mildmay sings neatly, prettily and with conscientious art, but somehow failed to charm me.

[3] *The Rape of Lucretia* and *Orfeo ed Euridice*, 1947

1947

THE RAPE OF LUCRETIA

Music by Benjamin Britten

Libretto by Ronald Duncan

Sung in English

Excerpts

Male Chorus	Peter Pears (tenor, English)
Female Chorus	Joan Cross (soprano, English)
Collatinus	Norman Lumsden (bass, English)
Junius	Dennis Dowling (bass, New Zealand)
Tarquinius	Frederick Sharp (bass, English)
Lucretia	Nancy Evans (mezzo-soprano, English)
Bianca	Flora Nielsen (mezzo-soprano, Canadian)
Lucia	Margaret Ritchie (soprano, English)

English Opera Group Chamber Orchestra

Conductor	Reginald Goodall
Recorded for The British Council	Studio No 1, Abbey Road under the supervision of the composer 16–19.7 and 19.10.1947
Mono recording	
Recording Producers	Lawrance Collingwood and David Bicknell
Balance Engineer	Douglas Larter

MATRIX/TAKE	DATE	STRAIGHT NOS/ AUTO NOS		MUSICAL ITEM	SINGERS
2EA12201–1–<u>2</u>	19.7.47	C	3699	Act 1 Sc 1	JC PP
		C	7706	Rome is now ruled	
2EA12193–<u>1</u>–2	17.7.47**	NOT ISSUED ON 78 OR LP		Act 1 Sc 1 Here the thirsty evening	DD NL FS PP
2EA12194–1–<u>2</u>	18.7.47	C	3699	Act 1 Sc 1	DD NL
		C	7707	Lucretia, Lucretia	PP

MATRIX/TAKE	DATE	STRAIGHT NOS/ AUTO NOS		MUSICAL ITEM	SINGERS
2EA12195–*1*–2	18.7.47	C	3700	Act 1 Sc 1	DD NL
		C	7708	With you two	FS
2EA12199–1–*2*	19.7.47	C	3700	Interlude	
		C	7709	Tarquinius does not wait	PP
				Act 1 Sc 2	
				Their spinning wheel	JC
2EA12192–*1*–2	17.7.47	C	3701	Act 1 Sc 2	NE FN
		C	7710	Till in one word	MR JC
2EA12185–1	16.7.47				
–2–3	17.7.47				
–4	19.7.47				
–*5*–6	19.10.47	C	3701	Act 1 Sc 2	NE FN
		C	7711	It is better	MR JC
2EA12186–*1*–2	16.7.47	C	3702	Act 1 Sc 2	NE FN MR
		C	7712	How quiet it is	JC FS PP
2EA12187–1–2	16.7.47				
–3	19.7.47				
–*4*–5	23.12.47*	C	3702	Act 1 Sc 2	NE FN MR
		C	7713	The Etruscan Palace	JC FS PP
2EA12200–1–*2*–3	19.7.47	C	3703	Act 2 Sc 1	JC PP
		C	7713	She sleeps as a rose	
2EA12196–1–*2*	18.7.47	C	3703	Act 2 Sc 1	FS NE
		C	7712	Lucretia! –	JC PP
				What do you want?	
2EA12197–1–2	18.7.47				
–*3*–4	8.10.47+	C	3704	Act 2 Sc 1	FS NE
		C	7711	See how the centaur	JC PP
2EA12188–1–*2*	17.7.47	C	3704	Act 2 Sc 2	FN MR
		C	7710	Oh what a lovely day	
2EA12189–1–2	17.7.47				
–*3*	19.10.47	C	3705	Act 2 Sc 2	NE FN MR
		C	7709	How hideous!	
2EA12190–1–*2*	17.7.47	C	3705	Act 2 Sc 2	NE NL
		C	7708	Too late Junius	
2EA12191–1–2	17.7.47				
–*3*	19.10.47	C	3706	Act 2 Sc 2	NL DD FN
		C	7707	This dead hand	MR JC PP
2EA12198–1–2–3	19.7.47				
–*4*–5	19.10.47	C	3706	Act 2 Sc 2	JC PP
		C	7706	Is all this suffering	

**This excerpt was recorded as a possible alternative to matrix 2EA 12194, which consisted of a different part of the same scene.

*Take *4* was a dubbing made on 23 December 1947 by transferring the first few bars of a pressing of take 2 and the remainder from a pressing of take 1.

+Take *3* was a dubbing made on 8 October 1947 by transferring the first few bars of a pressing of take 1 and the remainder from a pressing of take 2.

Original issue
Record Library Series 419
C 3699–3706	(8 12" 78s Straight Coupling)	3.1948
C 7706–7713	(8 12" 78s Automatic Coupling)	3.1948

This issue includes an explanatory booklet with a synopsis and musical examples.

Victor 12 0778–0785   (USA) (8 12" 78s)

Re–issues
MFP 2119	(1 12" LP)	5.1969

EMI CD CMS7 64727–2   (2 CD set) *The Rape of Lucretia* – Abridged recording of the revised version (1947): Scenes from *Peter Grimes*: and folk song arrangements – the complete early HMV and Decca recordings. [*Lucretia* excerpts 73'52"] 79'22"/76'36"   11.1993
The accompanying 60 page booklet contains essays by John Lucas, Eric Crozier and Philip Reed, reminiscences by Nancy Evans and Eric Crozier, a synopsis of *The Rape of Lucretia* and texts of the operatic scenes.

By the time that Glyndebourne re-opened in July 1946, with the première of Benjamin Britten's new opera *The Rape of Lucretia*, thought had already been given to making complete or abridged recordings of Glyndebourne productions. As early as October 1945, Sir Thomas Beecham had recommended to Rudolf Bing that Glyndebourne might consider approaching the Victor Company in the USA, because that company had a large worldwide distribution network – better, perhaps, than HMV's. Beecham felt this proposed relationship would be more successful commercially than continuing to record with The Gramophone Company, and suggested that *Carmen* or even a new *Figaro* might be recorded. These were two operas that had been discussed for possible production at Glyndebourne in 1946, with Beecham taking charge of the musical direction. Eventually, after falling out with Christie and Bing over casting suggestions, Beecham lost interest in the projects. He conducted Strauss's *Ariadne auf Naxos* for Glyndebourne at the 1950 Edinburgh Festival, but he never conducted opera in Sussex. In 1960 plans were made for him to conduct there and record *Die Zauberflöte*, but these never came to fruition either, because of the onset of the illness which led to his death in March 1961.

The Rape of Lucretia* was first performed on 12 July 1946, but even before the première, David Bicknell had written to Bing expressing great interest in making a recording of the new opera, either complete or abridged. Bing definitely preferred the former possibility. Naturally, Britten was also keen for a recording to be made and suggested that Bicknell and Lawrance Colling-wood, of the Artistes' Department at HMV, should visit Glyndebourne for discussions. Bicknell, particularly, was keen to renew the pre-war relationship that had proved so successful for both Glyndebourne and HMV.

The opera was performed with a double cast. Kathleen Ferrier sang Lucretia in the 'first cast' and Nancy Evans in the 'second'. Similarly, Peter Pears was the Male Chorus in the 'first' and Aksel Schiøtz in the 'second'. The two casts performed more or less alternately on alternate nights, both at Glyndebourne and on the subsequent tour of Britain and Holland. From time to time a member of one cast would sing his or her role with the other, making it a truly interchangeable opera. Which cast should be recorded? It was left to Britten to select the singers he preferred and a memo from Bicknell dated 27 June 1946 indicated that the composer's preference was for the first cast, with the exception of Frederick Sharp who would replace Edmund Donlevy as Junius in the recording.

It soon became clear that some of the singers Britten preferred would not be able to record for HMV. Peter Pears had been contracted to Decca for some time and in February 1946 Kathleen Ferrier had also joined Decca's ranks; she would not be free until October 1947 at the earliest. Ernest Ansermet, Swiss conductor of the first performance, was also a Decca artist, and it was evident that if the recording was to be made in the near future, ideas of using these three musicians would have to be forgotten. Britten seemed prepared to wait, as was HMV. Britten respected Ansermet and admired his understanding of the score; Ansermet seemed to like Britten, if finding him humourless. In his imperfect English, he confided to a Glyndebourne colleague that what Britten needed was ' . . . a little joke then and now. Yes, very sometimes.'

To add to the confusion, Decca wrote to Bing saying that *they* wanted to make a recording of *Lucretia*. As they had two leading singers and the conductor under contract, it might have been the best solution, but Bing replied that negotiations with 'another company' were already too far advanced to change now. After further correspondence, HMV offered to record *Lucretia* in an abridged form on four or five 78s with Nancy Evans (as Lucretia) and Peter Pears, who would be free from contractual obligations by the beginning of 1947. Bing was furious. He insisted that the opera be recorded complete, even if it meant waiting longer to do so. The eventual outcome was unsatisfactory from several points of view.

The Rape of Lucretia was finally recorded in an abridged form on eight 12" 78s in July and October 1947. Not only was it incomplete, but it lacked both the conductor and the contralto lead for whom Britten had expressed a preference in 1946. It was not issued until March 1948, by which time most of its topicality was lost.

The July sessions at Abbey Road took place immediately after three performances at Glyndebourne, but with a somewhat different cast. By this time the performances were under the control of the English Opera Group, which had been founded by Britten, Eric Crozier and John Piper. In 1947 Glyndebourne was simply the venue for the performances; it was no longer a Glyndebourne production as it had been in 1946. The English Opera Group had bought the scenery and costumes from Glyndebourne, and the work has never been performed there since. The single day of recording in October 1947 was the Sunday following three performances of the opera given by the EOG at Covent Garden, with a cast that included some of the singers on the recording. Four sides were re-recorded, requiring seven of the eight singers who appear in the opera; obviously the takes recorded in July had proved unsatisfactory.

Technical work on two of the July sides was also needed before release. Dubbing excerpts from two previously recorded sides on to a new wax was by no means unusual. Although it generally created a better side *artistically*, the sound quality was often markedly inferior. This was less likely to be heard on the playback equipment of the day, but with modern digital techniques for transferring 78s to CD the deterioration is usually more obvious.

In addition, one side was recorded on 17 July which was never issued. It consisted of music from Act 1 Scene 1, and was made as a possible alternative to matrix 2EA 12194. What the merits were of the one side over the other is not noted in the archives. The metalwork and EMI's test pressings of this matrix were destroyed several years after the other records were released.

Financial help for the recording was given by The British Council as HMV were seriously concerned about the commercial viability of the project. The Chairman of the British Council's Music Committee, Arthur Bliss, warned that the recording would only be supported if the opera were abridged to about half its length, but the compromise of sixteen sides was reached, representing appreciably more than half the music. So the project that started as an official Glyndebourne recording was, finally, no such thing. No mention is made on the record labels of Glyndebourne; the credits simply read *The English Opera Group*, and the sponsorship given by The British Council is acknowledged.

This set is most important historically, a creators' record indeed. It was the first recording of a Britten opera (even incomplete), and although not conducted by the composer, he was present at, and supervised, the sessions. Of its cast, three members appeared in the very first performance, (Pears, Cross and Ritchie) and three in the second (Nielsen, Evans and Sharp, although Sharp and Nielsen took different roles on the recording). The Collatinus, Norman Lumsden, has achieved new fame more recently as J R Hartley the fly-fishing expert in a television advertisement for *Yellow Pages*. As a singer he appeared with distinction in concerts and opera from the 1940s to the 1960s and created the role of Quince in Britten's *A Midsummer Night's Dream*. Dennis

Dowling, the Junius, was for many years a greatly admired member of the Sadler's Wells and English National Opera Companies.

The conductor, Reginald Goodall, took charge of several performances of the opera in both 1946 and 1947 at Glyndebourne and on tour; in July 1948 he conducted the first recording of excerpts of Britten's *Peter Grimes* for Columbia, an even more ill-fated project, which was never issued on 78s at all.

These excerpts of *The Rape of Lucretia* have been re-issued once on LP, in 1969, and three brief sections were included on the Glyndebourne *Fiftieth Anniversary Album* in 1984. Happily the recording has just appeared again, on CD, as part of a double set with Goodall's *Peter Grimes* excerpts and a selection of folk songs accompanied by Benjamin Britten. By great good fortune, a test pressing of take 1 of the previously unissued matrix 2EA 12193 has been traced in a private collection and is included on the CD.

Alec Robertson in *The Gramophone*, March 1948:

I was very glad to find the Chorus sung, in this recording, by Joan Cross and Peter Pears, who created the parts; . . . Peter Pears' excellent diction and feeling for words make every moment of his important part clear and intelligible . . . Dennis Dowling gives an outstanding performance as Junius. He has an admirable voice and can put a wealth of meaning into it. The others are excellent , although Norman Lumsden is never quite easy on his top notes. The duet between Junius and Tarquinius (side 3) is vividly realised and Junius' soft insinuations are enormously effective. . . On side 12 we have the 'lovely morning' scene. . . The florid duet is very well sung by Margaret Ritchie and Flora Neilsen [sic] and the eager rapture of Miss Ritchie's singing in particular carries the scene off successfully. Nancy Evans, whose Lucretia has been consistently good, fails to convince one in her outburst of hysteria (side 13) but both she and Miss Neilsen sing their two short arias, following on this, very well. . . Both the recording and the presentation of this opera are very well done. . . I should add a word of praise here for Reginald Goodall's fine handling of the orchestra, under the supervision of the composer.

Andrew Porter in *Record Review*, July 1969 (reviewing the LP re-issue):

Though some vital passages – notably Tarquin's address to the sleeping Lucretia and Lucretia's death scene – are missing, most of the opera's finest music is here; and the transfer to LP has been well made. Moreover, the cast is led by Joan Cross and Peter Pears, incomparable in the two chorus parts: to have this extended representation of Joan Cross in one of the major roles which Britten composed for her is specially valuable. . . The original Lucretia was Kathleen Ferrier but on this recording Nancy

Evans, who led the alternate cast of the Lucretia 'company' which was formed at Glyndebourne in 1946 . . . takes the title role: there is a ladylike quality about Miss Evans's enunciation which tends to draw attention to the more embarrassing aspects of the librettist's diction, but her singing is sensitive and the sound is good.

1947

ORFEO ED EURIDICE

Music by Christoph Willibald von Gluck

Libretto by Raniero de Calzabigi

Sung in Italian

Concise version

Orfeo	Kathleen Ferrier (contralto, English)
Euridice	Ann Ayars (soprano, American)
Amor	Zoë Vlachopoulos (soprano, Greek)

Glyndebourne Festival Chorus	Chorus Master Berthold Goldschmidt
Southern Philharmonic Orchestra	Leader David Martin

Conductor	Fritz Stiedry

Recorded	Kingsway Hall, London
	22, 23 and 29.6.1947
Mono recording	

Recording Producer	Harry Sarton
Balance Engineer	Arthur Haddy

MATRIX/TAKE	DATE	STRAIGHT NOS/ AUTO NOS		MUSICAL ITEM	SINGERS
Act 1					
AR 11392–_1_–2	22.6.47	K	1656	Ah se intorno	Chorus
		AK	1656	Euridice!	KF
				Amici, quel lamento	KF
AR 11393–1–_2_	22.6.47	K	1656	Ritornello	Orchestra
		AK	1657	Euridice!	KF
				Piango il mio ben	KF
				Io saprò	KF
AR11394–1–2–_3_	22.6.47	K	1657	Amore assisterà	ZV
		AK	1658	Della cetra	ZV KF
				Ascolta	ZV
				Che disse!	KF

MATRIX/TAKE	DATE	STRAIGHT NOS/ AUTO NOS		MUSICAL ITEM	SINGERS
Act 2					
AR 11395–*1*–2	22.6.47	K AK	1657 1659	Chaconne Ballet	Orchestra Orchestra
AR 11396–*1*–2	22.6.47	K AK	1658 1660	Chi mai dell'Erebo Deh! Placatevi	Chorus KF
AR 11397–*1*–2	22.6.47	K AK	1658 1661	Misero giovane Mile pene Men tiranne	Chorus KF Chorus KF Chorus
AR 11398–*1*–2	23.6.47	K AK	1659 1662	Dance of the Blessed Spirits E quest'asile	Orchestra AA Chorus
AR 11399–*1*–2	23.6.47	K AK	1659 1662	Che puro ciel!	KF Chorus
AR 11400–1–*2*	23.6.47	K AK	1660 1661	Vieni a regni	KF AA
Act 3					
				Ah vieni, o diletta Si, or il passo	KF AA KF AA
AR 11401–*1*–2	23.6.47	K AK	1660 1660	Sol uno sguardo Vieni, vieni con me	KF AA KF AA
AR 11402–*1*–2	29.6.47	K AK	1661 1659	Ah, potess'io Che fiero Avezzo al contento/ Qual dolor	AA AA KF AA KF
AR 11403–1–*2*	29.6.47	K AK	1661 1658	Ah! Per me il duol Qual pena Che feci mai Che farò	KF AA KF AA KF KF
AR 11404–1–*2*	29.6.47	K AK	1662 1657	Ah! Finisca Non più Frena, frena Usciam di qua Trionfi Amore	KF ZV KF ZV KF AA ZV ZV KF AA Chorus
AR 11405–1–*2*	29.6.47	K AK	1662 1656	Gaudio, gaudio Trionfi Amore	KF AA ZV Chorus

Original issue

Decca K 1656–62	(7 12" 78s Straight Coupling)		12.1947
Decca AK 1656–62	(7 12" 78s Automatic Coupling)		12.1947

Re–issues

Decca LXT 2898	(1 12" LP)	2.1954
Decca ACL 293	(1 12" LP)	11.1966
Decca 417 182–1DM	(1 12" LP)	5.1986
Decca 417 182–4DM	(1 cassette)	5.1986

Decca 433 468–2DM	(1 CD – 54'01")	4.1992

Includes a booklet containing a brief history of Ferrier's life and career by Maurice Leonard in English, French, German and Italian; a resumé of the story and the text in Italian and English, translated by Kenneth Chalmers.

London LLP 924	(USA) (12" LP)
London 5103	(USA) (12" LP)
London 433 468–2LM	(USA) (1 CD)

Excerpts
Che puro ciel

Decca LW 5225	(1 10" LP)	3.1956
Decca PA 172	(1 12" LP)	10.1971
Decca KCSP 172	(1 cassette)	6.1972
Decca ECSP 172	(1 stereo 8 cartridge)	9.1973
London LD 9229	(USA) (1 10" LP)	

The 1947 Glyndebourne season opened with a new production of Gluck's *Orfeo ed Euridice*, mounted especially for the contralto Kathleen Ferrier, who had enjoyed great success as Lucretia the previous year. As she was already contracted to Decca, there was no problem about her availability to record *Orfeo* for them; thus Decca were able to issue their only Glyndebourne recording in the sixty year history of the Festival. (Cavalli's *La Calisto*, released on Argo Records in 1972 was re-issued on Decca CDs in 1993, but the *Orfeo* from 1947 remains unique as an original Decca label recording.)

Ernest Ansermet, the conductor of the première of *The Rape of Lucretia* was contracted to take charge of all three operas being given during the 1947 Glyndebourne Festival. As well as *Orfeo*, there were to be performances of *The Rape of Lucretia* and *Albert Herring*. The latter was a new opera by Britten which received its world première on 20 June 1947. Only *Orfeo* was a true Glyndebourne production; the other two were *at* Glyndebourne under the control of the English Opera Group. By early March, Ansermet had cancelled, and Fritz Stiedry, the Viennese conductor who had made his home in the United States, was booked to take charge of *Orfeo*.

About Ferrier's appearance there was no doubt. It was to be her first appearance in a staged production of *Orfeo*. However, the two characters, Euridice and Amor were not easily cast and various singers were mentioned by Stiedry as suitable for the roles. Jarmila Novotna, the Czech soprano, was strongly recommended, but finally a young American, Ann Ayars, was cast as Euridice and a virtually unknown Greek soporano Zoë Vlachopoulos in the role of Amor. Ayars returned to sing Zerlina in the Glyndebourne production of *Don Giovanni* at the 1948 Edinburgh Festival, but Vlachopoulos never appeared with the Company again.

The version of *Orfeo* that Stiedry proposed conducting was, in his own word, the '*usual*' one, printed by Peters, edited by Dorffel. It is a blend of the Italian version for alto and the later French version for a high tenor Orfeo. 'In only one place I propose to use the old Italian version' wrote Stiedry, 'in the big C Major aria of Orfeo. It is longer than the version in French.' Stiedry was not, at least on this occasion, an easy man to work with. Ferrier, particularly, was upset by his attitude; he was impatient during rehearsals and more than once he insisted that she learn new words after he decided to alter the standard libretto. As this was her first experience of singing Italian, she found these demands increasingly annoying. A happier rapport was established with the Italian language coach, Renato Cellini; his help with the text was much appreciated by all the cast.

In May, shortly before the start of rehearsals, there were discussions between Bing, Stiedry and Decca about condensing the opera for a proposed recording. The plan was for the work to be issued on six 12" 78s (although this was increased to seven in the published set), but in creating a 'concise' version it was hoped to maintain the dramatic flow, rather than simply cutting whole sections and including only the big set pieces of the opera. Approximately an hour's music was to be recorded in this way – two thirds of the score. Three days after the first performance, recording started in Kingsway Hall, London, but a memo from Rudolf Bing to the cast only ten days earlier specifically mentions Decca's own studio in Broadhurst Gardens, West Hampstead. Either he was in error, or Decca realised at the last moment that the large chorus and orchestra could not be accommodated comfortably in the studio. Kingsway Hall had for many years been used by several companies for large scale works and continued to be an important recording venue until the early 1980s.

Orfeo was recorded on days when it was not being performed at Glyndebourne – two Sundays and a Monday. For Glyndebourne's and Decca's purposes the orchestra was called the Southern Philharmonic; it was, in fact, the Brighton Philharmonic, working under a temporarily assumed name.

Ferrier was invited to return to Glyndebourne to sing Orfeo again, but she always refused. Another invitation was to sing Ulrica in Glyndebourne's *Un ballo in maschera* at the 1949 Edinburgh Festival. She wrote that she didn't mind singing the role of a gipsy witch, but the part lay too high for her. Ferrier was never happy appearing in opera, finding it an unnatural medium, and was always more comfortable on the concert platform. In 1949 she wrote to a friend: ' . . . I think I'm lousy on stage. Can cope with expressing sorrow, happiness and fright on me old dial, but, oh! my large extremities! I fall upstairs, downstairs, even over my own feet . . . '

After its initial release on seven 78s, *Orfeo* did not appear on LP until February 1954. In that format it did not include all the music that had been issued on the original set. The orchestral section of the original fourth side was omitted, as was the whole of side seven and the chorus on side thirteen. Thus listeners have been deprived not only of a quantity of orchestral music, but also of Ann Ayars singing *Quest 'asilo* from Act 2. Even on Decca's most recent re-issue of this recording, (and it has been re-issued five times since 1947), as part of the ten CD set which commemorated the eightieth anniversary of Ferrier's birth, the absent parts have not been restored – a case of a good opportunity regrettably missed.

Critical comment after *Orfeo's* release in December 1947 generally approved of Ferrier's performance, but deplored unsatisfactory sound quality.

John Amis, writing in *The Tribune* on 28 November 1947 noted:

Emphatically, you can't rush disc-making, which I believe is what Decca have done with their concise version of *Orfeo*. For the recording is not up to standard, the acoustics are far from perfect, there is occasional shoddy playing, and there is someone humming very audibly on several sides (probably the conductor). . . But even so we must be grateful to Decca, for *Orfeo* is one of the world's finest operas, by a composer who is revered but rarely played. What a joy this set will be for someone hearing it for the first time, with those haunting recitatives and that fund of wonderful melodies. . . Final verdict: hear before buying.

The Times, 9 December 1947:

The chief merit of the concise edition on records is the glorious singing of Miss Kathleen Ferrier as Orpheus and the very attractive boyish voice of Miss Zoë Vlachopoulos as Amor. . . Mr Fritz Stiedry's tempi will provoke disagreement as they did at Glyndebourne in the summer. *Che farò* for instance is too fast, and a certain lack of sympathy with the music as Gluck wrote it may be detected again now and then.

1947–8

MACBETH

Music by Giuseppe Verdi

Libretto by Francesco Piave and Andrea Maffei

Sung in Italian

Two scenes

Lady Macbeth	Margherita Grandi (soprano, Tasmanian)
The Doctor	Ernest Frank (baritone, English)
Lady-in-Waiting	Vera Terry (soprano, Australian)

Royal Philharmonic Orchestra

Conductor   Sir Thomas Beecham

Recorded   Studio No 1, Abbey Road
                                             29.9.1947 and *16.1.1948
Mono recording

Recording Producer   Lawrance Collingwood
Balance Engineer   Arthur Clarke and *Douglas Larter

MATRIX/TAKE	DATE	RECORD NOS	MUSICAL ITEM	SINGERS
2EA12341–1–2	29.9.47			
–3–_4_	16.1.48	DB 6739	Vegliammo invan	EF VT
2EA12328–1–2	29.9.47			
3–_4_	16.1.48	DB 6739	Eccola!-Un lume	MG EF VT
2EA12329–1–2	29.9.47			
–3–_4_	16.1.48	DB 6740	Di sangue umano	MG EF VT
2EA12330–_1_–2	29.9.47	DB 6740	La luce langue	MG

Original issue
DB 6739–40   (2 12" 78s)   9.1948

Re–issues
Sir Thomas Beecham – A Musical Biography
A Centenary Tribute

Vegliammo invan   (The entire scene comprising the three original 78
                                sides.)
WRC SHB 100   (8 12" LP set Record No SH 1004)   5.1979
The set includes a hardback biographical tribute by Alan Jefferson.

Les introuvables du chant Verdien
Una macchia   (part of the second side and all the third side of the
                                Act 4 excerpt)
EMI 2910763   (1 12" LP included in an 8 Record Set
                                with an illustrated booklet included)

Glyndebourne's operatic activities in 1947 were not restricted to performances
in Sussex; two further operas, *Le nozze di Figaro* and *Macbeth* were seen at the
Edinburgh International Festival, which was in the first year of its existence, and
which Rudolf Bing, as Glyndebourne's General Manager, had helped to found.
    Carl Ebert had produced the first professional English performance of
Macbeth at Glyndebourne in 1938, conducted by Fritz Busch. The following
year the leading singers were the baritone Francesco Valentino as Macbeth

and Margherita Grandi as his Lady. Now, eight years later, they re-joined the Company and gave nine performances of the opera.

Rudolf Bing approached David Bicknell in May 1947 and suggested recording *Macbeth*. Bicknell had doubts, and replied that it would be impractical to record the opera complete, or even large extracts, but that individual scenes would certainly be suitable. Lawrance Collingwood was deputed to examine the score and suggest the best sections.

Two weeks before the Edinburgh Festival performances were due to open the conductor George Szell cancelled and the Italian Tullio Serafin was expected to replace him; he did not appear either and so Berthold Goldschmidt, the Chorus Master at Glyndebourne, took over. It may have been the lack of a big-name conductor that finally thwarted plans for extracts to be recorded under the Glyndebourne banner. The curse of *Macbeth* seemed to be at work. It was not the last time that plans for a Glyndebourne recording of this wonderful Verdi opera came unstuck at the last minute.

Bicknell was not going to allow the finest Lady Macbeth of the day to slip away without recording at least part of her role, and booked a session for Grandi on 29 September at Abbey Road with the Royal Philharmonic Orchestra under Sir Thomas Beecham. Two items were to be recorded for HMV – *La luce langue* from Act 2 and the 'Sleepwalking Scene' from Act 4, but despite the precaution of two takes being made of each side (one side was required for the former aria and three for the latter), things did not go well.

Writing to Audrey Christie at the end of October, Bicknell acknowledged that one side of *Macbeth* would have to be repeated. Although he did not specify which it was, it may be reasonably assumed to be the last side of the 'Sleepwalking Scene', with its taxing high D flat as Lady Macbeth makes her final exit. In her performances in 1939, and in Edinburgh, Grandi had used the services of another, off-stage, soprano to sing this note, and she would certainly need them for the recording.

On 16 January 1948 two more takes were made of each side of the 'Sleepwalking Scene', with a soprano and a baritone in the roles of the Lady in Waiting and the Doctor; Vera Terry had sung the former part in Glyndebourne's Edinburgh performances. The additional soprano who provided the final note for Grandi's exit was Dorothy Bond. She sang, as did Grandi, on the soundtrack of the Powell and Pressburger film *The Tales of Hoffmann* three years later. (It, too, was conducted by Beecham.) For her contribution to the recording Bond's fee was ten guineas, surely a rate of pay per note that would be the envy of many a soprano today.

From the non-consecutive matrix numbers, it may be inferred that HMV's original intention was to begin the 'Sleepwalking Scene' with what is now the second side. Perhaps it was only after recording two sides and the Act 2 aria that Lawrance Collingwood felt that the first part of the scene should be added; but by that time the next ten matrix numbers had been already been used for other waxes.

These recordings are two of the very few made of Beecham conducting Italian opera, and the complete 'Sleepwalking Scene' was included on a World Record Club centenary tribute to him in 1979, as a representative example of his work in the genre. Part of the scene was also included on a French EMI issue *Les Introuvables du Chant Verdien*. All of the first side and part of the second were omitted on this French release as the first side consists of orchestral introduction and a brief exchange between the Doctor and the Lady in Waiting. Lady Macbeth herself does not sing until well into the second side of the recording. These fragments of what might have been Glyndebourne's recording of *Macbeth* remain among the most effective and dramatic interpretations of the scenes from the opera; and the seamless change from Grandi to Bond in Act 4 has to be heard to be believed.

Alec Robertson in *The Gramophone*, October 1948:

I wish some attempt had been made to give the [Sleepwalking] scene its proper perspective, for the spectators and Lady Macbeth are all heard singing on the same plane and the Doctor in particular, once or twice ignores the injunction, which he should know, that it is dangerous to wake up a sleepwalker! How much more effective it would have been if the two spectators had whispered their comments. The vivid accompaniment, which suggests the washing of her guilty hands, is finely played and at all times the balance with the voice is excellent. On the third [and last side] Margherita Grandi, who possesses the dark tones, especially in the lower part of the voice that really do convey a sense of evil and tragedy, rises to the height of the occasion and her intonation is all it should be. . .

The reading of the second act aria *La luce langue* is very good and Signora Grandi is splendid throughout. . . The quality of the orchestral playing and its recording is so superb that the discs are worth buying for them alone.

[4]   Mozart Highlights

Così fan tutte, 1950 *and Idomeneo*, 1951

COSÌ FAN TUTTE

Music by Wolfgang Amadeus Mozart

Libretto by Lorenzo da Ponte

Sung in Italian

Excerpts

Ferrando	Richard Lewis (tenor, English)
Guglielmo	Erich Kunz (baritone, Austrian)
Don Alfonso	Mario Boriello (baritone, Italian)
Fiordiligi	Sena Jurinac (soprano, Yugoslav)
Dorabella	Blanche Thebom (mezzo-soprano, American)

Glyndebourne Festival Orchestra

Conductor	Fritz Busch
Recorded	Glyndebourne theatre
	12, 14 and 15.7.1950
Mono recording	
Recording Producer	Lawrance Collingwood
Balance Engineer	Douglas Larter

MATRIX/TAKE	DATE	ISSUE NOS	ISSUE DATE	MUSICAL ITEM	SINGERS
Act 1					
2EA 14958–1A–*1B*	12.7.50	DB 21115	6.51	La mia Dorabella Fuor la spada E la fede	RL EK MB
2EA 14959–*1A*	12.7.50	DB 21115	6.51	Scioccherie di poeti! Una bella serenata	RL EK MB
2EA 14960–1A–*1B*	14.7.50	DB 21116	1.53	Ah guarda sorella	SJ BT

MATRIX/TAKE	DATE	ISSUE NOS	ISSUE DATE	MUSICAL ITEM	SINGERS
2EA 14961–*1A*	14.7.50	DB 21117	10.50	Sento o Dio	RL EK MB SJ BT
2EA 14962–*1A*	14.7.50	DB 21117	10.50	Non v'è più Di scrivermi	RL EK MB SJ BT
2EA 14963–*1A*	14.7.50	DB 21118	3.51	Dove son? Soave sia il vento	MB SJ BT
2EA 14964–*1A*	15.7.50	DB 21118	3.51	Come scoglio	SJ

Act 2

MATRIX/TAKE	DATE	ISSUE NOS	ISSUE DATE	MUSICAL ITEM	SINGERS
2EA 14965–*1A*	15.7.50	DB 21119	12.50	Dunque fa Prenderò quel	SJ BT
2EA14966–1A–*1B*	15.7.50	DB 21119	12.50	Questa picciola Il core vi dono	EK BT
2EA 14967–*1A*	12.7.50	DB 21120	10.51	Ei parte Per pietà (Pt 1)	SJ
2EA 14968–*1A*	12.7.50	DB 21120	10.51	Per pietà (Pt 2)	SJ
2EA 14969–*1A*	15.7.50	DB 21116	1.53	Fra gli amplessi	RL SJ

Original issue
HMV numbers and dates as above.
Victor 12 3177–3182   (USA) (6 12" 78s)
Victor LM 1126   (USA) (1 12" LP)

Re–issue
WRC SH 397   (1 12" LP)   10.1981

Excerpts
Ah guarda, sorella – Come scoglio – Ei parte . . . Per pietà
EMI CDH7 63199–2   (1 CD-78'00")   11.1989

1950

COSÌ FAN TUTTE

Despina   Alda Noni (soprano, Italian)

MATRIX/TAKE	DATE	RECORD NOS	ISSUE DATE	MUSICAL ITEM
0EA 15018–*1*	22.9.50	DA 1986	7.51	In uomini, in soldati
0EA 15019–*1*	22.9.50	DA 1986	7.51	Una donna a quindicianni

UN BALLO IN MASCHERA

Music by Giuseppe Verdi

Oscar   Alda Noni

MATRIX/TAKE	DATE	RECORD NOS	ISSUE DATE	MUSICAL ITEM
0EA15020–*1*–2	22.9.50	DA 1954	12.50	Volta la terrea
0EA15021–*1*-2	22.9.50	DA 1954	12.50	Saper vorreste

Philharmonia Orchestra

Conductor   Walter Susskind

Recorded   Studio No 1, Abbey Road
                                   22.9.1950
Mono recording

Recording Producer   Unknown
Balance Engineer   Douglas Larter

Original issue
See details above.   (2 10" 78s)

In 1950 Glyndebourne was finally re-established on its pre-war basis. Two operas were presented in July in Sussex and two further productions were performed at the Edinburgh Festival. Thus, three operas by Mozart and one by Richard Strauss were given that summer and it was David Bicknell's firm intention that at least one of them would be recorded. No recording under the Glyndebourne banner had been made by HMV since *The Beggar's Opera* in 1940 and the opportunity of capturing on disc a well rehearsed ensemble of the quality of most of Glyndebourne's casts was not to be ignored.

Moran Caplat had joined Glyndebourne in 1946 as assistant to Rudolf Bing, the General Manager. When Bing left Britain for New York in 1949 to become General Manager of the Metropolitan Opera, Caplat succeeded him and remained in the post until 1981. Bicknell and Caplat became good friends, each with a natural understanding of the responsibilities and capabilities of the other. It was very largely due to the creative relationship that developed between these two men that HMV's fine recordings of Glyndebourne productions were made during the 1950s and early 1960s.

In February 1950 Caplat wrote to Bicknell with the news that Decca were planning to record *Die Entführung aus dem Serail* in Vienna with Endre Koréh, Glyndebourne's Osmin. Would that mean that The Gramophone Company would not think of recording it? After all, Koréh's contract would undoubtedly prevent him from singing the role for another recording company in the near future. Or might Decca be persuaded to change their minds and leave it to HMV to record the opera with the Glyndebourne Company?

Decca were not to be persuaded and the idea of that recording was soon forgotten; but on 3 July 1950 Bicknell wrote to Caplat, suggesting that HMV record excerpts from *Così fan tutte*, the other opera being performed in Sussex that season. It had a fine cast of singers; the Yugoslav Sena Jurinac; the Italian soprano Alda Noni; the tenor Richard Lewis and baritone Erich Kunz, all of whom had sung in Glyndebourne productions in Edinburgh in previous years. New to Glyndebourne were the American mezzo Blanche Thebom and the baritone Mario Boriello. At some performances, a young Welsh singer took over from Kunz as Guglielmo – Geraint Evans – but his name was not mentioned in connection with the recording. It was his first Glyndebourne season and he was very much the new man. Kunz was the established celebrity, thirteen years Evans' senior. The orchestra was the Royal Philharmonic, which played for Glyndebourne performances between 1948 and 1963. However, when recording Glyndebourne productions during the 1950s it was invariably known as Glyndebourne Festival Orchestra, and it was only with the 1962 recording of *Il barbiere di Siviglia* that it reverted to its real name.

Bicknell's suggestion was that excerpts should be recorded in the theatre itself. The recording van would drive down to Glyndebourne, as it had done before the war, but now tape would be used rather than waxes, allowing flexibility in editing. Bicknell had reservations about Alda Noni: '. . . I have omitted the Despina arias because they are not musically outstanding, and I do not believe that Noni will make very good records, excellent though she may be in the Opera House, and Kunz's arias because he has a Columbia contract, and I have been asked only to record him in concerted numbers, as he will probably record the solos later on in Vienna. . .' but with Jurinac's solos, several duets and concerted pieces, it would be easy to make twelve good sides. Apart from these excerpts of *Così*, Thebom had a busy time recording during her stay in England. RCA Victor commissioned The Gramophone Company to record six sessions with her at Abbey Road between 10 and 24 July 1950, which resulted in some fine discs including a luscious *Mon coeur s'ouvre à ta voix* from *Samson et Dalila*. Indeed, while her colleagues were recording parts of *Così* without her at Glyndebourne on 12 July, she was at Abbey Road making solo records for RCA.

The sessions took place at Glyndebourne on the mornings of 12, 14 and 15 July, days when *Così fan tutte* was not being performed. It was important, of course, that the day's recording was completed and all the equipment cleared away well before the audience for that evening's performance arrived. A piano was used to accompany the recitatives, but for the recording of excerpts from *Idomeneo* the following year Busch progressed to the stylistically preferable harpsichord; unfortunately two small cuts were made in order to accommodate the duet *Fra gli amplessi* on one 78 rpm side, but of some compensation is the horn playing of Dennis Brain, who accompanied Jurinac in her aria *Per pietà*.

On 28 July Busch visited Abbey Road to select the tape takes that he preferred; these were then transferred to wax during August and September and the matrices were prepared. The six 12" 78s were given consecutive issue numbers but were released over a frustratingly long period of time. The first appeared in October 1950 and consisted of *Sento, o Dio* and *Non v'è più – Di scrivermi*, featuring all five singers. The last was issued in January 1953, by which time one record of the 1951 *Idomeneo* had already been released. The complete set of twelve sides of *Così* was re-issued on a World Record Club LP in October 1981, an excerpt having been included on Glyndebourne's Twenty-Fifth Anniversary album in 1959. Two different selections were included on the Fiftieth Anniversary set in 1984 – the trio *Soave sia il vento* from Act 1 and the duet *Prenderò quel brunettino* from Act 2. It is a pity that these recordings have not enjoyed wider circulation, for they contain some lovely singing; but they remain overshadowed by the earlier complete version which has been re-issued on LP and CD.

Excerpts are seldom satisfactory and are often greeted with the call for a complete performance. That, certainly, is what happened in the case of *Idomeneo*, Busch's swan-song, recorded in 1951. To those he left behind it became something of a millstone.

Bicknell clearly had second thoughts about his comments on the recording quality of Alda Noni's voice, and when she returned to sing in London in September 1950, her request to record four arias from her repertoire was granted. Although these are not Glyndebourne recordings, (they were made with Walter Susskind and the Philharmonia Orchestra), they are of roles Noni sang in Glyndebourne productions – Oscar in *Un ballo in maschera* and Despina in *Così fan tutte*. The fact that they were released before some of the offical *Così* sides, from which she was excluded, may have given her some satisfaction.

Alec Robertson in *The Gramophone*, October 1950, reviewing DB 21117:

The adorable music is sung superbly by all concerned, but particularly by Sena Jurinac who has rapidly graduated from Dorabella to Fiordiligi to the astonishment of the snobs in Vienna. She has a rising phrase in the second quintet that is almost identical with one in Mozart's *Ave Verum* and I cannot imagine it more beautifully sung. My criticisms are that the baritone and bass do not tell sufficiently in the concerted portions of *Sento, o Dio!* and that one would not guess that these portions are directed to be sung sotto voce by all concerned. Other than that the recording is a sheer delight.

Alec Robertson in *The Gramophone*, March 1951, reviewing DB 21118:

Sena Jurinac gives a virtuoso performance of the difficult aria and it is not her fault if the highest notes have a tendency to blast. The trio, in which Dorabella, Fiordiligi and Don Alfonso pray for gentle winds and a calm sea is exquisitely done and very well recorded. Busch's accompaniment is perfection.

Alec Robertson in *The Gramophone*, January 1953, reviewing DB 21116:

The duet is very well sung, the only small defects being the too faintly recorded orchestral accompaniment (though the bassoons are clearly heard) and the slight unsteadiness of Blanche Thebom's florid phrases compared with those sung earlier by Sena Jurinac. Both artists are 'come scoglii' (firm as rocks) on the sustained notes each has in the Allegro and Jurinac negotiates her numerous high As very sweetly and is excellently recorded.

Alec Robertson in *The Gramophone*, July 1951, reviewing DA 1986:

In the first aria *In uomini*, taken at too quick a tempo, Alda Noni seems a little breathless and not pert enough. . . The second aria goes much better and although it, too, could be more saucy, the singer does get more characterisation into it. The really excellent thing here is the playing of the Philharmonia Orchestra under Susskind, which is not only very well recorded but surpasses the playing on the Glyndebourne records.

Well before the start of the 1951 season Bicknell and Caplat corresponded about the possibility of another Mozart recording based on a Glyndebourne production; the most likely contender was *Don Giovanni*. Caplat informed some members of the cast, which included Suzanne Danco, Léopold Simoneau and Geraint Evans, that discussions were taking place with David Bicknell and he hoped that the singers would be free to participate. The one uncertain factor was – who would sing Giovanni himself on the recording? Bicknell was very keen to use Ezio Pinza, the Italian born bass, and finest Don Giovanni of the 1930s and 1940s. Pinza had never sung at Glyndebourne and might not be free to sing there in the coming season, but perhaps he would be prepared to record the role. As the discussions continued during March and April Busch became increasingly unhappy at the prospect of using Pinza. Despite his undoubted 'star' quality, he was now aged nearly sixty and his best work in opera had been done over ten years previously, mostly at the Metropolitan in New York; within the last two years he had starred on Broadway in Rodgers and Hammerstein's *South Pacific*. Was he really right for a Glyndebourne recording? Another problem was Pinza's heavy schedule that summer, which made it difficult to arrange convenient dates. Busch's misgivings and

Pinza's schedule influenced Caplat and Bicknell, and the idea of a new recorded version of the opera was temporarily dropped; however, three years later, after Busch's death, there were further plans to record *Don Giovanni*, which came much closer to fruition.

1951

IDOMENEO

Music by Wolfgang Amadeus Mozart

Libretto by Giovanni Battista Varesco
Edited for performance at Glyndebourne by Hans Gal

Sung in Italian

Excerpts

Idomeneo	Richard Lewis (tenor, English)
Ilia	Sena Jurinac (soprano, Yugoslav)
Idamante	Alexander Young (tenor, English)
Electra	Dorothy MacNeil (soprano, American)
High Priest	Alexander Young

Glyndebourne Festival Chorus	Chorus Master John Pritchard
Glyndebourne Festival Orchestra Harpsichord continuo	John Pritchard
Conductor	Fritz Busch
Recorded	Studio No 1, Abbey Road 2 and 3.7.1951
Mono recording	
Recording Producer Balance Engineer	David Bicknell Douglas Larter

MATRIX/TAKE	DATE	ISSUE NOS	ISSUE DATE	MUSICAL ITEM	SINGERS
Act 1					
2EA15751–1–2	2.7.51	NOT ISSUED AS 78		Overture	Orchestra
2EA15752–1–2–*3*	2.7.51	DB 21527	9.53	Quando avran	SJ
2EA15753–*1*	2.7.51	DB 21527	9.53	Padre, germani	SJ
2EA15763–1–2–3	3.7.51	NOT ISSUED AS 78		Vedrommi intorno	RL
Act 2					
2EA15761–*1*–2	3.7.51	DB 21529	11.54	Se il padre perdei	SJ

MATRIX/TAKE	DATE	ISSUE NOS	ISSUE DATE	MUSICAL ITEM	SINGERS
2EA15764–1–2	3.7.51	DB 21529	11.54	Fuor del mar	RL
2EA15755–1–2	2.7.51	DB 21526	4.53	Sidoniè sponde Placido è il mar	SJ DM RL AY Chorus
2EA15757–1–2	2.7.51	DB 21528	11.53	Qual nuovo terrore Eccoti in me Corriamo, fuggiamo	Chorus RL Chorus

Act 3

MATRIX/TAKE	DATE	ISSUE NOS	ISSUE DATE	MUSICAL ITEM	SINGERS
2EA15762–*1*	3.7.51	DB 21525	11.52	Zeffiretti lusinghieri	SJ
2EA15754–1–2–*3*	2.7.51	DB 21525	11.52	Andrò ramingo	SJ DM RL AY
2EA15756–1–2	2.7.51	DB 21526	4.53	O voto tremendo!	AY Chorus
2EA15758–1–*2*–3	2.7.51	DB 21528	11.53	March Accogli o rè	AY Chorus

Original issue
HMV numbers and dates as above.
Victor LHMV 1021   (USA) (1 12" LP)
Victor WHMV 1021   (USA) (Set of 7" 45s)

Re–issues
WRC SH 294   (1 12" LP)   9.1979

Excerpts
Sena Jurinac – EMI Golden Voice Series
Quando avran . . . Padre, germani – Zeffiretti lusinghieri
EMI HQM 1024   (1 12" LP)   7.1966

Quando avran . . . Padre, germani – Se il padre – Zeffiretti lusinghieri
EMI CDH7 63199–2   (1 CD – 78'00")   11.1989

Glyndebourne has always been innovative in its approach to repertoire and the Festival has presented the world premières of several operas. On other occasions it has mounted productions of little-performed works (often by celebrated composers) and brought them success and popularity. In the latter category is Mozart's *Idomeneo*, which was first performed in Britain as late as 1934 by an amateur company in Glasgow.

Idomeneo was given its first professional English production during the 1951 season at Glyndebourne. There were six performances, prepared by the well established team of Fritz Busch and Carl Ebert; for these (and later) performances, the original score was drastically edited by Hans Gal. Ebert's production was revived during four seasons in the 1950s and the opera was given new productions at Glyndebourne in 1974 and 1983.

After the disappointment of the *Don Giovanni* recording project, Bicknell and Caplat put their energy into organising two days of recording excerpts from *Idomeneo* in July. By early June Bicknell had compiled a list of suitable numbers from the opera which would fill twelve sides of 12" 78s. The cast included two singers from the 1950 *Così* – Jurinac and Lewis – and two new-comers, Canadian tenor Léopold Simoneau and Swedish soprano Birgit Nilsson, who were both making their British débuts at Glyndebourne. For reasons which are not clear, Simoneau did not participate in the recording; and for reasons which are entirely clear, neither did Nilsson.

Nilsson first worked with Busch in Stockholm, when she had taken over the role of Lady Macbeth at short notice in a production which he was conducting, and it was his particular request that she should be offered Electra in *Idomeneo* at Glyndebourne. She recalled the circumstances in an interview with John Higgins, published in the June 1992 edition of *Gramophone*: 'Busch . . . became almost a father to me. He introduced me to the world. He gave me my first major engagement outside Sweden, Electra at Glyndebourne. My great regret was that I never recorded with Busch. Glyndebourne offered me the part on record, but the fee was pitiful –£40 or something like that. I asked for £75 and was refused. Such are the penalties of pride.'

Had Nilsson agreed, she would have appeared on two of the twelve sides that were taped at Abbey Road on 2 and 3 July 1951. At least, that is what the American soprano Dorothy MacNeil, who sang instead of Nilsson, recorded. MacNeil was also making her first Glyndebourne appearances in 1951, as Cherubino in *Le nozze di Figaro* in Sussex and as Donna Elvira in *Don Giovanni*, when that production was taken to the Edinburgh Festival.

Instead of Simoneau as Idamante, Alexander Young (who sang the High Priest in the same production) took the role for the recording, and also sang a fragment of the High Priest's music in the chorus *O voto tremendo*. Five years later, when HMV were planning a 'complete' recording of the opera, Simoneau was able to, and did, sing, despite the fact that he did not appear at all at Glyndebourne that season. Material for seven sides was recorded on 2 July 1951 by the four soloists and Glyndebourne Chorus; in addition, the orchestra recorded the overture, leaving two solos each for Jurinac and Lewis to be taped the following day. By 23 July, when Bicknell sent a set of test pressings to Caplat, the transfer from tape to wax had been completed. Bicknell was pleased with the results and hoped to start issuing the record in the autumn, but early in August Busch indicated that he wanted to hear pressings of different takes of several of the arias.

The use of tape naturally made the process of recording a great deal easier. The singers probably recorded a number of takes of their music and the best sections were spliced together. This master tape would then be recorded on to several different waxes, using different volume settings for each. Pressings were made of them all and the best was selected for issue. The take numbers shown against the matrices might, therefore, refer either to different performances of the given music or a different transfer to wax of the same version. The process of transferring taped performances to 78s was used for only two Glyndebourne recordings; *Così fan tutte* in 1950 and *Idomeneo* in 1951. Earlier recordings had been made directly on to wax in the traditional way and subsequent operas were originally issued only in LP form.

Bicknell's aim to start releasing the discs in the autumn of 1951 was overoptimistic. It was not until November 1952 that the first was issued, with catalogue number DB 21525. Four more followed at long intervals, the last being released in November 1954. Two sides were never issued at all as 78s – the overture and Lewis's *Vedrommi intorno*, although all twelve sides were included on a 1979 World Record Club issue. During the 1950s HMV planned to release all the sides in the new LP format; the record was even given its catalogue number, ALP 1048. The reason that it was never issued, and that the catalogue number remains unused, was perhaps due to Mrs Busch's subsequent correspondence.

After conducting performances of *Don Giovanni* and Verdi's *La forza del Destino* at the Edinburgh Festival in August and September, Busch returned to London. At the Savoy Hotel he suffered a heart attack and died four days later. The first performance of the 1952 season, *Idomeneo*, was dedicated to him and a memorial was unveiled in the Covered Way at Glyndebourne. His contribution to the founding and continued success of Glyndebourne Festival Opera was incalculable; and his legacy of recordings has set a standard in Mozart interpretation that is still held in high regard.

Moran Caplat hoped that Busch's widow, Greta, and her family, would come to Glyndebourne for the unveiling; but she was grievously upset about the recording of *Idomeneo* her husband had made only two months before his death. It had been reviewed (in an LP version already issued in the United States) in *The Evening Review* by music critic Irving Kolodin. He, and subsequently Greta Busch, complained that these excerpts did a great disservice to Busch's memory. On the LP version, one number followed immediately after another in a way not originally intended in the 78 format; there were jarring changes of key and mood from excerpt to excerpt. 'Nothing like a total picture of Mozart's creation can be ascertained from it' commented Mrs Busch. She emphasised that her husband had hoped to record the opera complete – he was clearly unhappy that only excerpts were considered suitable – and also questioned the participation of MacNeil and Young; they were not Busch's chosen singers. Both Caplat and Bicknell became involved in a lengthy and unhappy correspondence with Mrs Busch. Writing on behalf of HMV, Bicknell gently pointed out that Simoneau refused to take part and that Nilsson's voice was wholly unsuitable to recording. Whether he felt this last comment to be true, or whether he was trying to cover for Nilsson's refusal of the offered fee, can only be guessed. There was no possibility of a complete recording, continued Bicknell, although in 1956 that was exactly what he himself instigated. By that time *Idomeneo* was better known; it had enjoyed four series of performances at Glyndebourne and four BBC radio broadcasts.

The Record Guide, by Edward Sackville-West and Desmond Shawe-Taylor, published by Collins, 1955:

> In order to get *Zeffiretti lusinghieri* on to one side it has had to be shorn of its recitative (which is also omitted at Glyndebourne); moreover, the music is just a trifle hurried. The famous quartet on the reverse of DB 21525, where four different emotions run four separate courses, is well handled. DB 21526 couples two of the most beautiful choruses, the ravishing 6/8 E major farewell with its anticipation of calm sea voyage (it is probably no accident that Mozart should have reverted to the same key for a similar situation in *Così* and the solemn, almost Verdian *O voto tremendo*, with its impressive unisons. Both sides of this disc would have been double-starred but for some uncertainty of ornament in Dorothy McNeil's [sic] solo (as Electra) in the middle section of *Placido è il mar*.

1952 was the only year between 1950 and 1956 in which HMV did not record at least one Glyndebourne production, and that was not for want of trying. In February, Bicknell asked Caplat who would be singing Lady Macbeth in the revival of Verdi's opera, as RCA Victor were very interested in a recording of the production. The American soprano Dorothy Dow had already been booked, together with the Yugoslav baritone Marko Rothmüller as her husband. It would be the first commercially recorded version of the opera to be made, although a wartime broadcast from Vienna and the production featuring Maria Callas at La Scala Milan (also in 1952) were both subsequently released; but neither of these was recorded with the intention that they would be issued. (Indeed, *Macbeth* ultimately had to wait until 1959 to be commercially recorded, under Erich Leinsdorf.)

EMI and RCA Victor seemed very satisfied with the cast of *Macbeth* and several days were reserved towards the end of July to record at Abbey Road. Vittorio Gui was the conductor, the Irish tenor James Johnston was Macduff and Frederick Dalberg, Banquo. Bicknell assessed that the complete opera would require approximately thirty-six sides when issued on 78s, but it would also appear in the new Long Playing format in due course.

Everyone was ready and eager to start work on the project, but Bicknell took the precaution of writing to Caplat. He would decide after the dress rehearsal whether to go ahead with the recording – just a few days ahead on 30

June. By 8 July, when the production was under way, Bicknell cancelled the reservations he had made at No 1 Studio at Abbey Road. The recording would not take place.

Whether the decision was Caplat's or Bicknell's or both is not clear. The only salient comment was passed in a letter from Caplat to Bicknell in August, three weeks after the recording should have been completed: 'You know how jealous we are of the good name of Glyndebourne recordings . . . '

Although EMI's recording was never made, a pirate disc of excerpts from the 1952 performances of *Macbeth* was available for several years. Its label boasts a cast, conductor and orchestra that never existed, entirely fictitious names, invented, presumably, to disguise its source. It seems to be all that has survived of the performances of Dow, Rothmüller, Dalberg *et al* from that hot, frustrating summer of 1952.

Before the end of July 1952, undaunted by another disappointment, Bicknell was considering recording Gluck's *Alceste* in 1953 – its first Glyndebourne production. It seemed a strong possibility, with Jurinac tentatively cast in the name part. By March 1953 Magda Laszlo, the Hungarian soprano, was contracted to sing the role, but Bicknell was not impressed by her voice. He wanted to wait, as he had done with *Macbeth*, and see how the first few performances went before committing himself. Yet again the opportunity was allowed to pass and HMV recorded the opera with Kirsten Flagstad as Alceste and another cast entirely.

The planned recording of Rossini's *La Cenerentola* was scheduled for sessions at Abbey Road in September 1953, but in addition Glyndebourne was pressing EMI to complete Busch's *Idomeneo*. Perhaps this idea was in part due to the strong argument put up by Greta Busch in her correspondence in 1952. John Pritchard, Busch's former assistant, was conducting performances in Edinburgh, and it was hoped to record the remainder of the opera after the sessions for *La Cenerentola* were completed. Pritchard was asked to check the timings of individual numbers in case Glyndebourne's own performing version had to be cut further for reasons of economy – to enable it to be fitted on to a limited number of LP sides, for instance. Bicknell commented to his colleague Lawrance Collingwood that fifty-five minutes had been recorded in 1951; there were another eighty-five minutes left to record.

Exactly what cast he planned to use is not clear; Jurinac and Lewis were again in *Idomeneo* at the Edinburgh Festival and Alexander Young was in *Così* and *Ariadne auf Naxos*, but Dorothy MacNeil was not singing and might have to return to London to complete her part in the recording. The last reference to these planned sessions is dated January 1953 – a memo from David Bicknell to Mr Evans at EMI's Sales Promotion Department; in it, he cites contractual difficulties as the reason for the recording's cancellation, but still optimistic, he hoped it would take place next year . . . Fortunately, the plans for *La Cenerentola* continued as arranged.

The matter of *Don Giovanni* was re-assessed in November 1953, with a view to HMV's making a complete recording during the following summer. By February 1954 the principal roles had been cast: James Pease as Giovanni, Jurinac as Donna Elvira, Margaret Harshaw, Donna Anna, Anny Schlemm, Zerlina and Benno Kusche as Leporello. The conductor, making his first appearance at Glyndebourne, was the Hungarian born Georg Solti. For several years Solti had been (and at the time of writing still is) contracted to Decca Records; it was only his involvement in the recording project, booked for late July and early August, that cast any doubt upon its taking place. It was not the fact that he had a contract with a rival recording company, but that his schedule of concerts at Ravinia, in the USA, prevented his being free to record after the Glyndebourne performances. Solti was not prepared to cancel the American concerts in order to record unless he knew that the recording would definitely go ahead. EMI would not confirm that the recording could proceed until they were assured that Solti would make himself free for it. In order to obtain Solti's services, EMI were prepared to offer Hans Hotter to Decca for a recording of *Das Rheingold* that had been mooted. A warm spirit of co-operation, not always evident in this type of negotiation, augured well for the project; and yet, before finally committing himself to recording, Bicknell wanted to wait until he had seen the performance of *Don Giovanni* at Glyndebourne on 29 June.

Perhaps it was for musical reasons rather than clashes of dates that the recording of *Don Giovanni* failed to take place. On 12 July Bicknell wrote to Caplat at Glyndebourne: 'I have written to the singers and Solti telling them it has not been proved practicable to organise the recording of *Don Giovanni* this season. Just that and no more.' Bicknell immediately made arrangements to record Busoni's *Arlecchino* instead.

[5] Rossini Recordings

La Cenerentola, 1953
Le Comte Ory, 1956
Il barbiere di Siviglia, 1962

LA CENERENTOLA

Music by Gioachino Rossini

Libretto by Jacopo Ferretti

Sung in Italian

Clorinda	Alda Noni (soprano, Italian)
Tisbe	Fernanda Cadoni (mezzo-soprano, Italian)
Angelina	Marina de Gabarain (contralto, Spanish)
Alidoro	Hervey Alan (bass, English)
Don Magnifico	Ian Wallace (bass, Scottish)
Don Ramiro	Juan Oncina (tenor, Spanish)
Dandini	Sesto Bruscantini (bass, Italian)

Glyndebourne Festival Chorus	Chorus Master Leo Quayle
Glyndebourne Festival Orchestra	Leader David McCallum
Harpsichord continuo	Bryan Balkwill
Conductors	Vittorio Gui and *Bryan Balkwill
Recorded	Studio No 1, Abbey Road
	17–21.9.1953 and *15.2.1954
Mono recording	
Recording Producers	Lawrance Collingwood and David Bicknell
Balance Engineers	Douglas Larter and *Robert Beckett

Original issue
Record Library Series No 612
ALP 1147–9   (3 12" LPs)   7.1954
The accompanying 4 page leaflet includes a note on the opera and a synopsis in English by Stephen Williams. A separate line-by-line libretto was available at additional cost

Victor LHMV 600   (USA) (2 12" LPs)

Re–issues
Record Library Series No 688

HQM 1011–3	(3 12" LPs)	2.1966

The accompanying booklet contains a short history of the opera and a libretto in Italian, translated into English by Arthur Jacobs.

CMS7 64183–2	(2 CDs – 62'52"/54'23")	3.1992

The eighty-six page booklet includes notes on *La Cenerentola*: a synopsis in English, German and French: and the libretto in Italian and English.

CDMB 64183	(USA) (2CDs)

Excerpts
The Overture

7ER 5024	(1 7" 45)		9.1954
XLP 30042	(1 12" LP)		10.1965

Zitto, zitto, piano, piano	Oncina, Bruscantini	
SEOM 3	EMI The Enjoyment of Opera	11.1969
	12" Sampler record	

Vittorio Gui made his début with the Glyndebourne company at the 1948 Edinburgh Festival, when he conducted performances of *Così fan tutte*. This was very much Fritz Busch's musical territory, but it was not until 1950 that Busch returned to Glyndebourne, and took charge of two operas, after an eleven year absence. Whilst Busch's strength was generally acknowledged as being in the German musical tradition, Gui had established an important reputation as an expert on, and a fine conductor of, the music of Rossini. Before the second world war he had prepared new performing editions of several of Rossini's operas and conducted them frequently. He was determined to remove from these works the unauthorized alterations and accretions that generations of conductors and singers had imposed on them, and where possible he studied the original manuscripts. It was not surprising, therefore, that when Glyndebourne scheduled *La Cenerentola*, their first Rossini opera, for the 1952 season, Gui was asked to conduct. Indeed, it seems likely that his presence was a decisive factor in choosing the work.

The cast of the production was led by two Spanish singers – contralto Marina de Gabarain and tenor Juan Oncina; the baritones Sesto Bruscantini and Ian Wallace also took part, and, like Oncina, were to become mainstays of the Gui/Ebert Rossini operas during the 1950s and 1960s. Wallace was the only singer to take part in all three recordings of them made by EMI. He was fortunate enough not to be replaced, as were some of his colleagues, at the sessions for *Le Comte Ory* and *Il barbiere di Siviglia*. The character of Clorinda (one of Cenerentola's sisters) was sung by Alda Noni, and she, too, recorded her role in *La Cenerentola* for HMV. In 1953 the original cast was seen again, both in Sussex and at the Edinburgh Festival. During the rehearsal period in June 1953, Bruscantini and Sena Jurinac were married at St Pancras Church in Lewes. They first sang together at Glyndebourne in the 1951 performances of *Così fan tutte*, but the only Glyndebourne recording on which they both appear is the 1955 *Le nozze di Figaro*. Unfortunately, their own marriage was not so happy, and after some years they separated.

In June 1953 David Bicknell wrote to all the singers in the cast of *La Cenerentola*, telling them that HMV planned to tape the opera in September, (as part of HMV's new agreement with Glyndebourne to record at least one opera from the repertory each year), and he hoped they were free to participate. John Pritchard was again given the task of examining the score and suggesting where cuts might be made for the recording, particularly in the recitatives and in some of the very repetitive numbers. Bicknell's original aim was to issue the opera on two 12" LPs, but he soon realised that to do so would sacrifice too much of the music. Gui's performing version of *La Cenerentola* was already far from complete; it seems extraordinary that he, a Rossini scholar and purist, should have cut so much at Glyndebourne; of the three hundred and sixty pages of the score, forty were omitted from the edition he used. To be fair to Gui, some of the music thus lost was not composed by Rossini himself, but by Agolini, at Rossini's request; in editing the score so drastically, Gui cut some music that Rossini had not written, but had approved. For the recording itself, a recitative and an aria for Don Magnifico were also removed – perhaps the most damaging of the additional cuts made at Pritchard's suggestion and approved by Gui. When issued, the recording played for four minutes under the two hours that had been planned – an average of nineteen and a half minutes per side; in more recent years, thanks to improved technology, sides of well over thirty minutes became usual.

As arranged, the sessions took place at Abbey Road during September. They seem to have gone even better than planned, as the last two days were not required, and were devoted to recordings of Mozart and Haydn symphonies and Bizet's *Jeux d'enfants*, all conducted by Gui. Problems did not arise with *La Cenerentola* until the editing of the tapes was under way in October and November. It proved very difficult to put together a satisfactory version of Angelina's (the *Cenerentola* of the title) final aria and rondo, *Nacqui all'affanno* and *Non più mesta*. In early 1954 Bicknell was forced to acknowledge that the takes recorded in September could not be issued, and wrote to de Gabarain to book a session for repeats on 15 February at Abbey Road. Whilst de Gabarain herself was able to attend, most of the other members of the original cast were not. Gui was not in the country, and neither were Noni, Cadoni or Bruscantini, whose characters had lines to sing in the final scene; only Ian Wallace was free to repeat his role. Bryan Balkwill, Gui's assistant and player of the harpsichord continuo at the original sessions, conducted, and Eve Warren, Halinka de Tarczynska and Gwyn Griffiths replaced the original singers. A special chorus was similarly assembled, and, after a series of new takes, a satisfactory version of the last scene was put together. The set was first published in July 1954, re-issued on LP in 1966 and on CD in 1992. The overture was issued on a 45 in September 1954 and was included on a compilation LP of Rossini Overtures in 1965.

Since its original issue this performance of *La Cenerentola* has been regarded by some commentators as one of the finest available on record and is particularly noted for Gui's stylish conducting. It has also been severely criticised for being incomplete. Comparisons show that it contains nearly thirty minutes' less music than some other versions; how much of that music was by Rossini and how much by Agolini is, perhaps, hardly the point.

Dyneley Hussey in *Gramophone Record Review*. August 1954:

Marina de Gabarain's voice has just the right quality of gentleness and sweetness for the character of Cinderella and she possesses the technique to deal faithfully with the pyrotechnics of her music. . . This is a beautiful performance from the moment when she sings her simple ditty on her first entrance to the elaborate Rondo which ends the opera. She brings out the tenderness and pathos of the character, which differentiates it from the conventional heroines of *opera buffa*. . . There is Sesto Bruscantini in magnificent form as the valet in his royal master's clothes, and Ian Wallace who can match his Italian colleague in the quick and richly humorous enunciation of the words as the foolish, snobbish Baron Monte Fiascone. . . And there are the two silly daughters, the "ugly sisters" of the fairy tale, who are cleverly differentiated by Alda Noni and Fernanda Cadoni. Halfway between this crazy world and the world of romance, with a foot in each, stands the Prince, enjoying the fun and singing of love in the mellifluous voice of Juan Oncina. . . The precision of ensembles, every part exactly in place and yet seeming spontaneous, is quite breathtaking.

Thomas Heinitz in *Records and Recording*, March 1966 (reviewing the 1966 re-issue):

It is in the marvellous ensembles with which *La Cenerentola* is so richly endowed that HMV's performance scores so heavily: these are sung and played with a musical assurance and a dramatic bite which cannot simply be attained in the course of recording sessions. Listen, for example, to the sparkling duet between the Prince and Dandini in Act 1, or the superbly comic scene in Act 2 when Dandini reveals his true identity to Don Magnifico, the scintillating Act 1 finale or the delicious 'consternation' ensemble in Act 2, and you will surely agree that this is real 'theatre' of the most delightful sort.

1956

LE COMTE ORY

Music by Gioachino Rossini

Libretto by Eugène Scribe and Lestre-Poirson

Sung in French

Raimbaud	Michel Roux (bass, French)
Alice	Jeannette Sinclair (soprano, English)
Le Comte Ory	Juan Oncina (tenor, Spanish)
Ragonde	Monica Sinclair (contralto, English)
Le Gouverneur	Ian Wallace (bass, Scottish)
Isolier	Cora Canne-Meijer (mezzo-soprano, Dutch)
La Comtesse Adèle	Sari Barabas (soprano, Hungarian)
Young Nobleman	Dermot Troy (tenor, Irish)

Glyndebourne Festival Chorus	Chorus Master Peter Gellhorn
Glyndebourne Festival Orchestra	Leader Arthur Leavins
Conductor	Vittorio Gui
Recorded	Studio No 1, Abbey Road
	28–31.8 and 1, 2 and 5.9.1956
Mono recording	
Recording Producer	Lawrance Collingwood
Balance Engineer	Harold Davidson

Original issue
HMV ALP 1473–4   (2 12" LPs)   7.1957
The record sleeve has a note on *Le Comte Ory* by Philiberte Ory.

Angel 3565 B/L   (USA) (2 12" LPs)

Re–issues
Record Library Series RLS 694
HQM 1073–4   (2 12" LPs)   3.1967
The enclosed booklet contains historical notes on the opera, a synopsis in English and the French text with English translation.

Record Library Series RLS 744
HLM 7194–5   (2 12" LPs)   5.1980
The accompanying booklet contains the French text with English translation, and the notes include historical details about the opera and the original Comte Ory, and a synopsis in English.

CMS7 64180–2   (2 CDs – 56'27"/56'23")   3.1992
The accompanying eighty-five page booklet includes notes in English, German and French by Andrew Porter reprinted from *The Gramophone* in September 1954: a note by Philiberte Ory (as above): and a libretto in English and German translated by Joseph Allen.

CDMB 64180   (USA) (2 CDs)

At the 1954 Edinburgh Festival the Glyndebourne company gave its first performance of Rossini's *Le Comte Ory*, in the original French, produced by Carl Ebert with costumes and sets designed by Oliver Messel. *Ory* was Rossini's penultimate opera, succeeded only by *Guillaume Tell*, and is often considered the finest *opéra comique* of the first half of the nineteenth century. It was a natural successor to the Festival's *La Cenerentola* and *Il barbiere di Siviglia* (which also received its first Glyndebourne performance in 1954), and the presence of Vittorio Gui ensured that true Rossinian style would be respected. After seven performances of *Le Comte Ory* at Edinburgh in 1954, the production was revived in Sussex in 1955 and 1957. In 1958 it was taken to Paris for four performances before its final revival at Glyndebourne.

In the early summer of 1956, (one year that it was *not* performed), HMV decided that *Le Comte Ory* should be taped at the close of the Glyndebourne season. Caplat, too, was particularly keen on the idea because, as he pointed out to Bicknell, it would be the first time that the opera had been recorded in its original language.

Some members of the 1955 cast were not performing at Glyndebourne – Giuseppe Valdengo (Raimbaud), Halinka de Tarczynska (Alice) and Fernanda Cadoni (Isolier) – and their places in the recording cast were taken by singers appearing in other productions there. Before deciding on his replacements, Bicknell conferred with both Gui and EMI colleagues in Paris. Monique Linval was suggested for the role of Isolier, but, after an audition, the Dutch mezzo Cora Canne-Meijer, who was singing Cherubino in *Le nozze di Figaro* and Clorinda in *La Cenerentola*, was selected. She and Jeannette Sinclair required coaching specially for the recording, and Jani Strasser, Head of the Music Staff at Glyndebourne, acted as répétiteur. Bruscantini, who had appeared as Raimbaud when the production was new in 1954, was not used for the recording, (although he was singing in the 1956 season), and the role was sung by the French bass Michel Roux. The Glyndebourne chorus also needed re-training as several of their number had not sung in the opera the previous season.

In July 1956 David Bicknell consulted Gui about the length of the opera. As performed at Glyndebourne it was too long to fit on to two LPs and Bicknell asked Gui if it would be possible to make extra cuts of seventeen minutes without damaging the artistic shape of the work. Economic considerations were evidently very important when multi-record sets were being planned in the 1950s and, in this case, the extra cost of a third disc was thought likely to deter possible purchasers. Gui's response has not survived, but it seems likely that he would have considered seventeen minutes' worth of additional cuts to be extremely damaging. Perhaps he hoped that HMV would relent, as they had done with *La Cenerentola*, and issue the opera on three LPs after all. It was not until well after the opera was recorded, (on six consecutive days at the end of August and the beginning of September, plus one further session on 5 September to insert twenty seconds of orchestral playing), that serious consideration was given to what should, and what should not, be cut. In January 1957 Lawrance Collingwood of HMV wrote to Moran Caplat:

> Please give Maestro Gui my apologies for these horrible suggestions, but at any rate you have something to work on to get the opera down to four sides which seems to be most advisable.

Caplat replied:

> The cuts [Gui] proposes are rather different from yours because while he appreciated that to cut mainly repeats as you had done meant that most of the music got heard at least once, he felt that too much of the real style of Rossini was lost in this way and in particular he was loath to cut the first finale and even more the trio in the second act which he considers to be the most important thing in the opera, as did Berlioz. Instead we have cut mainly recitative and the whole of the Governor's aria which isn't very good . . .

Eventually *Le Comte Ory* was pared down to one hour fifty-two minutes, although appreciably more than that had been recorded. The whole of Scene 6 was omitted (consisting of one page in the score), a scene for La Comtesse, Isolier and Ragonde, several other short sections of recitative, and, of course, the Governor's aria. None of the cuts harm the finest scenes in the opera, but they disfigure the work as a whole – to the extent of about nineteen minutes' worth of music. Nevertheless this recording still holds its place among the finest, and in 1992 when it was re-issued on CD, Richard Osborne wrote in *Gramophone*:

> . . . As soon as the voices come into play it is clear how astutely the recording has been staged for the gramophone by Gui and the engineers.
> . . . The dramas of Act 2 – Ory and his followers disguised as nuns laying siege to the women and the cellars of Castle Formoutiers – are also staged with a tremendous sense of theatrical actuality. Like champagne and the works of P G Wodehouse, this recording is one of life's few infallible tonics.

Le Comte Ory was the last recording that EMI made of a Glyndebourne production in mono only; both *Le nozze di Figaro* (1955) and *Idomeneo* (1956) had already been recorded in the same studio at Abbey Road using stereophonic equipment. What criteria were used in deciding between mono only and mono/stereo sessions? Did not Rossini, no less than Mozart, deserve the best that current technology could provide?

Roger Dettmer in *Chicago American*, 29 March 1958:

We are fortunate that the Glyndebourne production is competent, though one misses the presence of bravura singers (Simionato, say, as the page Isolier, or Callas as the Countess). Still, there's mellifluous Juan Oncina as the Count; Sari Barabas as his prey; Cora Canne-Meijer as Isolier and Monica Sinclair (staunch!) as the Countess' companion.

Michel Roux, as the carousing Count's companion, has a hard time of it in fioriture passages (Gobbi fodder), and Ian Wallace's woody voice as the tutor is more serviceable than attractive. But Vittorio Gui conducts with spirit, recorded sound is vividly realistic, and the music sweeps all before it.

It was six years before another Glyndebourne production was recorded by HMV, and the choice again fell upon a Rossini opera – his most popular – *Il barbiere di Siviglia*. Before that, in 1958, discussions were held about a pro-jected recording of Handel's *Acis and Galatea*. It has never been produced at Glyndebourne, although at the time there were plans to present it there. Both Elsie Morison, the Australian soprano, and Richard Lewis were approached and dates in April 1959 were suggested for the sessions. Sir Thomas Beecham was asked to conduct and was very enthusiastic about the idea, but, like a number of previous projects, it came to nothing.

To mark the Festival's 25th anniversary in 1959 a new rehearsal stage was built at Glyndebourne and Moran Caplat suggested to David Bicknell that EMI might like to use it for recording. It offered excellent acoustics and was well away from traffic and aeroplane flight-paths that could cause serious problems in city-based studios. After an EMI engineer visited Glyndebourne to test the new stage, Bicknell regretfully turned down Caplat's offer. It was not, he wrote, a very practicable proposition 'to cart the orchestra down to the middle of the Sussex countryside, considering the return fare is £1. 1. 0d [£1.05 in decimal currency] per head, plus the bus ride of five miles.' Despite Bicknell's disappointing response, Beecham did use the stage for several days in May 1959 to rehearse the Royal Philharmonic Orchestra for his new recording of *Messiah*, which was subsequently issued by RCA.

Another project involving Beecham was Glyndebourne's production of *Die Zauberflöte*, which was scheduled for ten performances in 1960. Beecham had agreed to conduct and to record the opera for EMI in August. David Bicknell visited him in the south of France in April 1960 and on his return told Caplat that he looked far from well. Before either the performances or the recording started, Beecham was taken seriously ill. His place at Glyndebourne was filled by Colin Davis and the plans for the recording were cancelled. The opera was later recorded by EMI in London with an international cast under Otto Klemperer. No Glyndebourne recording of the work has been mooted since.

1962

IL BARBIERE DI SIVIGLIA

Music by Gioachino Rossini

Libretto by Cesare Sterbini after Beaumarchais

Sung in Italian

Rosina	Victoria de los Angeles (soprano, Spanish)
Count Almaviva	Luigi Alva (tenor, Peruvian)
Figaro	Sesto Bruscantini (baritone, Italian)
Basilio	Carlo Cava (bass, Italian)
Bartolo	Ian Wallace (baritone, Scottish)
Berta	Laura Sarti (mezzo-soprano, Italian)
Fiorello	Duncan Robertson (tenor, Scottish)
Ambrogio	Harold Williams (bass, English)
Uffiziale	John Rhys Evans (baritone, Welsh)

Glyndebourne Festival Chorus	Chorus Master Myer Fredman
Royal Philharmonic Orchestra	Leader Raymond Cohen
Conductor	Vittorio Gui
Recorded	Studio No 1, Abbey Road
	4–7, 9 and 10.9.1962
Recording Producers	Victor Olof and Ronald Kinloch Anderson
Balance Engineer	Christopher Parker

Original issue
Record Library Series RLS 904
AN 114–6   (3 mono LPs)   10.1963

Stereo Library Series SLS 904

SAN 114–6   (3 stereo LPs)   10.1963
The accompanying booklet includes the libretto in Italian and English, an essay *Tradition and Rossini's Barber* by Vittorio Gui and an essay *On a production of The Barber of Seville* by Peter Ebert.

Angel 3638 C   (USA) (3 mono LPs)
Angel S–3638 C   (USA) (3 stereo LPs)

Re–issues
Stereo Library Series SLS 5165
ASD 3718–20   (3 stereo LPs)   7.1979
Libretto as above

SCLX–3914	(USA) (3 stereo LPs)	
CFPD 4704	(2 stereo LPs)	8.1987
TC CFPD 4704	(2 stereo cassettes)	8.1987
CMS7 64162–2	(2 CDs – 71'16"/69'56")	3.1992

The accompanying 106 page booklet includes an historical note *Vittorio Gui and Rossini's Barber* in English, German and French by Richard Osborne, a synopsis by George Hall and a libretto.

Angel CDMB 64162	(USA) (2 CDs)

Excerpts

1. **Largo al factotum**	6. **A un dottor**
2. **All'idea**	7. **Fredda ed immobile**
3. **Una voce poco fà**	8. **Buona sera**
4. **La calunnia**	9. **Ah qual colpo**
5. **Dunque io son**	10. **Di si felice**

ALP 2307	(1 mono LP)	4.1967
ASD 2307	(1 stereo LP)	4.1967

A leaflet with the Italian text and English translation is included.

Angel 36207	(USA) (1 mono LP)
Angel S36207	(USA) (1 stereo LP)
Angel RL 32116	(USA) (1 stereo cassette)

Largo al factotum	Bruscantini	
TC2 MOM 112	(1 stereo cassette)	10.1980

Una voce poco fà	de los Angeles	
ALP 2274	(1 mono LP)	8.1966
ASD 2274	(1 stereo LP)	8.1966
SLS 5233	(3 stereo LPs)	3.1982
TC SLS 5233	(3 stereo cassettes)	3.1982
ASD 3915	(1 stereo LP)	11.1980
TC ASD 3915	(1 stereo cassette)	11.1980

Buona sera	Alva, de los Angeles, Bruscantini, Cava and Wallace	
ASD 2324	(1 stereo LP)	11.1967

Victoria de los Angeles first recorded *Il barbiere di Siviglia* for HMV with the conductor Tullio Serafin in 1952. Luigi Alva, the Peruvian tenor, recorded it for the first time in 1957 for Columbia, with Maria Callas as Rosina, conducted by Alceo Galliera; he also made later commercial recordings of the opera with the conductors Claudio Abbado and Arturo Basile. Neither de los Angeles nor Alva ever sang their respective roles at Glyndebourne – indeed, de los Angeles never sang there at all – but they were both asked by EMI to record the opera with Vittorio Gui in 1962, under the Glyndebourne banner.

Carl Ebert's production of *Il barbiere di Siviglia* (re-staged in 1961 by his son Peter) was not performed at Glyndebourne in 1962, but Sesto Bruscantini, Carlo Cava and Duncan Robertson from the 1961 cast were singing there, and were contracted for the recording. Ian Wallace, who had taken the role of Bartolo both when the production was new in 1954 and in the 1961 revival, was also engaged, although he was not appearing in the 1962 Glyndebourne season.

Juan Oncina and Alberta Valentini had sung the Count and Rosina in 1961, but, from the outset, EMI's recording producer Victor Olof made it clear that they would not be used on the recording. Both Alva and de los Angeles were at the height of their fame and vocal powers, and were already contracted to EMI. It was no surprise that they were chosen to perform on this new definitive version of *Il barbiere di Siviglia*, but the rejected Glyndebourne singers must have been extremely disappointed. Initially, Gui was reluctant to agree to the changes of cast. He particularly objected to the suggestion that 'his' Berta, the Italian mezzo Laura Sarti, should be replaced by Stefania Malagù and on this point he overruled Olof; but the final decision about the casting of the Count and Rosina remained with EMI. Singing the small role of the Officer was a young Welsh baritone, John Rhys Evans. He appeared in the 1961 performances, and Moran Caplat made a special point of informing Olof that he was the younger half-brother of Glyndebourne's more famous singing Evans – Geraint.

Plans for the recording were afoot at EMI as early as April 1961. In October, Olof informed Caplat that the sessions would take place at Abbey Road in the first two weeks of September 1962; de los Angeles was free – one of the few periods during the year that she was not already committed elsewhere – but it soon transpired that Gui was not available at the same time. Early in December, Olof wrote to Gui that de los Angeles had lost the baby she was expecting, and wanted to bring the date of the sessions forward to February. He also broke the news that Carlo Cava, Glyndebourne's Basilio, had already recorded the role for Deutsche Grammophon and would not be able to sing on EMI's version; Franco Ventriglia was suggested as a replacement. By February 1962 the situation had changed again. The sessions *could* take place in September, Gui *would* be free to conduct and Cava *was* available to sing after all.

In July 1962 John Christie, who to many had become synonymous with Glyndebourne, died at the age of seventy-nine. A Memorial Service was held for him on 3 September in Westminster Abbey and, as part of the tribute, Vittorio Gui conducted music from Mozart's *Requiem*, sung by Elsie Morison, Pamela Bowden, Richard Lewis and Carlo Cava; the March from Act 3 of *Idomeneo* was played as retiring music. The following day work began on taping *Il barbiere di Siviglia* at Abbey Road.

The recording was completed within a week – a total of eight sessions on six days. The last session, held during the evening of 10 September, was reserved for re-takes, for some of the recitatives (which were customarily recorded separately from the arias and ensembles they preceeded) and for 'Rosina's Lesson'. In the nineteenth and early twentieth centuries this aria was frequently omitted from performances of the opera so that the Rosina could give a short recital of her own choosing – no less brilliant, perhaps, and certainly no less popular, but nothing to do with Rossini or *Il barbiere di Siviglia*. Gui, of course, never allowed such a deviation from the original score, and naturally it was his new edition that was used both at Glyndebourne and for the recording. He wrote a short essay (in Italian, and translated by another hand) intended for inclusion in the booklet issued with the original records, which provides an insight into his research. The following extract explains his approach to the opera.

> The orchestral and vocal material used for this *Barber* of the Glyndebourne Theatre was taken direct from Rossini's manuscripts existing in the Italian libraries of Bologna with regard to the whole opera and of Pesaro with regard to the symphony [overture] which, as is known, had already been used by Rossini during the years preceeding 1815 for another two operas: *Aureliano in Palmira* and *Elisabetta di Inghilterra*. The original score of *Aureliano* having been lost, we have deemed it advisable to make use of the version used for *Elisabetta*, which presents a not inconsiderable difference to the usual edition published by Ricordi and still commercially available to this day.
>
> Thus the listener will be confronted with several passages which are different from what he was used to hearing in the more general performances which, unlike this recording, do not claim to be *critical* performances, ie match the original as closely as possible. HMV hopes to have rendered a service to Rossini's masterpiece by recording the performance taken from the repertoire of the Glyndebourne Theatre, where Maestro Gui, a devoted student of the works of Rossini, has endeavoured to remove all incrustations superimposed by a misguided tradition not always based on truly good taste, by approaching the author's (original) idea as closely as possible. As regards Rosina's part which, as is known, was originally written for mezzo-soprano, but has for more than half a century habitually been entrusted to a coloratura soprano instead, this recording is practically one hundred per cent faithful to the original version, as also, among the two arias of Don Bartolo's, that by Rossini has been chosen instead of the other one by Maestro Romani, which is usually preferred because it is less strenuous – and the same applies to the magnificent sextet in Act 2, where the score has been adhered to to the letter, for here Don Bartolo sings, while in conventional operatic performances he remains quite literally like a statue without singing, thus reducing the sextet to a mere quintet.

The principal omission was the Count's Act 2 aria *Cessa di più resistere*; a few bars of recitative were also cut. Basilio's *La calunnia* was sung by Cava in its original key of D, and was not transposed down to C as was, and is, frequently done in other performances and recordings.

On its first issue in October 1963 this set consisted of three LPs, and was one of the first of EMI's Angel series of 'luxuriously packaged recordings' (to use Bicknell's words). An informative booklet with essays and complete libretto with English translation was included – something of an innovation at the time. Previously, opera librettos had usually only been available separately, for an extra charge. The original records were issued in both mono and stereo formats simultaneously – another innovation. For some years after the advent of stereo recording it was customary for the mono LPs to be issued well in advance of the stereo. When re-issued in 1987, *Il barbiere di Siviglia* was expertly re-mastered on to two LPs and cassettes and, in 1992, on to two well-filled CDs.

Edward Greenfield in *The Gramophone*, October 1963:

This is the driest, most unatmospheric acoustic I have ever heard in a complete opera recording . . . Presumably to help make up for the lack of opera house atmosphere there is an enormous amount of movement from side to side on the stereophonic stage, but far from creating a genuinely dramatic aura it merely underlines the reality . . . Much will depend on one's attitude to the Rosina of Victoria de los Angeles. It is quite lacking in spite, the very antithesis of Callas's wonderful conception of the part . . . Los Angeles remains smiling throughout, and rather than thinking of the character one marvels at the richness of the voice . . . I have never heard Bruscantini in such splendid voice before. Every note is as firm and well focused as could be imagined, and the top Gs in *Largo al factotum* are gloriously rich . . . *La Calunnia* is not as comic as it might be, but better that than hamming of a kind which is more distracting each time the record is repeated. Cava is particularly careful about giving the opening phrase and the comparable phrase four bars later their exact note lengths, when most singers end with two crochets and not two quavers.

The Times, 19 October 1963:

. . . listeners can without difficulty imagine themselves back at Glyndebourne enjoying a live performance. Exits, entrances and in fact all positioning of voices were arranged with Peter Ebert's production in mind . . . the theatrical inspiration of this recording is also very apparent in the recitatives which trip off the tongue with a true-to-life alacrity and vividness of expression . . . The stereophonic engineering is superb so that it is difficult to envisage any future recording of *The Barber of Seville* that could possibly give more pleasure.

[6]   *Arlecchino,* 1954 and *The Soldier's Tale,* 1955

ARLECCHINO

Music by Ferruccio Busoni

Libretto by the composer

Eine theatralisches Capriccio in einem Aufzuge

Sung in German

Ser Matteo	Ian Wallace (bass, Scottish)
Arlecchino	Kurt Gester (spoken role, German)
Abbate Conspicuo	Geraint Evans (baritone, Welsh)
Doctor Bombasto	Fritz Ollendorf (bass, German)
Colombina	Elaine Malbin (mezzo-soprano, American)
Leandro	Murray Dickie (tenor, Scottish)

Glyndebourne Festival Orchestra	Leader Arthur Leavins
Conductor	John Pritchard
Recorded	Studio No 1, Abbey Road
	17–20.7.1954
Mono recording	
Recording Producers	Lawrance Collingwood and David Bicknell
Balance Engineer	Francis Dillnutt

Original issue

ALP 1223	(1 12" LP)	4.1955

Harold Rosenthal wrote biographical notes and a resumé of the plot for the record sleeve.

HTA 14	(1 'tape record')	7.1955
Victor LM 1944	(USA) (1 12" LP)	

At less than two weeks' notice in July 1954, John Pritchard, Glyndebourne Festival Orchestra (the name under which the Royal Philharmonic made Glyndebourne recordings) and six soloists prepared to record *Arlecchino.* David Bicknell had planned to record *Don Giovanni,* conducted by Georg Solti, but only three weeks before the sessions were due to begin he cancelled the project and rapidly substituted Busoni's one act theatrical *capriccio.*

The working agreement between Glyndebourne and EMI – the final contract had still to be drawn up – required that an opera be recorded each year, either from the current repertory or another that was mutually acceptable. EMI would have exclusive use of the Glyndebourne name for two years, renewable for another two. Hence there was considerable urgency to replace *Don Giovanni* with another opera and start recording before the casts dispersed at the end of the season.

Arlecchino was first performed in Zurich in 1917 with the composer conducting. Set to his own libretto, it introduces characters from *commedia dell'arte* and is divided into four sections – *Harlequin as Rogue, Harlequin as Soldier, Harlequin as Husband* and *Harlequin as Conqueror*. The work was first heard in Britain in January 1939 in a BBC studio broadcast, but its British stage première took place at Glyndebourne on 24 June 1954, where it was given six performances, as the 'curtain-raiser' to Richard Strauss's *Ariadne auf Naxos*. The production was revived for four performances in 1960 at the Edinburgh Festival as part of an opera triple bill, sharing the evening with Wolf-Ferrari's *Il segreto di Susanna* and Poulenc's *La Voix humaine*. Apart from one further performance in 1965, mounted especially for BBC television, *Arlecchino* has not been seen again at Glyndebourne.

In 1954, four members of the singing cast also appeared in its 'partner' opera *Ariadne*; Geraint Evans, Fritz Ollendorf, Elaine Malbin and Murray Dickie. Kurt Gester, the German baritone, played Arlecchino, a speaking role, and also sang Harlekin in *Ariadne*. The sixth member of the cast, who did not appear in *Ariadne*, was Ian Wallace. In addition to the six main characters, there is a silent role in *Arlecchino*, that of Annunziata, Matteo's wife. She is played by a ballerina, on this occasion Peter Ebert's wife Silvia Ashmole, and consequently is not heard on the recording.

The sessions took place over four days in July 1954 at EMI's Abbey Road studios, after John Pritchard, Jani Strasser and Lawrance Collingwood had hurriedly prepared a recording schedule. On 27 August, David Bicknell wrote to Moran Caplat about the successful completion of the project: 'I was delighted to hear on my return that you are very pleased with *Arlecchino* . . . I thought it sounded very well. I hope someone will buy it.'

Before the recording was issued, Caplat corresponded with Gwen Matthias of EMI about the musical and spoken textual cuts that had been made. In all, over forty bars of music were removed from Busoni's score, which reduced an already short '*capriccio*' to little over fifty minutes playing time – the maximum that one long playing record could accommodate.

The LP version of *Arlecchino* was issued in April 1955. During the same month special presentation copies of the record were sent to eighty members of the Glyndebourne Festival Society, at the suggestion of its Chairman, Lord Wilmot of Selmeston. It was a gesture that was evidently much appreciated by the recipients, whose 'thank-you' letters survive in Glyndebourne's archives. It is interesting to ponder how many of those special copies exist and are still played, nearly forty years later.

Three months after the LP was released, *Arlecchino* was issued in another format – the 'tape record' version. This consisted of a single mono reel-to-reel tape, for use on the increasing number of tape recorders in domestic use in Britain. Several other Glyndebourne recordings were also released in this form but none of them remained in EMI's catalogue for long.

Since its original LP and 'tape record' versions *Arlecchino* has never been re-issued. A single scene with Dickie, Malbin and Gester was included in EMI's *50th Anniversary Album* in 1984, but the only complete recording currently available with a Glyndebourne cast is a pirate one, with different singers, (except for Wallace as Matteo), made at an Edinburgh Festival performance in 1960. The 1954 *Arlecchino* is the one official Glyndebourne issue which includes the late Sir Geraint Evans in its cast. He sang at the Festival regularly between 1949 and 1961, but never took part in any further recordings of Glyndebourne productions. The three Gilbert and Sullivan roles he recorded with Sir Malcolm Sargent and the Glyndebourne Chorus were never part of his operatic repertoire.

In March 1956 Fred Grunfeld of New York's *Saturday Review* wrote of *Arlecchino*:

A carnival atmosphere prevails among the singers, for whom this is more of a test of character-building than vocal prowess. Kurt Gester endows the spoken role of Arlecchino with as much gusto as the part permits – though Busoni's decision to give his hero no music to sing is surely one of the opera's principal weaknesses, for the total amount of music is hardly enough to sustain so much stage business. Ian Wallace is suitably bumbly as the old tailor, first cousin to Pantaloon of the *commedia dell'arte:* Geraint Evans and Fritz Ollendorf radiate measured dignity in the stock *buffo* roles of the Abbate and the Dottore; the American soprano Elaine Malbin is a saucy and vocally attractive wench as Colombina, and Murray Dickie sounds like an eighteenth century Bertie Wooster . . . . When these four launch into their startling final quartet, they unfold a tour de force that belongs among the most intricate pieces of ensemble writing in all of opera. And the engineers have done it justice.

1955

THE SOLDIER'S TALE

Music by Igor Stravinsky

Libretto by Charles Ramuz
Translated into English by Michael Flanders and Kitty Black

In English

The Devil	Robert Helpmann (Australian)
The Soldier	Terence Longdon (English)
The Narrator	Anthony Nicholls (English)

Chamber Ensemble   Members of the Royal Philharmonic Orchestra

Arthur Leavins	Violin	Richard Walton	Cornet
Edmond Chesterman	Double Bass	Sidney Langston	Trombone
Jack Brymer	Clarinet	Stephen Whittaker	Timpani
Gwydion Brooke	Bassoon		

Conductor   John Pritchard

Recorded   Studio No 3, Abbey Road
                        12, 13, 25 and 28.4,
                        and 4 and 25.5.1955
Mono recording

Recording Producer   Lawrance Collingwood
Balance Engineer   Harold Davidson

Original issue
ALP 1377   (1 12" LP)   9.1956

This issue includes background notes and a synopsis by Felix Aprahamian.

Victor LM 2079   (USA) (1 12" LP)

Re–issue
HQM 1008   (1 12" LP)   12.1965

This issue includes the background notes and synopsis by Felix Aprahamian as well as brief biographical details about the composer.

During Glyndebourne's visit to the Edinburgh Festival in 1954 another work was performed by the company for the first time, in association with the Edinburgh Festival Society – Stravinsky's *The Soldier's Tale*. Like *Arlecchino*, its première took place in Switzerland during the first world war. Another similarity they share is that one of the characters is a silent ballerina, (although in the recording, and presumably also in the performances in Edinburgh, she is heard calling to the Soldier at the end of the work) but there the resemblance ends. Described simply 'to be read, played and danced in two parts', it is in no sense an opera, but, rather, a moral tale with four protagonists accompanied by a small chamber group of instrumentalists.

Stravinsky set a French text by Charles Ramuz (translated into English by Michael Flanders and Kitty Black) which tells the traditional Russian folk-tale of a soldier who forfeited his soul to the Devil. In his sleeve notes to the original issue of the recording, Felix Aprahamian wrote of the Edinburgh production:

> In the centre of the platform was a little stage for the actors (speaking parts for the Soldier and the Devil, who also dances, and the danced role of the Princess). On one side of the stage; the music, on the other, the narrator at his desk. The music was composed for seven players . . . a selection which would include the most representative types, in treble and bass, of the instrumental families.

There is no singing, but the spoken roles are partially notated with the rhythm of the music, and it is thus that the tale is told of the sad fate of Joseph the Soldier and his love for the Princess. Moira Shearer danced the role of the Princess and Robert Helpmann took the part of the Devil. Actors Terence Longdon and Anthony Nicholls were familiar to British audiences from their appearances on stage and television in the 1950s, and it was this cast which recorded the work in the spring of 1955.

A few days after the first performance in Edinburgh David Bicknell wrote to Moran Caplat: 'I have heard from Collingwood that *Soldat* was very well done and he would like us to record it. We are investigating the copyright position which is always most complicated in respect of Stravinsky.'

Hans Schmidt-Isserstedt had conducted the Edinburgh performances, but as he was not available for the recording, Bicknell invited John Pritchard to take his place. After a gap of seven months, five sessions were booked at studio 3, one of Abbey Road's smaller recording rooms. The majority of the text was recorded on 12 and 13 April, the remaining sessions being largely devoted to the purely instrumental parts of the work. By 4 May the recording was complete, except for a five minute section which was taped on 25 May.

Exactly two years after the idea of the recording of *The Soldier's Tale* was first suggested, it was issued on LP. Nine years later it was re-issued in HMV's HQM Everyman series, in which several other Glyndebourne recordings have also been released, but since 1965 it has not re-appeared.

Humphrey Searle in the *Gramophone Record Review*, September 1956:

> Robert Helpmann is admirable as The Devil and Anthony Nicholls is a most competent Narrator. Terence Longdon might have given more flavour to his part as The Soldier by adopting more of a regional accent . . .

The instrumental ensemble play most efficiently . . . Stephen Whittaker's handling of the tricky percussion part is particularly admirable. My only quarrel is with the ending, where the percussion solo is made to die away, instead of rising to a climax as in Stravinsky's recording, and in addition, the voice of the Princess, who is a silent character in the play, is suddenly heard calling for The Soldier. What justification is there for this? The recording is well up to standard . . .

[7] The 'Complete' Mozart Recordings

Le nozze di Figaro, 1955 and *Idomeneo,* 1956

LE NOZZE DI FIGARO

Music by Wolfgang Amadeus Mozart

Libretto by Lorenzo da Ponte after Beaumarchais

Sung in Italian

Figaro	Sesto Bruscantini (baritone, Italian)
Susanna	Graziella Sciutti (soprano, Italian)
Don Basilio	Hugues Cuenod (tenor, Swiss)
Marcellina	Monica Sinclair (contralto, English)
Cherubino	Risë Stevens (mezzo-soprano, American)
Count Almaviva	Franco Calabrese (bass, Italian)
Countess Almaviva	Sena Jurinac (soprano, Yugoslav)
Bartolo	Ian Wallace (bass, Scottish)
Antonio	Gwyn Griffiths (baritone, Welsh)
Barbarina	Jeannette Sinclair (soprano, English)
Don Curzio	Daniel McCoshan (tenor, Scottish)

Glyndebourne Festival Chorus	Chorus Master Peter Gellhorn
Glyndebourne Festival Orchestra	Leader Arthur Leavins
Harpsichord continuo	Raymond Leppard
Conductor	Vittorio Gui
Recorded	Studio No 1, Abbey Road
	4–9 and 11–12.7.1955
Recording Producer	Lawrance Collingwood
Balance Engineers	Harold Davidson/Christopher Parker

Original issue
Record Library Series 634

ALPS 1312 and	(1 single sided mono LP and	1.1956
ALP 1313–1315	3 mono LPs)	

A separate line-by-line libretto was available at additional cost.

Stereosonic Library Series 751

ASDS 274 and	(1 single sided stereo LP and	6.1959
ASD 275–277	3 stereo LPs)	
SAT 1003–4	(Act 2: 2 stereo 'tape records')	10.1955
SAT 1006–7	(Act 1: 2 stereo 'tape records')	5.1956
SAT 1009–11	(Acts 3&4: 3 stereo 'tape records')	9.1956
Victor LM 6401	(USA) (4 12" LPs)	

Re–issues

WRC OC 168–170 and	(3 mono LPs and	
OX 171	1 single sided mono LP)	6.1966
WRC SOC 168–170	(3 stereo LPs and	
SOX 171	1 single sided stereo LP)	6.1966
EMI EX 2900173	(3 stereo LPs)	6.1984
EMI EX 2900179	(2 stereo cassettes)	6.1984
CFP CDB7 67261–2	(2 CDs 79'21"/78'53")	7.1991
TC CFPD 4724–4	(2 stereo cassettes)	7.1991

The Classics for Pleasure re-issues include a 10 page booklet with a synopsis by Peter Avis.

Excerpts

1. **Cinque, dieci**
2. **Se vuol ballare**
3. **La vendetta**
4. **Non so più**
5. **Non più andrai**
6. **Porgi amor**
7. **Voi che sapete**
8. **Crudel ! Perchè finora**
9. **Hai già vinta**
10. **E Susanna – Dove sono**
11. **Aprite un po'**
12. **Giunse alfin – Deh vieni**
13. **Tutte e tranquillo**

WRC OH 172	(1 mono LP)	6.1966
WRC SOH 172	(1 stereo LP)	6.1966
Victor LM 2053	(USA) (1 LP)	

Sena Jurinac – EMI Golden Voice Series
Porgi amor – E Susanna . . . Dove sono

HQM 1024	(1 LP)	7.1966

To commemorate the bi-centenary of Mozart's birth in 1756, EMI made plans to record Glyndebourne's productions of two of his operas. Carl Ebert's 1950 production of *Le nozze di Figaro* was to be revived in 1955, with new designs by Oliver Messel, and *Idomeneo*, also designed by Messel, was to be performed in 1956. These were the works that David Bicknell and Moran Caplat agreed to record in what have sometimes been called 'complete' versions; in fact, the former was not quite complete and the latter was heavily cut.

At Glyndebourne the cast of *Figaro* was headed by Sesto Bruscantini, Sena Jurinac and the Italian soprano Elena Rizzieri, who sang Susanna; the conductor was Vittorio Gui. Caplat was generally enthusiastic about the singers and recommended to Bicknell that they should, with two exceptions, participate in the recording. He expressed doubts about Frances Bible as Cherubino and, as a result, in December 1954 Bicknell invited the American mezzo Risë Stevens to replace Bible at the recording sessions. Stevens accepted the offer to record but stipulated that she should appear in at least two performances of the role which she had previously sung at Glyndebourne sixteen years earlier in 1939; Caplat agreed.

Finding a replacement for Rizzieri, who was contracted to the Italian record company Cetra, was a more difficult proposition. Graziella Sciutti, the Italian soprano, was suggested, but Caplat wrote to Bicknell, only five weeks before the sessions, that he was 'convinced that her voice is not of the right type to be successful on the records.' Sciutti had made her first appearance at Glyndebourne the previous year as Rosina in *Il barbiere di Siviglia*, and was contracted to sing there again, and at the Edinburgh Festival, repeating Rosina and adding Zerlina in *Don Giovanni*. If chosen to record, she would be readily available for the *Figaro* sessions in London and could rehearse her role with Jani Strasser and Gui as required. At the time of her scheduled performances Sciutti was heavily pregnant and it was perhaps no surprise that, at short notice, she cancelled her appearances in both operas, and was replaced by Gianna d'Angelo. In spite of Caplat's misgivings, Sciutti was selected to record Susanna for HMV, and in early July travelled to London specifically for the nine days of sessions. Her performance as Susanna has since been praised by many reviewers and is one of the delights of the set; she did not sing the role at Glyndebourne until 1958.

Among the *comprimario* singers who appeared in both the performances and the recording of *Le nozze di Figaro*, special mention must be made of the veteran Swiss tenor, Hugues Cuenod, who sang the role of Don Basilio. Cuenod made his stage début in Paris in 1928 and took part in the famous series of Monteverdi madrigal recordings conducted by Nadia Boulanger in the 1930s. After his first Glyndebourne appearances in 1954 he continued performing there with notable success, predominantly in comedy-character roles, until 1987, when he sang in *Capriccio* at the age of 85. After *Le nozze di Figaro* he took part in three further Glyndebourne recordings, *L'incoronazione di Poppea*, *L'Ormindo* and *La Calisto*, distinguishing all his performances with great vocal refinement and individuality; so it is regrettable that his only solo in *Figaro* has been cut from the set's most recent re-issue.

During preparations for the recording, Basilio's aria was one of the numbers in the opera that Bicknell considered might be omitted. On 13 June he wrote that he planned to cut both it and Marcellina's aria in Act 4, but within four days he had re-instated Basilio's. It was included in the original issue and all subsequent releases until 1991, when it was removed in order to accommodate the remainder of the opera on two well filled CDs and cassettes. Marcellina's aria *Il capro e la capretta*, which is frequently cut in stage performances, was not recorded and was the major omission from the original set; a few bars of *secco* recitative were the only other victims of the editor's pencil.

Bicknell was most enthusiastic about the development of Stereosonic Sound recording – EMI's early name for stereophony – which had been developed at HMV over the previous two years, and was publicly launched at the 1955 Radio Show in London. He planned to record *Le nozze di Figaro* using both single and double track tape machines, so that a Stereosonic version of the opera could be issued. In due course it proved to be the first stereo recording of a Glyndebourne production, a landmark in the technological advances masterminded by Bicknell and his colleagues.

A few weeks before the sessions began, Bicknell consulted Carl Ebert about technical points in his production of the opera; the directional quality that is the principal feature of stereophony lends itself to effective use of space and distance, and Bicknell was determined to make the most of every opportunity in this recording. He soon realised that the sound effects should be those actually used at Glyndebourne, and an assortment of contraptions used to simulate breaking glass, opening and closing doors and windows and other noises was transported from the theatre to Abbey Road studios for several of the sessions.

HMV had not yet designed a purpose-built stereo tape recorder for use in their studios and, as opportunities arose to make stereo recordings, used an adapted mono recorder with an added second recording head. The two heads were staggered, a short distance apart, and the tape passed over each separately, one head for each channel. Although the system worked well, it made subsequent editing extremely difficult; the matching signals from the two heads were not adjacent to each other on the tape, and a cut at one point affected two slightly different parts of the performance, a fraction of a second apart. Nothing daunted, EMI engineers used this equipment at several recording sessions between 1954 and 1957, often with spectacular success. Some years later, many of the original tapes recorded in this way were carefully transferred to new ones using modern in-line head recorders to facilitate future editing and re-mastering for LP. In these early days of stereo, mono was still considered by far the more important format, and priority was given to obtaining a good mono master tape. Stereo tapes were recorded in a separate and less convenient recording suite.

Thirteen sessions between 4 and 12 July 1955 had been booked, six months in advance, for *Le nozze di Figaro* at Abbey Road, but they were reduced to twelve when the one on the morning of 10 July was cancelled at short notice, an indication, perhaps, that they were proceeding satisfactorily, and ahead of schedule. Even at the end of the final session on 12 July, sufficient time was available for Gui and the orchestra to record Bizet's *Jeux d'enfants*, the only stereo orchestral recording made by the Glyndebourne Festival Orchestra.

The continuo was played at the *Figaro* sessions by Raymond Leppard, taking part in his first Glyndebourne recording, using a Goff harpsichord. The recitatives were taped separately from the arias and ensembles which they introduced, standard practice at recording sessions. Special credit for excellent studio production and sound quality achieved on this set must go to Lawrance Collingwood, the recording producer, and the balance engineers Harold Davidson and Christopher Parker. Collingwood's career in the studios began in the 1920s, when he first participated in recording sessions conducted by Sir Edward Elgar and other celebrated musicians. He continued to assist Elgar with his recordings until 1934, when he actually conducted the last session supervised by the dying composer. He prepared scores for recording, suggested 78 side breaks and cuts where necessary and, as conductor, made many records of operatic and orchestral music in his own right from the 1920s onwards. In 1957 Moran Caplat wrote this tribute for a dinner given in Collingwood's honour:

> Glyndebourne owes much of its renown to the confirmation that recordings have given to the tales of returning travellers in many parts of the world. We think it is true to say that Lawrance Collingwood has been involved in every one of our pre- and post-war recordings and we are eternally grateful to him for the sympathy he had shown to the works themselves and to our aims in performing them.

Collingwood's last contribution to a Glyndebourne issue was the preparation of the twenty-fifth anniversary commemorative LP in 1959 *Memories of the first Twenty-five Years*.

The first part of *Le nozze di Figaro* to be released was issued three months after completion of the recording. It was of Act 2 only, and was in EMI's 'tape-record' format. Only a handful of recordings were published in this reel-to-reel tape version, generally those in demonstration-quality sound. The series included four others using Glyndebourne forces; Mozart and Haydn symphonies conducted by Gui, Busoni's *Arlecchino* (both of which were in mono only), Bizet's *Jeux d' enfants* and *The Gondoliers* which, like *Figaro*, were early stereo recordings. The second part of *Le nozze di Figaro* to be issued as 'tape-records' was Act 1 in May 1956, followed by Acts 3 and 4 (together on three tapes) in September 1956 – a frustratingly fragmented way to release a prestigious commemorative recording. The mono LP version was issued on seven sides in January 1956, just in time for the Mozart bi-centenary, but its stereo counterpart did not appear until 1959; in the United States the set was released on four Victor LPs. Ten years after its first British release the opera was re-issued, again on seven sides, on World Record Club; WRC also produced the first highlights selection, in both mono and stereo, in June 1966. There have been two further re-issues by EMI, the first in 1984 on LP and cassette, the second in 1991 on cassette and CD. At budget price the 1991 set offers exceptional value and wears its nearly forty years lightly.

Three of the singers in this performance of *Le nozze di Figaro* took part in other recordings of the opera during the 1950s. Jurinac recorded the role of

Cherubino under Karajan for Columbia in 1950. A Cetra issue, taken at a live performance at La Scala, Milan in 1954, also preserves her interpretation of that part. She had sung it with Glyndebourne at the Edinburgh Festival in 1950, before being elevated to the role of the Countess in 1955, the year of Gui's recording. As the Countess she sang in another complete recording, on Philips under Karl Böhm, released shortly after Mozart's bi-centenary month of January 1956. Jurinac's husband, Sesto Bruscantini, recorded the role of the Count with the Milan Radio Chorus and Orchestra under Fernando Previtali in 1951, a performance in which Graziella Sciutti also took part, as Barbarina.

Gui's *Le nozze di Figaro* has become one of the classic recorded performances of the opera, comparable to its Glyndebourne predecessor of 1934/5 in the quality of its ensemble work. In critical review it is often compared to Decca's contemporary stereo version, also issued to celebrate Mozart's bicentenary conducted by Erich Kleiber with a cast that included Cesare Siepi, Lisa della Casa and Hilde Gueden.

Nation, New York, 17 March 1956:

As against the old Glyndebourne Festival *Marriage of Figaro* that Busch made mercurially swift and light, suave and elegant, the new Glyndebourne performance conducted by Gui is slow-moving and sharply pointed up for dramatic sense. But Gui not only lessens the effect of the section of the second act finale beginning with the Count's *Vostre dunque saran questa carta* by pacing it too slowly; he also destroys the effect of the Count's and Countess' spellbound amazement, which Susanna comments on with her *Signore! Cos'e quel stupore?* by playing the passage too fast. The most beautiful singing is Jurinac's as the Countess; Cuenod creates an outstanding Basilio with his remarkable inflection and coloring of his voice; and Ian Wallace's Bartolo and Monica Sinclair's Marcellina are good. But Graziella Sciutti's Susanna is a little sharp-edged; Bruscantini is a dry and rough voiced Figaro; Calabrese is a rough sounding Count; and Risë Stevens is a plushy-sounding Cherubino. A feature that calls for mention is the dramatically pointed and witty harpsichord accompaniment of the recitative by Raymond Leppard. But another is the dry recorded sound. The performance is, then, not without attractive features; but as a whole it is one I advise against.

David Hunt in *Records and Recording*, November 1959:

This stereo version of the Glyndebourne *Figaro* is a great success. So too were the stereo tapes of the same performance which have been commercially available for some time; but of course it did not automatically follow that the quality would be maintained in the transfer to disc. The acoustic, without being at all dry, is much less resonant than in the Decca stereo recording of the opera, and this results in a marked gain in clarity . . . In keeping with the style and character of the respective performances, HMV's stereo projects a livelier sense of stage movement than the Decca and is better 'stage-managed' from the point of view of sound effects . . . The voices are reproduced without the occasional edginess of the Decca, though there is some roughening in the Act 2 finale towards the end of side 4.

1956

IDOMENEO

Music by Wolfgang Amadeus Mozart

Libretto by Giovanni Battista Varesco
Edited for performance at Glyndebourne by Hans Gal

Sung in Italian

Idomeneo	Richard Lewis (tenor, English)
Ilia	Sena Jurinac (soprano, Yugoslav)
Idamante	Léopold Simoneau (tenor, Canadian)
Electra	Lucille Udovick (soprano, American)
Arbace	James Milligan (bass, Canadian)
High Priest	William McAlpine (tenor, Scottish)
Voice of Neptune	Hervey Alan (bass, English)

Glyndebourne Festival Chorus   Chorus Master Peter Gellhorn
Glyndebourne Festival Orchestra   Leader Arthur Leavins

Conductor   John Pritchard

Recorded   Kingsway Hall
                                      6 and 30.7.1956
                                      Studio No 1, Abbey Road 7.7 and
                                      4, 6, 8, 13, 26 and 27.8.1956

Recording Producer   Lawrance Collingwood
Balance Engineers   Harold Davidson and Douglas Larter

Original issue
Record Library Series 642
ALP 1515–7   (3 mono LPs)   10.1957
The twenty-four page accompanying booklet includes an introductory essay by Dyneley Hussey and a libretto in Italian and English, translated by M and E Radford.

Angel 3574 C/L   (USA) (3 mono LPs)

Re–issues

WRC OC 201–203	(3 mono LPs)	5.1968
WRC SOC 201–203	(3 stereo LPs)	5.1968

The sleeve notes contain background information on the opera and a synopsis in English by Virgil Pomfret.

Seraphim SIC–6070   (USA) (3 stereo LPs)
A libretto with the original Italian text as sung, and English translation, is included.

EMI CHS7 63685–2   (2 mono CDs – 72'05"/71'21")   12.1990

The accompanying thirty-eight page booklet includes an historical note in French, English and German by André Tubeuf: a synopsis in French, English and German by John Steane; and a libretto in Italian.

Excerpts

1. **Padre, germani**
2. **Non ho colpa**
3. **Tutte nel cor**
4. **Vedrommi intorno**
5. **Il padre adorato**
6. **Se il padre**
7. **Fuor del mar**
8. **Placido è il mar**
9. **Pria di partir**
10. **Zeffiretti lusinghieri**
11. **Andrò ramingo**

WRC OH 204	(1 mono LP)	12.1968
WRC SOH 204	(1 stereo LP)	12.1968

The excerpts of *Idomeneo*, recorded in 1951, had proved something of a mixed blessing when they were issued between 1952 and 1954. The quality of the singing, particularly that of Sena Jurinac, and Fritz Busch's conducting, had earned high praise, but the distress that the record's issue caused to Greta Busch, the conductor's widow, created considerable difficulties at EMI. Busch himself was said to be very hurt not to have had the opportunity to record the work complete, (or complete in Glyndebourne's performing version), but to have done so would have been a great commercial risk on EMI's part at a time when the opera was so little known. Undoubtedly prompted by the success of the original 78s, David Bicknell and Lawrance Collingwood hoped to record the remaining eighty-five minutes of the opera in 1953, at seven sessions in mid-September, before work started on *La Cenerentola* at Abbey Road, but their plans did not come to fruition. The contractual difficulties surrounding the project (to which Bicknell referred in a memo in 1954) are not mentioned in detail in EMI's archives; whilst Jurinac, Lewis and Young were all appearing at Glyndebourne in 1953, and could probably have taken part in the proposed completion, Dorothy MacNeil was not – the English soprano Jennifer Vyvyan was singing Electra. Would Bicknell have been obliged to ask MacNeil to complete her role, or would he have considered a different singer to be acceptable? A complete recording with two singers performing one role would surely be unsatisfactory, so the two sections on which MacNeil originally sang, at least, would have had to be re-made; and to merge two different performances, recorded two years apart, on to an LP issue would be fraught with technical difficulties. Plans for completion sessions, rather than a totally new recording, were mooted again by Bicknell in 1954, but were similarly abandoned.

Perhaps the prospect of a 'Stereosonic' recording, to be made in Mozart's bi-centenary year, was the spur that encouraged Bicknell to approach the members of his proposed *Idomeneo* cast in February 1956, with a view to making a completely new version of the opera. Of the seven singers whom Bicknell finally selected, two (Jurinac and Simoneau) were not appearing in the opera at Glyndebourne that year, and one – William McAlpine – had never sung his role there at all.

Bicknell's chosen cast was not assembled without considerable difficulty and several changes of plan. Despite having offered Jurinac a contract to record Ilia in February 1956, on 12 March he telexed the German soprano Elisabeth Grümmer, who was due to sing the role at Glyndebourne that season, and invited her to record it. There is no trace of either Jurinac's or Grümmer's response to his offers, but obviously suitable terms and a convenient schedule were in due course arranged with the former.

Léopold Simoneau, the Canadian tenor, had sung Idamante when Ebert's production was new in 1951, but had declined the offer to take part in the highlights recording conducted by Busch – whether for personal or contractual reasons is not clear. Now, five years later, he was prepared to record the role, but was available in London only between 4 and 8 July – although he could return at the end of the month if necessary. Detailed planning was required to arrange his sessions with other singers at times when they were all available.

Lucille Udovick, the American soprano who made her only Glyndebourne appearances as Electra in the 1956 season, was asked by Bicknell to make a preliminary test recording of parts of her role at Abbey Road. He had heard her sing early in the series of performances of *Idomeneo* but was not convinced that she was the ideal interpreter for the recording. On 21 June, Jani Strasser suggested that Lois Marshall, another American soprano, would be a suitable alternative, so Bicknell also arranged a test session for her; the previous month she had, with great success, recorded the role of Constanze in *Die Entführung aus dem Serail* with Simoneau under Sir Thomas Beecham. After Bicknell had heard playbacks of both sets of tests, he decided that Udovick was, after all, the better choice and on 28 June he wrote to Moran Caplat telling him of his preference.

David Galliver, Glyndebourne's High Priest, was originally invited to take part in the recording, but subsequently Bicknell realised that he would be unsuitable; his place was taken by William McAlpine, Glyndebourne's Idamante. This situation was a reversal of that in 1951 when Alexander Young, High Priest in Ebert's original production, had graduated to the role of Idamante for the recording. Richard Lewis, who sang the opera's title role in seven Glyndebourne and Edinburgh Festival seasons between 1951 and 1974, was a clear choice for the recording and was sufficiently free of other commitments in July and August 1956 to enable him to participate. It is worth recalling that just a month earlier he had completed EMI's recording of *The Mikado*; the journey from Nanki-Poo to Idomeneo is one that few singers ever make and it indicates the musical range of this most versatile and popular of Glyndebourne tenors.

With a satisfactory cast contracted for the recording, session planning was the next problem that Bicknell had to resolve. He originally hoped that studio No 1 at Abbey Road would be available for all nine dates, but he found that on 6 and 30 July it had already been booked for other sessions, including Geza Anda's recording of Chopin's *E Minor Piano Concerto* with Alceo Galliera. On those two days there was no alternative but to transfer *Idomeneo* to Kingsway Hall, a compromise he was prepared to make 'provided the musical numbers are complete in each studio and this applies also to the recitatives', as he wrote to Moran Caplat. Both studio No 1 and Kingsway Hall were excellent recording venues, but it was far from ideal to have to divide the sessions between them, with their different layout and acoustic properties.

EMI's archives indicate the scenes and arias that were recorded at the two Kingsway Hall sessions. The sections taped on 6 July were: *The Processional March* in Act 1; the duet *Padre, mio caro padre* in Act 3, running into *No la morte*, and the short duet *Ma, che più, tardi?* William McAlpine may have sung his phrase *Deh non turbar il sacrifizio*, but it is not clear at what point recording stopped at the end of Scene 9. On 30 July the following sections were recorded: Act 1 Scene 8, beginning *Ecco ci salvi alfin* including Idomeneo's *Vedrommi intorno*; Idomeneo's recitative and aria *Qual mi conturba* and *Fuor del mar* in Act 2 Scene 3: *Eccoti in me* in Act 2 Scene 7, and Idomeneo's *Popoli!* to the end of his aria *Torna la pace* in the opera's final scene.

Can a perceptive ear discern a difference in the recorded sound of these sections? Does Kingsway Hall have greater reverberation than studio No 1 at Abbey Road? Perhaps it is the stereo production that seems to give a marginally different focus to the sound in these scenes, but bearing in mind the difficulty of the task, the sessions' producer and engineers were able to match the acoustics of the two halls very successfully.

Hans Gal prepared the edition of *Idomeneo* that was used at Glyndebourne for its first production in 1951 and for all subsequent revivals until 1964. It was based on Mozart's original score composed in 1781 for performance in Munich, and also included a duet for Ilia and Idamante *Spiegarti non poss'io* that he composed for Vienna in 1786. The role of Idamante was given to a tenor and not to a soprano or mezzo – the original singer in Munich in 1781 was the male soprano Vicenzo Del Prato – which required the transposition of much of the character's music. Gal's score is preserved at Glyndebourne, and a mere glance shows how much he cut for performance. This mutilated version was also used by EMI in 1956, and whilst accepting that cuts may be acceptable in the theatre, particularly in a work of this length, reviewers have consistently criticised its use for the recording. Of all Glyndebourne's 'complete' recordings, *Idomeneo* suffered the most from damaging editing. The converse of this, of course, is that what *was* recorded reflected very faithfully the opera as performed at Glyndebourne, and probably represents better than *Le Comte Ory* or *La Cenerentola*, for instance, what the audience actually heard in the theatre.

The cuts are too numerous to list in full detail. They comprise some whole scenes; Act 2 Scene 4, (which consists of only eighteen bars), Act 3 Scenes 4 (fifteen bars) and 5, which included one of Arbace's two arias (both of which were cut); ballet music, and smaller excisions within many recitatives and arias that change the whole balance and shape of Mozart's work. In some cases Gal opted for Mozart's own condensed versions of arias, including Idomeneo's *Fuor del mar* and *Torna la pace*. As a brief example, in the first twenty-seven pages of the score, up to the end of Idamante's *Non ho colpa*, the following cuts were made:

Page 9:	4 bars cut in Ilia's recitative;
Pages 9/10:	6 bars;
Pages 14/15:	10 bars cut in *Padre, germani;*
Pages 16/17:	5 bars cut in the opening of Scene 2;
Pages 17/19:	29 bars;
Page 23:	7 bars cut in *Non ho colpa;*
Page 25:	6 bars;
Pages 26/27:	22 bars;

Perhaps too much can be made of what does *not* appear on this recording of *Idomeneo*. What *does* appear is some of the finest singing of Mozart's music recorded up to that time; Jurinac, Lewis and Simoneau in particular have been praised by many reviewers. More stylistically authentic and more complete versions have been issued since 1957 (when this set first appeared in the UK) but the elegance and passion of the interpretations are undeniable. John Pritchard's conducting has been complimented for its gentle shaping of the score and the sweetness of the orchestral sound. For some, it lacks the vitality and urgency that Busch brought to the 1951 excerpts.

Pritchard's *Idomeneo* has had a chequered career on record. It was originally issued on three mono LPs in the UK and the USA, on HMV and Angel respectively. For unspecified technical reasons it was not at that time available in stereo. Its first stereo issue in the UK was in 1968 on World Record Club (which also released highlights LPs in both mono and stereo), and in the USA in 1971 on Seraphim, Angel's mid-price label. More recently, *Idomeneo* has been released on two EMI CDs, for which the mono tapes were again used. The quality of the original stereo tapes was found to be too poor for re-issue.

Frank Granville Barker in *Records and Recording*, November 1957:

HMV's recording with Glyndebourne artists gives us the opera virtually as it has been presented at the "Sussex Salzburg" in the past seven years. This means, unfortunately, that *Idomeneo* is ruthlessly pruned. Cuts include Arbace's arias, though evidently one of them, *Se il tuo duol*, was originally to have been included as it has been listed in the booklet that accompanied these records . . . We lose a little, then, through being given the existing Glyndebourne version. But we gain tremendously, too. The conductor, singers and players are now so familiar with the opera that the interpretation has much more maturity and authority than could otherwise have been the case . . . this Idomeneo deserves high praise on every account: so much so, in fact, that any criticism sounds like mere carping.

Stanley Sadie in *The Gramophone*, August 1969 (reviewing the World Record Club Reissue):

There is much to be said in favour of this old Glyndebourne set, which must have given many people their first taste of Mozart's richest opera. The weakest thing about it is the text it follows: along the lines of worst German opera-house practices, many little cuts are made, often within lyrical items, distorting their form, reducing their scale: there are also many cuts in the recitative, including some very ill-advised ones in the big, dramatic accompanied recitatives . . . There is some excellent singing. Sena Jurinac is a fine Ilia, firm and clear, a real classical princess rather than the gentle girl we are sometimes given – I've heard performances with more tenderness, but perhaps none better sung. Léopold Simoneau makes a most elegant Idamante, singing very stylishly and coping easily with the florid music, though occasionally he tends to sing minutely flat. Richard Lewis is characteristically solid and efficient as Idomeneo. The Elektra [sic], Lucille Udovick, is quite capable, and has the right kind of incisive tone; the fierce arias come off pretty well, but she lacks the control for *Idol mio* . . . John Pritchard conducts competently, with a good deal of fire, but less emotional weight than the score can (and should) bear.

[8]   Glyndebourne's Baroque Era

L'incoronazione di Poppea, 1963
L'Ormindo, 1968
La Calisto, 1971
Il ritorno d'Ulisse in patria, 1979
Orfeo ed Euridice, 1982

L'INCORONAZIONE DI POPPEA

Music by Claudio Monteverdi

Libretto by Gian Francesco Busenello
An abridged version realised for performance at Glyndebourne by Raymond Leppard

Sung in Italian

Poppea	Magda Laszlo (soprano, Hungarian)
Nerone	Richard Lewis (tenor, English)
Arnalta	Oralia Dominguez (contralto, Mexican)
Drusilla	Lydia Marimpietri (soprano, Italian)
Ottone	Walter Alberti (bass, Italian)
Seneca	Carlo Cava (bass, Italian)
Ottavia	Frances Bible (soprano, American)
Valetto	Duncan Robertson (tenor, Scottish)
Damigella	Soo-Bee Lee (soprano, Chinese)
Liberto	John Shirley-Quirk (baritone, English)
Lucano	Hugues Cuenod (tenor, Swiss)
Littore	Dennis Wicks (bass, English)
Primo Soldato	Dennis Brandt (tenor, English)
Secondo Soldato	Gerald English (tenor, English)
Pallade	Elizabeth Bainbridge (soprano, English)
Amor	Annon Lee Silver (soprano, Canadian)

Continuo Players

Raymond Leppard	Harpsichord I	Courtney Kenny	Flue Organ
Martin Isepp	Harpsichord II	John Bacon	Reed Organ
Freddie Phillips	Guitar	Terence Weil	Cello
Maria Korchinska	Harp	Joy Hall	Cello
Robert Spencer	Lute	Robin McGee	Double Bass

Glyndebourne Festival Chorus	Chorus Master Myer Fredman
Royal Philharmonic Orchestra	Leader Raymond Cohen

Conductor | John Pritchard

Recorded | Studio No 1, Abbey Road
1, 3 and 31.7 and 1–3, 6 and 8.8.1963

Recording Producers | Ronald Kinloch Anderson and Peter Andry
Producer for Stereo Movement | John Cox
Recording Engineer | Robert Gooch

Original issue
RLS 908
HMV AN 126–7 (2 mono LPs) 6.1964

SLS 908
HMV SAN 126–7 (2 stereo LPs) 6.1964

The accompanying booklet to the original issues includes an historical note and synopsis by Raymond Leppard, who also translated the Italian text into English.

Angel 3644 (USA) (2 mono LPs)
Angel S–3644 (USA) (2 stereo LPs)

Re–issues
EMI SLS 5248 (2 stereo LPs) 6.1982
EMI TC SLS 5248 (2 stereo cassettes) 6.1982

The accompanying booklet includes an essay on the opera and a synopsis and the Italian text with English translation by Leppard.

Seraphim S–6073 (USA) (2 stereo LPs)

Excerpts
Non morir Seneca Glyndebourne Festival Chorus
EMI The Enjoyment of Opera
SEOM 3 12" sampler record 11.1969

Günther Rennert's 1962 production of *L'incoronazione di Poppea* broke new ground; Monteverdi's final opera, which was first performed in Venice in 1642, had never previously been staged professionally in England. In the ten years following Glyndebourne's production, three further Venetian baroque operas were given there, sung, like *Poppea*, in versions newly realised by Raymond Leppard.

Before Glyndebourne's production, the operas of Monteverdi were so little known that in October 1961, when planning recording schedules for the coming year, David Bicknell was prepared to write: '... I would not recommend the recording of *L'incoronazione di Poppea*, as I'm sure we couldn't give it away, let alone sell it ...' But by the time he came to prepare his schedule for 1963, recording the opera had become one of his priorities.

Leppard's musical preparation for Glyndebourne's production involved detailed research into the early manuscripts of the opera that survive in Italy – and these were incomplete. He had to reconstruct the music of the missing sections and orchestrate appropriate musical lines, re-creating as far as he could Monteverdi's intentions. Every scholar who has approached this task – and several have attempted it, including Gian Francesco Malipiero, Ernst Krenek, Walter Goehr and, more recently, Nikolaus Harnoncourt and Steuart Bedford – has come to different conclusions, but how nearly any of them has succeeded in preparing a truly authentic version remains a matter of conjecture. Leppard also had to make difficult decisions about textual cuts, as the opera was considered impracticably long for an evening's performance at Glyndebourne. Thus his performing version omits four scenes, containing music for Seneca, Ottone, Amor, Nerone and Poppea. In the thirty years since its first performance, Leppard's edition has been superseded by the research of other musicologists, but the extraordinary impact that it made at its première at Glyndebourne cannot be overestimated. There were twelve performances of *L'incoronazione di Poppea* in 1962 with a further ten the following year; on the morning of 1 July 1963, during the opera's run at Glyndebourne, the first recording session was held at Abbey Road's No. 1 studio.

Whilst Bicknell now wholeheartedly supported the recording project, he, and Peter Andry its co-producer, believed that a complete Glyndebourne version on disc was not commercially viable, even though the opera was already severely cut. They decided that the set would consist of two LPs, necessitating further heavy excisions. Jani Strasser, Head of Music at Glyndebourne, wrote to the conductor John Pritchard on 3 March 1963:

> According to our time sheet, the total duration of music in both acts is a hundred and forty eight and a half minutes. The amount that can be recorded on four sides is, to reckon safely, a hundred minutes. We are faced with the task of cutting out music totalling forty eight and a half minutes . . . Mr Andry says it may just be possible to record one minute more one each side, but that cannot be foretold with any assurance . . . I hope we shall be able to keep in at least part of the opening Sinfonia, and the part of the Seneca/Liberto scene which contains *Solitudine amata*, one of the most beautiful bits of the whole score. As it is, we manage to keep in all the most important features both from the dramatic sequences and the music aspect. One necessary loss is the final *Ritornello* of Act 1.

So one third of the music of Glyndebourne's production was cut from the recording, fully justifying its later description as an 'Abridged Version' of the opera. No further complete scenes were omitted, but almost every scene suffered to some extent. For example, in the first scene four cuts were made, in the third scene five, and a further five in the fourth scene of the second act;

only the final two scenes of the opera were recorded complete. The following explanation was printed in the libretto booklet included with the records –

> This recording of the Glyndebourne version has been abridged in such a way that no complete scenes have been omitted. Many scenes have been reduced in length but the continuity of the music and the story has been maintained.

– exactly the same principle used by Decca when recording *Orfeo* with Ferrier in 1947.

Peter Andry was invited to Glyndebourne in June to see some early rehearsals, and to discuss movements for the stereo production of the recording with John Cox, Rennert's assistant. Andry wrote to Moran Caplat:

> I should very much like to come to the pre-dress rehearsals on the mornings of 13 and 14 June and I should like to bring with me Mr Kinloch Anderson who will actually supervise the recording sessions, and our engineer Mr Gooch . . . Also I should be very grateful if you could lend us one or two scores of this work if you have them spare.

Difficulties are often encountered scheduling recording sessions to suit the availability of the performers, particularly when they are in the country for only a limited period. *L'incoronazione di Poppea* was no exception, and the first two sessions had to take place a month before the remainder. Oralia Dominguez was available only on 1 and 3 July, Walter Alberti was not free after 5 August and Richard Lewis could not record on 31 July or 2 August. Indeed, Lewis was very fully occupied at Glyndebourne during the recording period, singing in two productions in addition to *Poppea*. He appeared as Florestan in *Fidelio* and Tom Rakewell in *The Rake's Progress* – a total of twenty-seven performances during the season. Carlo Cava, the Italian bass, was equally committed. He sang Sarastro in *Die Zauberflöte* and Bartolo in *Le nozze di Figaro* as well as Seneca in Monteverdi's opera.

As at Glyndebourne, Raymond Leppard and Martin Isepp played harpsichord for the recording; there were eight further continuo players including Maria Korchinska the harpist and Robert Spencer the lutenist. The recording, with the Royal Philharmonic (whose last season this proved to be as Glyndebourne's resident orchestra), and the Glyndebourne Festival Chorus, was conducted by John Pritchard.

The recording was first released in Britain on the EMI Angel Record Library Series in both mono and stereo in June 1964; in 1982 it was re-issued in stereo on two LPs and equivalent cassettes. The duet *Pur ti miro* for Poppea and Nerone was included on EMI's *50th Anniversary Album* in 1984, and the chorus *Non morir Seneca* appeared on a Grand Opera Gala LP in 1969.

When the recording was originally issued it was compared by several critics with the only other version then available – a three record set, with different cuts, conducted by Rudolf Ewerhart on the Vox label. Whilst opinions differed, most reviewers felt that Leppard had over restored the instrumental lines, creating a sound that was more lush and fussy than his rival's; and, understandably, they deplored the destruction of the balance of the original, caused by the many cuts. But this set of *L'incoronazione di Poppea* has taken its place among HMV's pioneering recordings of Glyndebourne productions. With several more recent versions now available, it is generally considered neither a definitive nor an authentic performance, but it remains a potent reminder of the first English professional production of a work that has been taken into the international repertoire. It also proved to be the last Glyndebourne recording made by EMI for twenty-one years, excepting only the Classics for Pleasure highlights of *Die Entführung aus dem Serail* in 1972. It was not until 1984 that the next collaboration – *Don Giovanni*, conducted by Bernard Haitink – was taped, and by then David Bicknell and Moran Caplat, who together had been responsible for so many successful Glyndebourne issues, had both retired.

Bernard Jacobson in *Records and Recording*, June 1964:

> . . . HMV's recording obscures some of the textural detail in places, and in the mono it sometimes surrounds the voices with a degree of fuzz, but it conveys most of the colour of Leppard's scoring, and above all it captures the ambience of the theatre, especially in the spacious and natural sounding stereo version . . . The final love-duet, added by Monteverdi himself in place of Busenello's chorus of cupids and what-not, perfectly sums up the characteristics of the two versions: in the Vox it was grateful, crisp, melodious, "authentic" with a hint of the inverted commas; in the HMV it tears at the heart – this is the truer, deeper authenticity of Monteverdi's passion.

1968

L'ORMINDO

Music by Francesco Cavalli

Libretto by Giovanni Faustini
A version realised for performance at Glyndebourne by Raymond Leppard

Sung in Italian

Ormindo	John Wakefield (tenor, English)
Amida	Peter-Christoph Runge (baritone, German)

Nerillo	Isabel Garcisanz (soprano, Spanish)
Sicle	Hanneke van Bork (soprano, Dutch)
Melide	Jean Allister (mezzo-soprano, Irish)
Erice	Hugues Cuenod (tenor, Swiss)
Erisbe	Anne Howells (mezzo-soprano, English)
Mirinda	Jane Berbié (mezzo-soprano, French)
Ariadeno	Federico Davià (bass, Italian)
Osmano	Richard Van Allan (bass, English)

Continuo players

Jonathan Hinden	Harpsichord	Ian Harwood	Lute
Martin Isepp	Harpsichord	Freddie Phillips	Guitar
Courtney Kenny	Organ	Terence Weil	Cello
Elisabeth Fletcher	Harp	Christopher Irby	Cello
Robert Spencer	Theorbo	Peter Vel	Viola da Gamba
Desmond Dupré	Lute	William Webster	Bass
		David James	Bass

London Philharmonic Orchestra	Leader Rodney Friend
Conductor	Raymond Leppard
Recorded	The Organ Room, Glyndebourne 6–11.8.1968
Recording Producer	Michael Bremner
Balance Engineers	Kenneth Wilkinson and Trygg Tryggvason

This recording was made possible with funding from the Glyndebourne Arts Trust.

Original issue

Argo NF 8–10	(3 mono LPs)	2.1969
Argo ZNF 8–10	(3 stereo LPs)	2.1969

The enclosed booklet contains an essay *Francesco Cavalli and his opera L'Ormindo* and a libretto in English and Italian.

Raymond Leppard's next restoration of a baroque opera for Glyndebourne was first seen in 1967. Francesco Cavalli's *L'Ormindo*, also produced by Günther Rennert, was given its first performance of modern times there on 16 June. Composed in 1644, two years after *L'incoronazione di Poppea*, it was originally presented at the Teatro San Cassiano in Venice, the first public opera house in the world. Cavalli sang for a number of years in the choir of St Mark's, and later became its organist and *Maestro di Capella*; he began a successful career as a composer in 1640, completing over forty operas during his long life.

Following *L'Ormindo*'s success at Glyndebourne in 1967, twelve further performances were scheduled the following year with an almost identical cast; the only change was that in 1968 Irmgard Stadler, who sang Sicle, was replaced by the Dutch soprano Hanneke van Bork. Singers who appeared in both seasons included the mezzo-soprano Anne Howells, John Wakefield in the title role, Hugues Cuenod and Richard Van Allan. Van Allan enjoyed particularly close connections with Glyndebourne; he first appeared there as a chorister and an Apparition in *Macbeth* in 1964 having been a pupil both of Jani Strasser and of David Franklin, the Commendatore in Ebert's production of *Don Giovanni* in 1936. His solo début was in 1966, the year in which he received the John Christie Award from the Worshipful Company of Musicians.

Negotiations between Argo Records (part of the Decca group of companies), Donald Mitchell of Faber's (who had published Leppard's realisation of *L'Ormindo*), and Glyndebourne began in the late autumn of 1967. On 8 January 1968 Moran Caplat wrote to Michael Bremner of Argo with the decision on which the whole project depended.

> We had a board meeting today . . . [and] were told that John Christie Ltd were prepared to advance the £4,000 to make the recording of *L'Ormindo* possible. We can therefore go ahead and as soon as I have had confirmation of the availability of the artists for the period of 6–11 August I will let you know.

From a purely commercial point of view, a recording of an unfamiliar opera by a virtually unknown composer would have been unthinkable. Argo's enthusiasm and the support of John Christie Ltd, the fore-runner of Glyndebourne Productions Ltd, made it not only possible, but a viable proposition. One innovation that was readily agreed was that the sessions would take place in the Organ Room at Glyndebourne, the splendid music room added to the main house in 1920. Before the recent re-building, audiences were able to walk through the Organ Room on their way from the red foyer of the theatre to the terrace in front of the house. Now, although detached from the theatre, this room is still open on performance days. Over the years it has also been used extensively for rehearsals and concerts, but never before for a recording. Being far smaller than the old theatre, its acoustics suited Argo's purpose ideally. The rather complex layout for the sessions was planned well in advance. Bremner suggested that the orchestra and continuo should be placed facing away from the organ, spreading into the large bay window that overlooks the garden on one side, and the fireplace recess on the other. The singers should face them from the gallery end, actually singing from the gallery itself if a particular spatial effect were required for the recording.

Moran Caplat prepared a provisional timetable for the sessions, pointing out to Bremner that:

> . . . the first session cannot start before 10.20 am as some people arrive by train and we cannot get them here earlier . . . The second session should start at 2.45 to 5.45, with the statutory hour between the second and third

sessions, we arrive at 6.45. With the start of the third session a difficulty occurs here, insomuch as the last direct train from Lewes [to London] leaves at 9.25. I think you will have to cater for this when you plan your sessions and keep the continuo only perhaps for the latter part of the evening . . . I expect those artists who have gone back to London during the season [which closed on 4 August] will stay in the neighbourhood, but even so I need not tell you that the strain is considerable and it is therefore very important that they should, if possible, only take part in two sessions a day, or leave earlier on one session and come only for the second half of the next . . . The most vulnerable in this respect are Anne Howells and John Wakefield who unfortunately have the lion's share.

Between fifteen and twenty minutes of recorded material was expected to result from each of these three hour sessions, an indication of the labour intensive nature of the recording process.

Once the recording was under way in August 1968, Caplat wrote to Bremner:

As the Organ Room has proved to be such an acceptable studio for this sort of music, this is perhaps the moment to say that any time of the year when it is not needed as a public room for the opera, we should be happy to act as hosts if anyone wished to make recordings here of other music. In fact, it might even be worth considering recording a special series of chamber works if anyone has any bright ideas and, of course, cash.

The final edit of the tapes of *L'Ormindo*, completed by Michael Bremner a few days earlier, was heard at Kingsway Hall in London on 8 October, when Jani Strasser, Donald Mitchell and Raymond Leppard were invited to attend. It was clear immediately from the excellent recorded sound that the choice of the Organ Room as a studio was a wise one; and the musical performance under Leppard had been faithfully preserved.

In June 1969, four months after the three-LP set's release, Michael Bremner wrote with delight to George Christie at Glyndebourne: 'I thought you might be interested to hear that our recording of *L'Ormindo* has won an Edison Award in Amsterdam. This should help sales considerably . . .'

The records certainly gave reviewers a great deal to ponder. Again, the two principal questions were those of cuts (which in *L' Ormindo* were severe) and Leppard's realisation of the score. Cavalli's original three acts were reduced to two, and several complete scenes were omitted, including the Prologue, and much of the recitative. The characters of Love, Destiny and the Messenger, among others, were cut, and several scenes were moved within the opera, altering its original shape and balance. Whether or not Leppard had over-restored the instrumentation and continuo parts was discussed in detail – and the feeling was that he had destroying some of Cavalli's musical effects in the process. He had also transposed much of the music, the better to suit the voices of the singers. For example, originally Ormindo himself was sung by an alto castrato, whilst at Glyndebourne the role was taken by a tenor. Leppard made many other changes to Cavalli's score in matters where there was no doubt as to the composer's intentions. His was not so much a reconstruction of the opera as a re-writing.

Jeremy Noble, *Musical Times*, August 1969:

There is some charming singing here, especially by the women; in fact, Isabel Garcisanz as the page Nerillo nearly steals the show, although Anne Howells conveys much of the heroine Erisbe's fascination, vividly painted in the music. Even if some of the men are a little unwieldy (both Peter-Christoph Runge as Amida and Federico Davià as Ariadeno), the singing as a whole is never less than lively. Sometimes a little more, perhaps: there are exaggerations of rhythm, tempo and charcterization (not to mention the too-obtrusive continuo realisation) that strike me as vulgar, though it is interesting that Hugues Cuenod as Erice manages to be funny without ever being embarrassing, simply because of his impeccable musical taste.

1971

LA CALISTO

Music by Francesco Cavalli

Libretto by Giovanni Faustini
A version realised for performance at Glyndebourne by Raymond Leppard

Sung in Italian

La Natura	Marjorie Biggar (mezzo-soprano, Canadian)
L'Eternità	Enid Hartle (mezzo-soprano, English)
Il Destino	Teresa Cahill (soprano, English)
Giove	Ugo Trama (bass, Italian)
Mercurio	Peter Gottlieb (baritone, French)
Calisto	Ileana Cotrubas (soprano, Rumanian)
Endimione	James Bowman (counter-tenor, English)
Diana	Janet Baker (mezzo-soprano, English)
Linfea	Hugues Cuenod (tenor, Swiss)
Satirino	Janet Hughes (mezzo-soprano, English)
Pane	Federico Davià (bass, Italian)
Sylvano	Owen Brannigan (bass, English)
Giunone	Teresa Kubiak (soprano, Polish)
The Echo	Isla Brodie (soprano, Scottish)

Glyndebourne Chorus	Chorus Master Kenneth Cleveland
London Philharmonic Orchestra	Leader Rodney Friend
Conductor	Raymond Leppard

| Recorded | The Organ Room, Glyndebourne |
| | 10–13.8.1971 |

| Recording Producer | Michael Bremner |
| Balance Engineers | Kenneth Wilkinson and Stanley Goodall |

Original issue

| Argo NF 11–12 | (2 mono LPs) | 2.1972 |
| Argo ZNF 11–12 | (2 stereo LPs) | 2.1972 |

The accompanying sixteen page booklet includes a synopsis and note on Cavalli by Raymond Leppard, and the libretto in English and Italian.

Re–issues

| Serenata 436216–2DM02 | (2 CDs 62'18"/57'32") | 3.1993 |

The booklet contains a synopsis by Raymond Leppard and full libretto.

Excerpts
Janet Baker Recital
Ardo, sospiro – Ululi, frema

| Decca SDD 368 | (1 stereo LP) | 5.1973 |

The international success of *L'Ormindo* prompted Argo to begin discussions with Glyndebourne in 1970 about a recording of Leppard's next baroque realisation, *La Calisto*, even before the opera had been produced. Composed seven years after *L'Ormindo*, *La Calisto* had remained similarly unseen since performances in Venice in 1652. Peter Hall was invited to produce the opera at Glyndebourne, the first of many productions that he was to undertake there; the designer was John Bury.

The Philips Record Company had already expressed an interest in recording *La Calisto* when Moran Caplat wrote to Michael Bremner on 13 February 1970:

I have heard from Philips regarding the possible recording of *La Calisto*. From a practical point of view no recording of this piece could be made by us until the early winter, and only then if all the forces could be got together. More probably, any recording would have to be made just before or just after our 1971 season . . . I rather doubt whether I could raise the money as I did for *L'Ormindo* though an up to date estimate of how our outlay may be expected to return from this source would help me, if such money raising had to be done. Can you give me any information?

The following month Bremner replied:

... I am interested, though hardly surprised to learn that Philips have been after *La Calisto*, and the situation is, quite frankly, fairly complicated. *L'Ormindo*, which we recorded without any member of the cast being of star quality has done quite well, but it was only the Glyndebourne financial co-operation which has made it viable. In *La Calisto* the main part is to be taken by Janet Baker, who, I understand through the grapevine, is about to sign a new exclusive contract with EMI. This will naturally run a coach and horses through anybody's plans to record *La Calisto* with the original Glyndebourne cast, however well the production is received by the public and the critics. My own attitude is therefore this: if Janet Baker does not let herself be inextricably tied up with EMI, and if *La Calisto* is received with the same enthusiasm as was *L'Ormindo*, I would be interested in recording it using Argo funds alone. I am sure you will understand that, before I make any definite proposition, I must wait and see how these two problems resolve themselves. At this particular moment I will only plead that you do not commit yourselves to Philips, since our own recording of *L'Ormindo* has received such critical acclaim ...

Glyndebourne did not commit itself to Philips in this matter, but five months later members of the chorus did take part in Leppard's recording of some of Monteverdi's *Madrigals* and other shorter pieces – the first and only occasion on which the Glyndebourne name has appeared on the Philips label.

The question of Janet Baker's appearance was resolved in June, when Bremner wrote: ' ... I was very pleased to hear that Janet Baker will definitely make herself free to record *La Calisto* for us at the beginning of August next year. This being so, I would like to confirm that it is our definite intention to make a recording of this work ...'

In July, Bremner contacted Eric Bravington of the London Philharmonic Orchestra, regarding the orchestral forces to be used:

When we booked the orchestra for *L'Ormindo*, too many *tutti* strings were ordered and they could not be physically fitted into the Organ Room. Furthermore, after having had several very careful post mortems on the sound we have come to the conclusion that a better string sound could be obtained by further reducing the number of *tutti* strings. This will give more focus and a less boomy effect. We will therefore only be able to ask members of the LPO to take part in the following strength for the *tutti* strings; six first violins, six second violins, six violas, two cellos and one bass ... The continuo players of course remain exactly as they are.

La Calisto made further technical demands on the recording crew, and Bremner made the following comment and suggestion: 'One of the problems is going to be that so much of the chorus is off-stage and I have suggested to the engineer that we use the rehearsal stage for the off-stage chorus in conjunction with closed-circuit television or other similar electronic aids.'

The layout in the Organ Room suggested by Bremner in 1969 for *L'Ormindo* was reconsidered, and the positions of the orchestra and singers were altered. This conveniently placed the offstage chorus behind the soloists rather than behind the conductor, a more logical arrangement. A photograph in the booklet supplied with the records of *La Calisto* clearly shows Leppard conducting by the gallery, facing the soloists who were placed at the far end of the room behind the orchestra. Despite the reduction in the *tutti* strings, there still seems too little room for all the musicians to be accommodated comfortably.

Diana in *La Calisto* was Janet Baker's second solo role at Glyndebourne; she had previously appeared in fourteen performances of Purcell's *Dido and Aeneas* (including a television recording), and had sung in the chorus during the 1956 and 1957 seasons. Ileana Cotrubas, the Rumanian soprano, first came to the Festival in 1969 and made her British début as Mélisande in Debussy's opera *Pelléas et Mélisande*. The following year she sang Pamina in *Die Zauberflöte* and took the name part in *La Calisto*; in 1971, the year of the recording, she returned for eight more performances of Cavalli's opera. The cast was further distinguished by the presence of the counter-tenor James Bowman in his first role at Glyndebourne, of Hugues Cuenod, and of Owen Brannigan who, in 1971, celebrated the twenty-fifth anniversary of his first appearance at the theatre as Collatinus in *The Rape of Lucretia*.

Perhaps it goes without saying that Leppard's reconstruction of *La Calisto* attracted similar critical comment to that given to *L'incoronazione di Poppea* and *L'Ormindo*. The cuts were, not surprisingly, considered damaging and Leppard's realisation of the orchestral lines was felt often to be out of keeping with the composer's wishes; but of the three baroque operas so far recorded it was the most admired. The singing of Janet Baker and Ileana Cotrubas was particularly praised. Originally released in both mono and stereo on the Argo label, at the price of £4.50 for the set of two LPs, the opera was re-issued in the UK in March 1993 on two Decca Serenata CDs at mid-price.

In September 1972 the set of *La Calisto* was awarded the Montreux Grand Prix Mondial by an international jury of record critics, of which the chairman was Felix Aprahamian. Hugues Cuenod, the only Swiss member of the cast, collected the award on behalf of Argo.

Peter Branscombe in *Hi-Fi News and Report Review*, February 1972:

. . . . Whether the recording will appeal to people who have not seen the production, or to purists who have is less certain. If you can relish Hugues

Cuenod's brilliant cavortings as an eldery and would be lascivious nymph, you are safe in buying the set. On a more serious level, if you aren't sure you could take Janet Baker in the twin roles of the chaste Diana and as the sly, no-holds barred Jupiter disguised as Diana – I wager your doubts will be spirited away once you hear Miss Baker's marvellously apt and subtle vocal timing. Side 2 is perhaps the one to sample but she is in superb voice throughout. I don't think she has ever appeared to finer advantage.

The recording is technically extremely fine. As its producer Michael Bremner said when introducing a playback for critics, the aim was to achieve as natural a performance as possible . . . In the case of James Bowman's lovely counter-tenor singing in the important part of Endymion the gramophone has the advantage over the stage, that in terms of volume as well as musicianship, Bowman is the equal of Baker.

Shortly after the sessions for *La Calisto* were completed in August 1971, the question of recording yet another baroque opera – Monteverdi's *Il ritorno d'Ulisse in patria* – was raised by Michael Bremner; a new production was scheduled for the 1972 Glyndebourne season. In September Bremner wrote to Caplat:

> I have now been able to go into the question of *Il ritorno d'Ulisse*. Unfortunately we have run into a major snag. As you may have read, Decca have released a recording of this work on the Turnabout label at a cheap price. What is more, it has had very good reviews. The result of all this is that I doubt whether we would be granted the funds to make a new recording, even though it would include Janet Baker and might be more complete than the one they've just issued. I'm afraid this means that I must back out of the project, which I do most regretfully.

It was not until eight years later, when both Janet Baker and Benjamin Luxon (who sang Ulisse) had left the production of *Il ritorno d'Ulisse in patria*, that a recording was made, and then not by Argo, but by CBS.

The final collaboration between Glyndebourne and Argo took place in late 1971. On 13 October Miss Greenwood wrote on behalf of Michael Bremner to Caplat:

> In November we have a Rameau recording scheduled with George Malcolm, harpsichord, William Bennett, flute and Ambrose Gauntlet, gamba. Unfortunately the studio has just let us down and at this stage all our other usual studios are booked. I gather you and Michael did discuss the possibility of using the Organ Room for recordings other than the operas and I wondered if this would be feasible. The dates are 16-19 November. I know Michael would be delighted if this were possible, not only because it would get us out of a jam, but because of the high quality

of the Organ Room as a recording studio.

The chamber music sessions took place as Miss Greenwood requested but the recording was never considered to be a Glyndebourne project as such, and Argo made no further use of the Organ Room.

1979

IL RITORNO D'ULISSE IN PATRIA

Music by Claudio Monteverdi

Libretto by Giacomo Badoaro
A version realised for performance at Glyndebourne by Raymond Leppard

Sung in Italian

Penelope	Frederica von Stade (mezzo-soprano, American)
Ulisse	Richard Stilwell (baritone, American)
Telemaco	Patrick Power (tenor, New Zealand)
Ericlea	Nucci Condò (mezzo-soprano, Italian)
Eumete	Richard Lewis (tenor, English)
Melanto	Patricia Parker (mezzo-soprano, English)
Eurimaco	Max-René Cosotti (tenor, Italian)
Minerva	Ann Murray (mezzo-soprano, Irish)
Nettuno	Roger Bryson (bass, English)
Giove	Keith Lewis (tenor, New Zealand)
Giunone	Claire Powell (mezzo-soprano, English)
L'Humana fragiltà	Diana Montague (mezzo-soprano, English)
Il Tempo	Ugo Trama (bass, Italian)
La Fortuna	Lynda Russell (soprano, English)
Amore	Kate Flowers (soprano, English)
Antinöo	Ugo Trama
Pisandro	John Fryatt (tenor, English)
Anfimono	Bernard Dickerson (tenor, English)
Iro	Alexander Oliver (tenor, Scottish)

Continuo Players

Jonathan Hinden	Harpsichord	Tim Crawford	Lute
Jean Mallandaine	Harpsichord	Freddie Phillips	Guitar
Aniko Peter-Szabo	Organ	Mark Jackson	Cello
Stephen Wilder	Organ	Catherine Wilmers	Cello
David Watkins	Harp	John Lowdell	Cello
Robin Jeffrey	Lute	William Webster	Double Bass
Jakob Lindberg	Lute	Stephen Crabtree	Double Bass

Glyndebourne Chorus	Chorus Master Nicholas Cleobury
London Philharmonic Orchestra	Leader David Nolan
Conductor	Raymond Leppard
Recorded	Henry Wood Hall, London
	4, 5, 14, 17–19 and 22.6.1979

Recording Producer   David Mottley
Balance Engineers   Robert Auger and Mike Ross-Taylor

Original issue
CBS Masterworks 79332   (3 LPs)   11.1980
The accompanying forty-four page booklet includes the text and translations in English, French
and German, and an essay on the opera by Raymond Leppard, reproduced from the
Glyndebourne Programme, 1972.

CBS Masterworks 40–79332   (3 cassettes)   11.1980
CBS M3–35910   (USA) (3 LPs)

After the inconclusive discussions in 1971 about recording *Il ritorno d'Ulisse in patria*, the subject lay dormant for several years. The opera was given at Glyndebourne in three seasons – 1972, 1973 and 1979 – in a famous production by Peter Hall, designed by John Bury.

Ulisse dates from 1641, when its composer was seventy-four, but for many years there was doubt among scholars that it was by Monteverdi at all. A single contemporary manuscript has survived, and this is not in his own hand; Leppard discovered that it contained so many obvious errors that it raised doubts about the accuracy of the remainder. As with the other baroque operas that he realised for production at Glyndebourne, little detail is given about instrumentation, and in parts where the music for a scene is missing entirely, Leppard chose to compose replacement sections based on other works by Monteverdi that he considered appropriate. These included parts of *Madrigali guerrieri* and *Scherzi musicali*, both of which he had recorded for Philips two years before Glyndebourne's first peformance of *Ulisse*.

As Leppard himself pointed out in his extensive notes in the 1972 Glyndebourne Festival Programme, *Il ritorno d'Ulisse* is a comparatively short opera, and he needed to cut little purely for reasons of timing; only the long archery scene (Act Two, Scene Eight) was 'tautened', to use his own word. At a playing time of two hours forty-five minutes, the six sides of the recording run for longer than the staged performances of *L'incoronazione di Poppea* at Glyndebourne in 1962. In the sixteen years between the recordings of these two works, public enthusiasm for the operas of Monteverdi had increased enormously, and by 1979 David Bicknell's refusal to record the 'complete' version of *Poppea* looked, with hindsight, over-cautious.

In addition to Janet Baker and Benjamin Luxon, the cast of the 1972 performances of *Il ritorno d'Ulisse* at Glyndebourne included several notable young British singers; John Wakefield, Anne Howells, Alexander Oliver, Robert Lloyd and David Hughes. Only one Italian – Ugo Trama – took part; he was one of the five principals who also appeared in the 1979 revival, in which Frederica von Stade assumed the role of Penelope and Richard Stilwell that of Ulisse. Richard Lewis, at the age of sixty-five, made his final appearance at the Glyndebourne Festival in the role of Eumete, thirty-two years after his first performance there as the Male Chorus in *The Rape of Lucretia*.

In February 1977 CBS Records made the first formal approach to Brian Dickie, Glyndebourne's Opera Manager, who was later to succeed Moran Caplat as General Administrator, about the possibility of recording *Il ritorno* during its run of performances in May and June 1979. Dickie was impressed by the enthusiasm of Paul Myers, Chief Producer of Classical Records at CBS, and his assistant Vivienne Taylor, and in March 1977 reported to Caplat and George Christie that: 'They have already tied up Frederica von Stade and Richard Stilwell in principle, and I have told them that we would expect them to use the rest of the Glyndebourne cast, and this in principle they are very happy to do. The first thing to find out now is whether Faber [publisher of Leppard's new realisation] and Raymond Leppard are prepared to co-operate . . .'

Provisional recording sessions were planned over a year in advance, and in May 1978 Vivienne Taylor forwarded to Dickie her proposals. She suggested five sessions for the whole orchestra and three for the continuo alone, with one further session free to be used in whatever way was required. Raymond Leppard disagreed and wrote to Dickie:

> You will see that we need three continuo alone and seven with orchestra, thus some have only strings- only three use the wind band. By my definition:
>
> Full orchestra means Strings, Trombones and Continuo, and where indicated, wind band.
>
> Strings and continuo means what it says (ie no trombones and no wind band).
>
> Continuo means what it says (including the celli and bassi continuo).

Finally ten sessions were agreed upon for 4, 5, 14, 17–19 and 22 June 1979 at the Henry Wood Hall in London. The producer was David Mottley. The problem of space for the instrumentalists did not arise as it had in the Organ Room; the converted church is large and easily accommodated the strings and trombones of the London Philharmonic Orchestra and the fourteen continuo players. The recording was issued on three LPs and cassettes in November 1980, and it serves as a valuable reminder of the innovative production and highly praised musical performance.

Arthur Jacobs in *Hi-Fi News and Record Review*, December 1980:

> Some of the finest, most affecting singing I have ever heard in a baroque opera performance (recorded or 'live') comes from Frederica von Stade as Penelope – lamenting, at the opening of the first act, the cruel loneliness

imposed on her by the 20-year absence of her husband, Ulysses. Her interpretation of the role, coupled with Richard Stilwell's equally powerful Ulysses, would be enough reason in themselves to commend this set . . .

    This is, however, Raymond Leppard's considerably edited version of the score as opposed to the attempts made more than a decade ago to get near to an original scoring. These were the recordings conducted by Rudolf Ewerhart on Turnabout and, using 'period' instruments, by Nikolaus Harnoncourt on DG. The main point is that during long stretches of recitative Leppard makes frequent 'dramatic' changes between the accompanying continuo instruments (harpsichord, organ, reed-organ, harp etc) and even gives over certain sections to a fully orchestrated sound of strings or a consort of trombones. To listen to that opening soliloquy of Penelope's first on Ewerhart's recording, then on Leppard's, is to hear first a concentration on the voice with an almost monochrome background, and then a voice whose emotional changes are reinforced and even seemingly prompted by instrumental colour. Leppard's work is masterly in its effectiveness, and without doubt will give most modern listeners the stimulus of variety they like. But is this, perhaps, painting the lily?

1982

ORFEO ED EURIDICE

Music by Christoph Willibald von Gluck

Libretto by Raniero de Calzabigi

Sung in Italian

Orfeo	Janet Baker (mezzo-soprano, English)
Euridice	Elisabeth Speiser (soprano, Swiss)
Amor	Elizabeth Gale (soprano, English)
Glyndebourne Chorus	Chorus Director Jane Glover
London Philharmonic Orchestra	Leader David Nolan
Harpsichord continuo	Jean Mallandaine
Conductor	Raymond Leppard
Recorded	Brent Town Hall 12–15 and 18.8.1982
Producer	John Rushby-Smith
Balance Engineer	Pierre Lavoix

Original issue
Erato NUM 750423   (3 LPs-5 sides)   1.1983
A booklet including a synopsis of the opera by Raymond Leppard, from the 1982 Glyndebourne

Programme Book; the libretto in Italian with translations into English and French; and interviews with Dame Janet Baker, Raymond Leppard and Sir Peter Hall, was issued with the set.

RCA Erato NUM 750423   (USA) (3 LPs)

Re–issue
Erato 2292 45864–2   (2 CDs TPT 127")   12.1992
The booklet contains the libretto in Italian, English, French and German; interviews by Edward Greenfield with Dame Janet Baker, Raymond Leppard and Sir Peter Hall, and the synopsis, by Raymond Leppard (taken from the 1982 Glyndebourne Festival Programme Book), in English, French and German.

In October 1980, even before the set of *Il ritorno d'Ulisse in patria* was issued, CBS intimated to Glyndebourne that they would be interested in recording the forthcoming production of Gluck's *Orfeo ed Euridice*. For both Glyndebourne and the record company it would be a most prestigious venture. The French label Erato had also expressed interest in the project and for eight months preliminary discussions took place with both companies. By December CBS decided not to proceed with the project, and during the following eighteen months detailed negotiations over contractual and financial arrangements were held with Michel Garcin of Erato and his colleagues in Paris.

Dame Janet Baker was required for five of the seven sessions that were arranged for August 1982 in Brent Town Hall. Recording started on the day following a Promenade Concert performance at the Royal Albert Hall, and understandably, Dame Janet preferred not to sing at the first session. Instead it was used to record the overture and some of the ballet music in Acts 1 and 2. A further 'orchestra-only' session was held on the morning of 14 August, when the Dance of the Heros from Act 2 and the Chaconne and all the third act ballet music was taped. Raymond Leppard himself conducted the London Philharmonic Orchestra, as he had done at Glyndebourne, and Jean Mallandaine, for many years a valued member of his group of continuo players, was the harpsichordist.

In order to accommodate all the ballet music that Leppard had decided to retain, five 33rpm sides were required, making this perhaps the longest recorded version of the opera. Ten years after the set's original issue it was released for the first time on CD.

When preparing *Orfeo ed Euridice* for the Glyndebourne production, Raymond Leppard decided to base his version on Berlioz's 1859 adaptation of the opera for Pauline Viardot. Sung in Italian, it included many of the improvements to the score that Gluck made for the first Paris production in 1774 (twelve years after the première in Vienna), although some post-Berliozian alterations to the recitatives were also incorporated. One particularly attractive feature of Leppard's version was the inclusion of the ballet music, much of which is frequently cut from stage productions. He also included the bravura aria which closes the first act (of which Gluck's authorship was once doubted) *Addio, addio, o miei sospiri*. His '. . . intention to remain true to Gluck's inspired, mature version of the piece' was triumphantly realised.

Dame Janet Baker first sang Orfeo at performances at Morley College in 1958, but the role had never been as important to her as, for example, Dido in *Les Troyens*, nor as central to her career in opera as it had been to Kathleen Ferrier, her only predecessor in the part at Glyndebourne. Neither was it a favourite role, a point that she made clear during an interview with the critic Edward Greenfield, published in the booklet issued with the recording.

In her autobiographical journal *Full Circle* [*Full Circle* – An autobiographical journal by Janet Baker. Julia MacRae, 1982], Dame Janet relates the story of her final year as an operatic singer, including, of course, the seven week rehearsal and performance period of *Orfeo* at Glyndebourne. In a most personal way she reveals the stress that production caused her:

> The utter turmoil and desolation which has assailed me during these weeks of rehearsing it is far from simple, and only I can ever know what this desperate journey of Orfeo's has done to me; in the process of entering Hades and conquering the Furies, in the test of will and discipline involved in bringing Euridice back from the dead and obeying the god's [sic] demand not to look at her, Orfeo fails. The gods know the fatal weakness in all of us and choose the very thing they know we cannot do. Of course Orfeo fails the test. Of course everybody does. The myth says Euridice stays dead; I think this a true picture of the situation.

There were ten performances of *Orfeo* in 1982 with Elizabeth Gale as Amor and Elisabeth Speiser as Euridice. These were Dame Janet's last appearances in opera and brought to a close her remarkable twenty-six year stage career. The production also marked the end of the special partnership between Baker, Leppard and Hall which dated back to *La Calisto* in 1970. *Orfeo ed Euridice* was the third opera at Glyndebourne that combined their talents and all three were notable productions. As Dame Janet wrote in 1982: 'To work with Peter, one of the great directors of our time, coming as he does from that other world [of theatre], has been the peak experience for me as a singer-actress. He has brought much to us.'

Max Loppert in *Opera*, April 1983:

[Leppard's] performance possesses a quite splendid vigour, marrying to best advantage modern instruments (plus *chalumeaux* and *cornetti*) and pre-Romantic styles of execution. Dramatic intention is palpable in almost every one of his tempo choices. The character of the performer is, of course, at one with the character of its hero – in itself a mark of quite special achievement. Some claim to hear in Dame Janet's mature voice signs of wear; some detect hints of mannerism. I accept the criticisms while being myself profoundly moved by her every utterance. Like all the great Gluck singers on record, she moulds a strongly personal manner of utterance into a serene line . . . Elisabeth Speiser's Eurydice [sic] introduces a sad let-down – after the long build-up, the flutter of her first phrases momentarily imperils the whole enterprise, and though her soprano gains somewhat in focus thereafter, the difficult role needs far cleaner voicing than this. Elizabeth Gale's Cupid had the right keen touch, marred by a similar (if less serious) infirmity of tone. Most *Orfeo* sets, even the best, have some point of weakness; I would not let those of the Erato issue prevent it from joining my own *Orfeo* shortlist.

This chapter almost returns to where it began in 1963, with *L'incoronazione di Poppea*. Having decided against recording *Orfeo ed Euridice* in 1982, CBS expressed interest in taping the new Glyndebourne production of *Poppea* scheduled for 1984. The cast was to include Dennis Bailey, Maria Ewing, Frederica von Stade, Dale Duesing, and Robert Lloyd. Considerable research was undertaken by the Music Staff at Glyndebourne into the 1962 production and a detailed correspondence about timings and orchestration was begun; the project seemed well on the way to being confirmed by CBS. But as tentative enquiries were made about the availability of singers and orchestral players, the expenses of the project began to mount and by January 1983 the earlier excitement had cooled noticeably. The last traced correspondence on the topic was from Brian Dickie on 9 May 1983, writing to Martin Campbell-White of Harold Holt Ltd, who was assisting with negotiations:

Dear Martin,

Whatever is happening about the *Poppea* recording? . . .

[9] *Die Entführung aus dem Serail*, 1972

DIE ENTFÜHRUNG AUS DEM SERAIL

Music by Wolfgang Amadeus Mozart

Libretto by Johann Gottlieb Stephanie

Sung in German

Excerpts

Belmonte	Ryland Davies (tenor, Welsh)
Constanze	Margaret Price (soprano, Welsh)
Blonde	Danièle Perriers (soprano, French)
Pedrillo	Kimmo Lappalainen (tenor, Finnish)
Osmin	Noel Mangin (bass, New Zealand)

London Philharmonic Orchestra	Leader Rodney Friend
Conductor	John Pritchard
Recorded	The Organ Room, Glyndebourne 22–24.7.1972
Recording Producer	John Boyden

Act 1

1. Overture	Orchestra
Wer ein Leibchen	NM
2. Constanze!. . . . . O wie ängstlich	RD
3. Ach ich liebte	MP

Act 2

4. Welche Kummer	MP
5. Welche Wonne	DP
5. Vivat Bacchus	KL and NM
6. Wenn der Freude	RD
8. Ach Belmonte	MP DP RD and KL

Act 3

9. Im Mohrenland	KL
10. O! Wie will ich	NM
11. Welch ein Geschick!	MP and RD

Original issue

Wills Embassy Master Series		
CFP 40032	(1 LP)	11.1972
Vanguard VSD–71203	(USA) (1 LP)	
Vanguard LC 75–761987	(USA) (1 cassette)	

John Pritchard enjoyed a long and very successful career at Glyndebourne between 1947, when he joined the music staff as répétiteur, and 1977, when he retired from the post of Musical Director, which he had held for eight years. The range of works that he conducted for the company was extremely wide and included three notable English premières; Henze's *Elegy for Young Lovers* in 1961, Monteverdi's *L'incoronazione di Poppea* in 1962 and von Einem's *The Visit of the Old Lady* in 1973.

Pritchard prepared the scores for many Glyndebourne performances which he did not actually conduct; he played harpsichord continuo (and can be heard doing so on the 1951 excerpts of *Idomeneo*), had the unenviable task of advising on the cuts to be made when recordings were being edited, and himself conducted five commercial Glyndebourne recordings. The first of the five was *Arlecchino* in July 1954, followed closely by *The Soldier's Tale* in the spring of 1955. The next year he taped *Idomeneo* in the far-from-complete version then performed at Glyndebourne, and, in 1963, an abridged version of *L'incoronazione di Poppea*. All these performances appeared on the HMV label in the UK, and on Victor (*Arlecchino* and *The Soldier's Tale*) and Angel (*Idomeneo* and *L'incoronazione di Poppea*) in the USA.

In 1972 John Cox's new production of Mozart's *Die Entführung aus dem Serail* was given at Glyndebourne in two separate groups of performances. In the second group Belmonte was sung by the Welsh tenor Ryland Davies, Constanze by the Welsh soprano Margaret Price, and the role of Osmin, keeper of the seraglio, was taken by Noel Mangin (who had taped the part for HMV under Yehudi Menuhin in a recording issued in 1968); the Blonde and Pedrillo who sang in all performances in 1972 were Danièle Perriers and Kimmo Lappalainen, both making their British débuts. These were the five singers who took part in Pritchard's fifth and final Glyndebourne recording, which was issued in the Wills Embassy Master Series, on Classics for Pleasure in the UK, and on Vanguard in the USA.

Selected highlights of several operas were issued by Classics for Pleasure in the 1970s, including *Un ballo in maschera*, *Fidelio* and *Der Rosenkavalier*, but this *Entführung* was the only Glyndebourne production recorded by CFP. The series was in a budget price range, and when issued in November 1972 this single LP sold for just 89 pence.

The 'excerpts only' format was not, of course, unfamiliar to Glyndebourne and its Music Directors – certainly not to Pritchard himself. The recordings of *The Beggar's Opera, Orfeo* (1947), *Così fan tutte* (1950), *Idomeneo* (1951) and *L'incoronazione di Poppea* made no claim to be anything other than highlights or 'concise' versions of the operas, even though in some cases they included most of the music; (the occasions when a recording was cut, but still appeared to be a complete version, are in a different category, which includes *La Cener-*

entola, *Le Comte Ory* and the 1956 *Idomeneo*).

John Boyden of CFP corresponded with Moran Caplat and John Pritchard about the selection of excerpts to be recorded over the three days, 22-24 July 1972. On 7 March Pritchard wrote:

> I think this [*Die Entführung*] is a good choice in that it does not have such a large cast of stars as, for example, *Figaro* or *Don Giovanni* or even *Così*. Thus I imagine we could make a record consisting of the overture, one aria for the tenor, two arias for the soprano (one must have *Martern aller Arten*), the 'Triumph' aria for Osmin, one aria for Blonde and preferably the big quartet. I suppose one might economise and leave out Pedrillo and Blonde altogether, but then you cannot do the quartet and would have to replace it with one of the long duets for soprano and tenor.

It was soon decided that the chorus would not take part, as their participation would make the venture too costly. As the letter above implies, everyone involved in the project took it for granted that Constanze's *Martern aller Arten*, would be included; it is, after all, one of Mozart's great soprano arias – perhaps the best known number in the score. As late as 11 July a decision had still not been reached as to which of the character's other arias should also be included – either *Ach ich liebte* from Act 1 or *Welche Kummer* from Act 2. After discussions, the extraordinary decision was taken to drop *Martern aller Arten* altogether but to include the other two. This was a matter of great regret, not only to reviewers when the LP was issued, but also to its many purchasers who particularly hoped to hear Price sing it. The other singers are fairly represented on the recording; Davies and Mangin have two solos each and Perriers and Lappalainen one. Osmin and Pedrillo's duet *Vivat Bacchus*, the extended quartet at the end of Act 2, and Constanze and Belmonte's final duet are all included. The recording opens with a stylish performance of the overture by the LPO.

Following Argo's recent example, Boyden and Caplat arranged for the sessions to be held in the Organ Room at Glyndebourne, where both *L'Ormindo* and *La Calisto* had been recorded. The season was still in progress, and care had to be taken that all signs of the recording equipment were removed before the audience's arrival during the afternoon. The acoustics clearly suited the small musical forces employed, but despite several opportunities, and its apparently convenient location, the Organ Room has not been used for a commercial recording since *Die Entführung aus dem Serail*.

Alan Blyth in *The Gramophone*, December 1972:

> A potted *Entführung* must inevitably sound a bit like a series of concert arias and ensembles, but as such this disc is quite compelling, especially for

the superlative singing of Margaret Price, who has every attribute for the ideal Constanze; creamy but dramatic tone, brilliant attack, impeccable coloratura and a perfect sense of Mozartian style, taking in, and justifying beyond question, *appoggiaturas*. In view of the quality of Miss Price's singing it is sad that *Martern aller Arten* could not have been included. It is still more regrettable that the great G minor aria is horribly truncated, bad practice even in stage performances . . . but inexcusable on disc. What is left of the aria receives a poised elegiac reading from Miss Price, for whom the earlier *Ach ich liebte* holds absolutely no terrors.

We miss Haitink's virile, pointed conducting and have in its place Pritchard's more leisurely account of the music . . . We have Ryland Davies's ardent, lyrically sung Belmonte. If only Mr Davies could perfect his technique in coloratura passages, which here sound rather perilous, he would be a match for all present-day Mozartian tenors, except possibly Peter Schreier.

Since original publication in November 1972, this recording has not been re-issued.

John Pritchard's work at Glyndebourne continued for another six seasons, but he made no further commercial recordings there. He can, however, be heard conducting several broadcasts preserved by the BBC, the NSA and the MPRC. The earliest is the double bill *Arlecchino* and *Ariadne auf Naxos*, dating from 16 July 1954, and the latest *Le nozze di Figaro* at a Promenade Concert performance on 6 August 1974. He conducted two further Glyndebourne broadcasts, both in 1975, but these were not kept. Pritchard also conducted a number of performances for television, of which *Macbeth*, recorded two weeks after Classics for Pleasure's *Die Entführung*, is the earliest to have been issued commercially on video. But it seems appropriate that his last Glyndebourne audio recording should be Mozart. He was a Mozartian through and through, a natural successor to Fritz Busch, whom he so greatly admired, and from whom he learned so much.

[10] Anniversary Albums

Twenty-fifth, Fiftieth and Sixtieth Anniversary Albums
1959, 1984 and 1994

GLYNDEBOURNE FESTIVAL
1934–1959
Memories of the first Twenty-five years

Original issue
HMV ALP 1731   (1 mono LP)   8.1959
With sleeve notes by David Bicknell.

Le nozze di Figaro – 1935
Non più andrai   Domgraf-Fassbaender
Porgi amor   Rautawaara

Così fan tutte – 1935
La mia Dorabella   Nash, Domgraf-Fassbaender and Brownlee
Ah guarda sorella   Helletsgruber and Souez

Don Giovanni – 1936
Madamina   Baccaloni
Finch' han dal vino   Brownlee
Batti, batti   Mildmay
Deh vieni alla finestra   Brownlee

Così fan tutte – 1950
Non v'è più tempo
Di scrivermi   Jurinac, Thebom, Lewis, Kunz and Boriello

La Cenerentola – 1953
Zitto, zitto   Noni, Cadoni, Oncina and Bruscantini

Le nozze di Figaro – 1955
Riconosci in quest'   Sciutti, M Sinclair, Bruscantini,
amplesso   Wallace, McCoshan and Calabrese

Idomeneo – 1956
Andrò ramingo   Jurinac, Udovick, Simoneau and Lewis

Le Comte Ory – 1956
Venez amis   J Sinclair, M Sinclair, Canne-Meijer, Barabas, Oncina,
                               Wallace and Troy

In the spring of 1959, the industrious David Bicknell wrote to Moran Caplat saying that EMI was planning to issue a special LP to celebrate the twenty-fifth anniversary of Glyndebourne Festival Opera, which fell on 28 May. The record would include scenes from several of EMI's Glyndebourne recordings, and Lawrance Collingwood, who had been closely associated with the original production of most of them, was to select appropriate excerpts.

Collingwood must have found his task as fascinating as it was perplexing. There were twelve recordings which qualified for inclusion, but at a total playing time of about fifty-five minutes, the record would not be able to represent them all fairly. His final choice included excerpts from eight. *The Beggar's Opera*, *Idomeneo* (1951), *Arlecchino* and *The Soldier's Tale* were omitted from the selection.

In making his decisions, Collingwood was keen to include as many of Glyndebourne's best known singers as he could. By his judicious choice of solos, duets and ensembles he was able to feature almost every prominent artist who had spent more than one season at the Festival during the previous twenty-five years, and who had recorded a Glyndebourne production for EMI. Some names come to mind as regrettable absentees from the selection – Roy Henderson, Irene Eisinger, Constance Willis, Marina de Gabarain and Risë Stevens – but this was partially amended when Henderson, Willis, de Gabarain and Stevens were subsequently included on the fiftieth anniversary set in 1984.

David Bicknell wrote the sleeve notes for this issue. He recalled being asked by Fred Gaisberg to take charge of the sessions at Glyndebourne in 1934, when the recording van from HMV's headquarters drove down and parked outside the theatre; and the difficulty of trying to record eighteen takes of *Le nozze di Figaro* in one day – the session that led to the first *Mozart Society* issue the following year. He, more than anyone, was responsible for the wealth of fine Glyndebourne recordings that were made by EMI during the Festival's first twenty-five years.

Every Glyndebourne enthusiast would relish the opportunity to compile his or her own list of representative recordings in the way that Collingwood did in 1959, but any who attempted it would soon understand the difficulties involved – less than an hour was simply not long enough. The LP *Memories of the first Twenty-five years* was issued, in mono only (although two of the extracts included had been recorded in stereo) in August 1959.

Alec Robertson in *The Gramophone*, September 1959:

. . . the final impression of listening straight through the disc is to confirm that Glyndebourne has maintained its high standards throughout the twenty-five years here covered. Good casting, intensive rehearsal, a desire on the part of all concerned to give first place to the composer, have led to an engagement at Glyndebourne being regarded as a hallmark of artistic ability and to a perfection of ensemble rarely to be found elsewhere . . . Everyone, I think, will enjoy this delightful disc which shines like a good deed in a naughty world and must give great satisfaction to John Christie, whose vision and that of his wife Audrey Mildmay, whose charming *Batti, batti* is included, has been so amply rewarded.

50th ANNIVERSARY ALBUM
An Anthology of historic recordings from Glyndebourne Productions 1934–1963

Original issue

EMI SLS 2900233	(3 mono/stereo LPs)	5.1984
EMI TC SLS 2900235	(3 mono/stereo cassettes)	5.1984

The accompanying booklet includes articles by Spike Hughes and David Bicknell and texts of the extracts in the original language and English translation.

Le nozze di Figaro – 1934/5

Overture	Orchestra
Se a caso Madama	Mildmay and Domgraf-Fassbaender
Dunque – O cielo!	Mildmay, Domgraf-Fassbaender, Rautawaara, Willis, Henderson, Allin, Nash and Jones

Così fan tutte – 1935

Ah guarda sorella	Helletsgruber and Souez
Donne mie	Domgraf-Fassbaender
Fra gli amplessi	Souez and Nash

Don Giovanni – 1936

Guardate! – Madamina	Baccaloni
Vedrai carino	Mildmay
Che grido	Helletsgruber, Brownlee, Baccaloni, Franklin and Chorus

Die Zauberflöte – 1936

Grosser Sarastro	Ebert

The Beggar's Opera – 1940

How happy could I be	Redgrave
I'm bubbled	Gray and Mildmay
Cease your funning	Mildmay
The modes of the court	Redgrave, Flegg and Chorus
Would I might be hanged	Gray, Mildmay and Chorus

The Rape of Lucretia – 1946

Tarquinius does not wait	Pears
She sleeps as a rose	Cross
Flowers bring	Evans and Nielsen

Orfeo ed Euridice – 1947
Deh, placatevi   Ferrier and Chorus

Così fan tutte – 1950
Soave sia il vento   Jurinac, Thebom and Boriello
Prenderò quel brunettino   Jurinac and Thebom

Idomeneo – 1951
Placido è il mar   MacNeil and Chorus
Zeffiretti lusinghieri   Jurinac

La Cenerentola – 1953
Miei rampolli   Wallace
Nel volto estatico   de Gabarain, Oncina, Bruscantini, Wallace and Alan
Nacqui all'affanno   de Gabarain and Chorus

Arlecchino – 1954
Mit dem Schwerte   Malbin, Gester and Dickie

Le Comte Ory – 1955
 A la faveur   Barabas, Canne-Meijer and Oncina

Idomeneo – 1955
Andrò ramingo e solo   Jurinac, Udovick, Lewis and Simoneau
O smania!   Udovick

Il barbiere di Siviglia – 1961
All'idea di quel metallo   Alva and Bruscantini
La calunnia   Cava

L'incoronazione di Poppea – 1963
Pur ti miro   Laszlo and Lewis

Le nozze di Figaro – 1955
Se vuol ballare   Bruscantini
Canzonetta sull'aria   Jurinac and Sciutti
In quegl'anni   Cuenod
Pace, pace   Jurinac, Sciutti, Bruscantini, Cuenod, Stevens,
                         M Sinclair, J Sinclair, Calabrese, Wallace, Griffiths
                         and McCoshan

The compilation prepared by Keith Hardwick of EMI for Glyndebourne's fiftieth anniversary in 1984 was altogether more comprehensive than its predecessor. It was a boxed set of three LPs/cassettes, and was issued in HMV's Treasury series in May 1984. The enclosed booklet contained the texts of the excerpts in their original language with English translations, a foreword by Spike Hughes and articles by Hughes and David Bicknell, which supplied fascinating background information. It was illustrated with photographs of many of the productions. Recording dates, names of the producers and engineers and original matrix and issue numbers were also given. Confusingly, the dates given against the titles of the operas in the booklet do not always refer to the year of recording, but to the year of the most recent performances of the work at the time that the recording was made. For example, *Le Comte Ory* is shown as 1955 (not 1956) and *Il barbiere di Siviglia* as 1961 (not 1962). To add further confusion, *The Rape of Lucretia* is given as 1946, although the recording was made in 1947, immediately following three performances of the opera at Glyndebourne. Fortunately, the recording session dates, given in an adjacent note, are correctly listed.

Sixteen different Glyndebourne recordings were represented, including two which were not originally made by EMI, and one – *The Rape of Lucretia* – which was not truly a Glyndebourne recording. All four of the operas that had originally been recorded in stereo appeared in that format. Although entitled *Glyndebourne Festival – 50th Anniversary Album*, the recordings actually covered only twenty-nine years – from 1934 to 1963 – the earliest being Busch's *Le nozze di Figaro* and the latest Pritchard conducting *L'incoronazione di Poppea*.

As well as an excerpt from Decca's recording of Gluck's *Orfeo ed Euridice* with Kathleen Ferrier and the Glyndebourne chorus, a fragment of a BBC broadcast of *Die Zauberflöte*, given on 30 June 1936, was included. Carl Ebert, the producer, invariably played The Speaker in Act 2 of his pre-war production of the opera – (in Act 1 the role was taken by other singers, Ronald Stear and John Brownlee among them) – and the short speech *Grosser Sarastro* represents Ebert's contribution to the success of Glyndebourne Festival Opera. The provenance of the excerpt is a mystery. No copy of the broadcast is listed as surviving in the BBC archives and no recording of further extracts of the performance has been traced.

As in the 1959 compilation, *The Soldier's Tale* was omitted; so were the recordings made by Argo, CBS and Erato of the four operas by Cavalli, Monteverdi and Gluck between 1968 and 1982 – contractual difficulties may have prevented their inclusion. More surprisingly, the 1972 *Die Entführung aus dem Serail* was unrepresented, despite Classics for Pleasure's association with EMI.

The early 78 sections sound as good as new, excellently transferred and virtually free of surface noise; the whole set is a wonderful tribute to Glyndebourne's artistic achievement during its first thirty years. It is a tribute, too, to the skill of the original recording technicians and of Keith Hardwick, all of whom helped to make its issue a success.

John Steane in *Gramophone*, May 1984:

House, grounds and coat of arms grace the box front, essays by Spike Hughes and a memoir by David Bicknell distinguish the booklet within, and 12 operas, 15 productions, are recalled by the records. We begin and end with *Le nozze di Figaro* . . . Curtain rises, and there before us are

Audrey Mildmay and Willi Domgraf-Fassbaender, vivid as video in their acting with the voice . . . The last item of the whole set of records has the end of the opera, 20 years later, the tradition of fine ensemble work surviving, even if something of the exuberance of that 14 side day, June 6th 1934, is missing . . . Old favourites from the cast lists are remembered – Ian Wallace's Don Magnifico, for instance, and (oldest and most favourite of all) Hugues Cuenod, who carries his age rather better than does the sound quality of some of the recordings. All in all, rich gleanings from a golden half-century.

GLYNDEBOURNE RECORDED
Sixtieth Anniversary Compact Disc
Recordings from 1934–1988

Original issue
CDH 5 65072 2   (1 CD – 75'14")   3.1994
The CD booklet includes an introduction by Sir George Christie and notes on Glyndebourne's 60 year association with EMI by Paul Campion.

Le nozze di Figaro – 1934
Canzonetta sull'aria –   Rautawaara and Mildmay
Ricevete o padroncina   Chorus

Così fan tutte – 1935
Una bella serenata   Nash, Domgraf-Fassbaender and Brownlee

Don Giovanni – 1936
Epilogue Act 2   Helletsgruber, Mildmay, Souez, Pataky, Henderson
                                      and Baccaloni

The Beggar's Opera – 1940
O Polly, you might have toyed   Mildmay, Willis and Henderson
My heart was so free   Redgrave
Were I laid on Greenland's coast Redgrave and Mildmay

Così fan tutte – 1950
Questa picciola   Thebom and Kunz
Il core vi dono

Idomeneo – 1951
Vedrommi intorno   Lewis

La Cenerentola – 1953
Signor . . . Una parola   de Gabarain, Wallace, Bruscantini and Oncina

La nozze di Figaro – 1955
Riconosci in quest' amplesso   Sciutti, M Sinclair, Bruscantini, Wallace, McCoshan
                                      and Calabrese

Le Comte Ory – 1956
O bon ermite   Barabas, Canne-Meijer, Oncina and Chorus

Idomeneo – 1956
Ah perchè pria
Spiegarti non poss'io   Jurinac and Simoneau

Il barbiere di Siviglia – 1962
Ah qual colpo   de los Angeles, Alva and Bruscantini

L'incoronazione di Poppea – 1963
Pur ti miro   Laszlo and Lewis

Die Entführung aus dem Serail – 1972
Ach ich liebte   Price

Don Giovanni – 1984
Là ci darem la mano   Gale and Allen

Così fan tutte – 1986
Dove son
Soave sia il vento   Vaness, Ziegler and Desderi

Le nozze di Figaro – 1987
Cinque, dieci   Desderi and Rolandi

Porgy and Bess – 1988
Bess you is my woman now   White and Haymon

The Festival's sixtieth anniversary provides another wonderful opportunity to issue a compilation of excerpts of Glyndebourne opera recordings, the first such on CD.

EMI invited Paul Campion to choose extracts which would represent the recorded repertoire of Glyndebourne's first sixty years and would feature many of the singers and conductors who have appeared at the Festival with particular success. This was a delightful, if daunting task, as both Lawrance Collingwood and Keith Hardwick had already discovered. With a maximum CD playing time of under eighty minutes, each extract would necessarily have to be short – certainly no more than six minutes and ideally considerably less. Only the sextet from *Le nozze di Figaro* of 1955 and the duet from *L'incoronazione di Poppea* of 1963 have previously been included on Glyndebourne compilations. *Arlecchino* is the sole EMI opera recording that is not represented.

The CD *Glyndebourne Recorded* includes excerpts from seventeen commercial recordings beginning with *Le nozze di Figaro* in 1934. The Act 3 duet is delightful; Mildmay and Rautawaara sparkle in the brief recitative and only the chorus sound perhaps a little faded sixty years on. In the trio from *Così fan tutte* Nash, Brownlee and Domgraf-Fassbaender are in romantic high spirits; how sweet is their deceptive scheming. Alas, it has still not proved possible to represent the highly-praised Despina of Irene Eisinger, the one especially regretted omission from the CD.

In the Epilogue to Act 2 of *Don Giovanni* all the principals, save the eponymous rake himself, are heard; particularly pleasing are the lyrical Don Ottavio of Pataky and the two Donnas – Anna and Elvira. Souez and Helletsgruber are superb and the re-mastered sound of the 1936 recording is astonishingly good.

Three excerpts from *The Beggar's Opera* introduce Mildmay, Willis, Redgrave and Henderson. Redgrave's light baritone is heard to advantage in both his solo *My heart was so free* and his duet with Mildmay *Were I laid on Greenland's coast*, a tune as familiar today as it was to Pepusch and John Gay over two hundred and sixty years ago. In the trio *O Polly, you might have toyed and kissed* Mildmay, Willis and Henderson are hardly authentic low-life characters, but are properly 'English and correct' – and none the worse for that!

Moving on ten years, to *Così fan tutte* in 1950, Thebom and Kunz sing their palpitating second act duet with warmth. Neither was a 'Glyndebourne regular' although Kunz had been a chorister at the Festival before the second world war and returned to sing Guglielmo (in Edinburgh) in 1948. The 1950 season was his last and Thebom's only one at Glyndebourne. Richard Lewis's 1951 version of *Vedrommi intorno* from *Idomeneo*, never issued as a 78, is heard here with all his youthful freshness of tone. He was to sing the role at several Glyndebourne seasons for a further twenty-three years!

The exuberant first act quartet from *La Cenerentola* introduces four singers who, in 1952, took part in Glyndebourne's first production of a Rossini opera. Angelina was de Gabarain's only Rossini role at Glyndebourne, but Wallace, Bruscantini and Oncina also sang there in both *Le Comte Ory* and *Il barbiere di Siviglia*. Sinclair, Sciutti, Calabrese, Bruscantini, McCoshan and Wallace are heard in the brilliant sextet from the third act of *Le nozze di Figaro*, surely the finest ensemble from any of Mozart's comic operas. Under Gui's guidance the singers bestow on it both the gravity and the wit that it needs to make its full effect; this was one of EMI's first commercial stereo recordings and it still sounds exceptionally good.

The trio from *Le Comte Ory* offers Sari Barabas an opportunity to display her bright-toned soprano. She sang Countess Adèle in all four seasons that the opera was produced at Glyndebourne in the 1950s and Oncina sang Ory in all these performances. Canne-Meijer never sang Isolier at the Festival, but learnt the role for the recording. *Idomeneo* was also recorded in 1956 and the recitative and duet from Act 3 feature Glyndebourne's supreme Mozartian soprano of the decade, Sena Jurinac. She and Simoneau sing with tender, ardent tone in their declaration of love.

The inclusion of de los Angeles and Alva in *Ah qual colpo* from *Il barbiere di Siviglia* may be cheating slightly, as they never sang the roles of Rosina and Almaviva at Glyndebourne, but Bruscantini was a much admired Figaro there. Together they make the elopement trio a marvellously funny, urgent scene as they are on the point of being discovered.

Glyndebourne's productions of baroque opera are acknowledged by the closing duet from *L'incoronazione di Poppea*, with Lewis and Laszlo. A more recent 'authentic' recording might sound very different from this lush realisation by Raymond Leppard, but the beauty of the singing and instrumentation cannot be denied.

EMI's only Glyndebourne recording of the 1970s – CFP's *Die Entführung aus dem Serail* excerpts – is represented by Margaret Price's singing of *Ach ich liebte* from Act 1. She sang in two productions of the opera at the Festival to great acclaim, and her creamy soprano, with its outstanding flexibility, was ideally suited to the role of Constanze.

Sir Peter Hall's productions of Mozart's da Ponte operas provide the next three items on the CD. Don Giovanni, in the person of Thomas Allen, tries a little persuasion on an *almost* innocent Zerlina (Elizabeth Gale), and surely more nearly gets his own way than any other singer on record, such is his seductive charm. The Fiordiligi and Dorabella of Vaness and Ziegler are joined by Don Alfonso, sung by Claudio Desderi, in the celebrated trio from *Così fan tutte* – *Soave sia il vento* – and the ladies bid farewell to their lovers, as the men's deception begins. Next, Desderi and Rolandi sing the opening duet of *Le nozze di Figaro* as Figaro and Susanna prepare, in their different ways, for their forthcoming wedding.

Finally, two more lovers express their feelings in a duet from *Porgy and Bess*. *Bess you is my woman now* is one of the best known numbers from Gershwin's score, and is generously and lovingly sung by White and Haymon on EMI's most recent recording of a Glyndebourne production.

The conductors who are featured on the CD are Fritz Busch, Michael Mudie, Vittorio Gui, John Pritchard, Bernard Haitink and Simon Rattle, and the orchestras the London Symphony, and the Royal Philharmonic (both of which recorded as the Glyndebourne Festival Orchestra) and the London Philharmonic.

[11]   The Haitink Mozart Recordings

Don Giovanni, 1984
Così fan tutte, 1986
Le nozze di Figaro, 1987

DON GIOVANNI

Music by Wolfgang Amadeus Mozart

Libretto by Lorenzo da Ponte

Sung in Italian

Don Giovanni	Thomas Allen (baritone, English)
Donna Anna	Carol Vaness (soprano, American)
Donna Elvira	Maria Ewing (soprano, American)
Leporello	Richard Van Allan (bass, English)
Don Ottavio	Keith Lewis (tenor, New Zealand)
Commendatore	Dimitri Kavrakos (bass, Greek)
Zerlina	Elizabeth Gale (soprano, English)
Masetto	John Rawnsley (baritone, English)

Glyndebourne Chorus	Chorus Director Jane Glover
London Philharmonic Orchestra	Leader David Nolan
Harpsichord continuo	Martin Isepp
Mandolin	James Ellis
Conductor	Bernard Haitink
Recorded	Studio No 1, Abbey Road
	3–12.1.1984
Recording Producer	John Fraser
Balance Engineer	Stuart Eltham

This recording, to commemorate the 50th anniversary of Glyndebourne, was made possible by the generosity of friends and relatives of Dawson and Cyril Miller, who were longstanding members of the Glyndebourne Festival Society.

Original issue

EMI SLS 143665–3	(3 LPs)	6.1984
EMI SLS 143665–9	(2 cassettes)	6.1984
EMI CDS7 47037–8	(3 CDs 63'35"/63'44"/44'17")	8.1984

The accompanying booklet includes an essay *The Opera of Operas* by John Higgins: an introduction in English, French and German and the libretto in English, French, German and Italian.

CDCC 47036   (USA) (3 CDs)

In October 1981, after a break of eighteen years (with the exception of *Die Entführung* on CFP), Glyndebourne and EMI came together again to discuss the possibility of a joint recording. Brian Dickie, who had just succeeded Moran Caplat as General Administrator, met Peter Andry and Mike Allen, respectively Director and General Manager of EMI Classical Division. A new Mozart recording to celebrate fifty years of the Glyndebourne Festival was discussed, the obvious choice being *Le nozze di Figaro*. Dickie wrote to Allen after the meeting:

> I think I have emphasised enough to you the enthusiasm we have for EMI recording the two other da Ponte operas. *Don Giovanni* will be conducted here next year by Bernard Haitink, and I have no doubt that we could assemble the forces sometime between September 1982 and April 1983. He will also be conducting *Così fan tutte* in 1985 or 1986 and it would give us great satisfaction if HMV were to repeat with Bernard Haitink in the 80's what they did with Fritz Busch in the 30's.

Because of the schedule of performances at Glyndebourne in 1984, the wisest course seemed to be to split the twelve sessions that *Figaro* required between early June and late July/early August.

By November, Brian Dickie's feelings about the choice of the *Figaro* recording had changed, as Haitink's commitments in the summer of 1984 made the inclusion of twelve sessions virtually impossible. Equally difficult was the fact that the casting of the performances at Glyndebourne was not yet complete:

> . . . we have serious doubts about the wisdom of committing ourselves to a recording in advance of contracting the cast. On the other hand, we are not prepared to allow our casting of the 1984 performances to be influenced by recording considerations.

Three months later Dickie wrote to Bernard Haitink, whose enthusiasm as Musical Director of Glyndebourne was, naturally, essential to the project:

> It would, of course, be wonderful to record *Idomeneo* but I feel that it would be wrong to commit ourselves to recording immediately after the 1983 season when the piece and the cast, in recording terms, are unknown quantities. I favour very strongly an examination of the possibility of recording *Don Giovanni*. We have a pool of distinguished singers who have sung the roles at Glyndebourne over the last six years to choose from, and

I believe that we could get together a very impressive combination for a fortnight in January . . . I really feel that to record after your last *Idomeneo* performance in 1983 would be unsatisfactory since the orchestra will have further performances at Glyndebourne. However, if EMI can get the orchestra and singers for two weeks in January 1984 it would be possible to recreate the conditions for a real Glyndebourne performance.

Among the distinguished singers whom Dickie listed as possible choices for the recording were Benjamin Luxon, Thomas Allen and Brent Ellis as Don Giovanni, Leo Goeke, Philip Langridge and Keith Lewis as Don Ottavio, and Rosario Andrade, Rachel Yakar and Elizabeth Pruett as Donna Elvira. Over the next few months the artists under consideration continued to change. Thomas Allen emerged as a clear preference, but Gösta Winbergh, who was also booked to record with Herbert von Karajan, was now proposed as a possible Don Ottavio. As Elvira, both Lucia Popp and Kiri Te Kanawa were mentioned, but the name of Maria Ewing received the most support, although she had never sung the role at Glyndebourne. Referring to Leporello, Dickie wrote to Peter Andry:

> . . . I believe that [Richard Van Allan's] inclusion in the cast is extremely important if we are to produce a real Glyndebourne *Don Giovanni* performance . . . I think you should know that close though both Sam Ramey and Donald Gramm are to Glyndebourne, we cannot in all conscience include them in the recording and attempt to pass it off as a Glyndebourne performance – it would not be.

In May 1982 both George Christie and Brian Dickie had reservations about other suggestions made by EMI. The proposed cast was becoming less and less like a genuine Glyndebourne performance, and Christie noted in a memo: '. . . let's forget it and think instead of doing *Figaro* after the 1984 season, for issue in 1985 . . . It would be the genuine article, with a real Glyndebourne cast.'

But *Don Giovanni* was not to be forgotten, and by January 1983 almost the entire cast of the 1982 performances was engaged for the recording. The two exceptions were the Masetto, Gordon Sandison, who was replaced by John Rawnsley, (who had sung the role in the 1978 season), and the Donna Elvira, Elizabeth Pruett, replaced by Maria Ewing.

The detailed schedule of sessions at Abbey Road studio was prepared a year in advance, and had to take special note of the fact that Carol Vaness, the Donna Anna, was available only from 3 to 8 January 1984, and Dimitri Kavrakos, the Commendatore, on only 3 and 4 of the month. Thus, while Vaness was free, there needed to be at least three days with two three-hour sessions per day, with an average of fifteen minutes of music recorded at each.

A few minutes of rehearsals and a short section of one of the recording sessions at Abbey Road were filmed for BBC Television, who were preparing a fiftieth anniversary tribute, entitled *Glyndebourne – A Celebration of 50 Years* (q.v. p. 207). The extracts relating to the recording also included comments by Martin Isepp, the Head of Music Staff, Sir Peter Hall, and Bernard Haitink. The film, which was broadcast on 30 June 1984, provides a fascinating glimpse of the cast with their répétiteur, producer and conductor.

The release of the set on LP and cassette was planned for 28 May 1984, the fifitieth anniversary of the first performance of the Festival. Copies were on sale at the shop at Glyndebourne and, according to Brian Dickie on 31 May: '. . . it is selling quite well, though not nearly as well as the Anniversary album [see Chapter 10] which is going like hot cakes.'

Mike Allen was justifiably proud of the speed with which the records had been issued:

> . . . it always was the intention that it should be a June release, with its first appearance in public being at Glyndebourne on 28 May. I am sure you will appreciate that we have, in fact, brought out the record in an exceptionally short space of time. As regards the CD release, two months from now is my best guess. It will be our very first opera on CD, and we are currently going through the process of learning how to put the normal twelve-inch libretto into a four-inch multi-page book. There is no problem about the discs: they have already been mastered for CD.

Edward Greenfield in *The Guardian*, 30 May 1984:

The new set shows at almost every point just how well Glyndebourne keeps it place even in the highest international league. Unlike Busch's 1937 [sic] version, this one has a dozen or so rivals in the current catalogue, many of them with casts notably more star-studded, yet this is the most consistent and satisfying of recent versions. Thomas Allen's Giovanni is amongst the best and most stylish ever put on on record, and certainly the most winning . . . Above all, with Haitink rising to the challenge too, the closing scene of Giovanni's descent to hell has never been so powerfully, chillingly gripping on record. It is not just the result of spacious digital recording.

Carol Vaness as Anna is magnificent in Act 1, but then falls a little short over *Non mi dir* in Act 2, while similarly Maria Ewing, a vibrant Elvira, is more effective in ensembles than in her arias . . . Of the others, Keith Lewis makes an excellent, heady-toned Ottavio, superb in *Dalla sua pace*, Richard Van Allan an agile Leporello, who avoids unmusical *buffo* tricks, Dimitri Kavrakos, a light but still threatening Commendatore, and Elizabeth Gale and John Rawnsley endearing as the plebeian pair of Zerlina and Masetto.

1986

COSÌ FAN TUTTE

Music by Wolfgang Amadeus Mozart

Libretto by Lorenzo da Ponte

Sung in Italian

Ferrando	John Aler (tenor, American)
Guglielmo	Dale Duesing (baritone, American)
Don Alfonso	Claudio Desderi (baritone, Italian)
Fiordiligi	Carol Vaness (soprano, American)
Dorabella	Delores Ziegler (soprano, American)
Despina	Lillian Watson (soprano, English)

Glyndebourne Chorus	Chorus Master Ivor Bolton
London Philharmonic Orchestra	Leader David Nolan
Harpsichord continuo	Martin Isepp
Cello continuo	Robert Truman

Conductor	Bernard Haitink

Recorded	Studio No 1, Abbey Road
	16–21, 23, 26 and 27.2.1986

Recording Producer	John Fraser
Recording Engineer	Stuart Eltham

This recording was made possible with sponsorship from Vincent Meyer

Original issue
EMI EX 270540–3	(3 LPs)	5.1987
EMI EX 270540–5	(3 cassettes)	5.1987
EMI CDS7 47727–8	(3 CDs 73'32"/59'02"/53'33")	5.1987

This issue includes an accompanying booklet with essays in English, French and German: *The neglect and rediscovery of a masterpiece* by William Mann: *The Enigma of 'Così fan tutte'* by David Cairns (reproduced from the 1978 Glyndebourne Programme Book); and a synopsis and libretto in English, French, German and Italian.

CDCC 47727	(USA) (3 CDs)

After a visit to Glyndebourne on 2 July 1984, Mike Allen wrote to Brian Dickie:

> As promised, I will discuss with my colleagues your question about further recordings of the Hall/Haitink productions. I appreciate the importance to Glyndebourne of foreseeing such recordings before the end of Bernard Haitink's distinguished tenure of the Music Directorship. As I told you, he is held in very high esteem by all of us at EMI . . . As you will appreciate, our commitments elsewhere and the economics of recorded opera do mean that sponsorship could be the key to the situation. If Glyndebourne were able to find generous sponsors for these recordings, it would take us quite a long way towards solving the difficulties.

Allen's notes of a subsequent meeting re-stated EMI's interest in continuing the series – but not with *Le nozze di Figaro*, which Riccardo Muti was due to record for EMI in 1986 with the Vienna Philharmonic Orchestra. *Così* seemed more promising, although a Salzburg production had recently been recorded by EMI, also conducted by Muti. Possible casts were suggested, which, Allen emphasised, should be based on actual Glyndebourne performances and not simply assembled and marketed under the Glyndebourne name. The crucial matter was that of financial support without which the project could not be considered. Within a year an enthusiastic supporter was found in Mr Vincent Meyer, who offered to sponsor recordings of both *Così* and *Figaro*, to be made in 1986 and 1987 respectively. With this generous financial backing, plans proceeded apace and in July 1985, Allen's suggested schedule for recording *Così fan tutte* in February 1986 was sent to Brian Dickie.

In 1984 the cast of the fiftieth anniversary performances of *Così* had consisted of Carol Vaness, Delores Ziegler, Jane Berbié, Ryland Davies, J Patrick Raftery and Claudio Desderi; the conductor was Gustav Kuhn. For the recording EMI retained Vaness, Ziegler and Desderi, but contracted two Americans, Dale Duesing and John Aler, and the English soprano Lillian Watson, to replace the other three. Naturally, Bernard Haitink was to conduct. Both Aler and Watson had sung in previous Glyndebourne productions of *Così fan tutte*, but Duesing was new to his role there. Haitink, of course, was familiar with the work and had conducted it in two previous seasons. So while the recording was not cast from a single series of Glyndebourne performances, as its predecessor in 1935 had been, it was reasonably representative of Sir Peter Hall's production.

The fourteen sessions were interspersed with rehearsals, largely for the benefit of those members of the cast who flew in after the recording had begun. Duesing and Ziegler taped arias and a duet on 16 February and were joined the following day by Watson, who recorded two arias. Aler and Vaness had two sessions to themselves on 18 and 19 February and Desderi's first day at the studio was 20 February when the sextet *Alla bella Despinetta* was set down. Unusually for an operatic recording, the end of the opera was actually recorded at the final session, on 27 February, with all six soloists and the chorus. Two customary cuts were made – Guglielmo's *Rivolgete a lui*, an alternative aria to *Non siate ritrosi*, and a short internal excision in Ferrando's *Ah! lo veggio*.

Così fan tutte took much longer to issue than its predecessor *Don Giovanni*. It was released fifteen months later in May 1987, by which time the next in the series, *Le nozze di Figaro*, had already been cast and successfully recorded at Abbey Road.

Rodney Milnes in *Opera*, August 1987:

There is a strong sense of ensemble so essential to this of all operas. The recitative, inventively accompanied by Martin Isepp, preserved the variety of pace and inflection that has always been so notable a feature of Peter Hall's production in the theatre. It is as though one is listening to a really well directed play, which is not always the case in recordings of 18th century opera.

Crispness of ensemble is also the hallmark of Haitink's conducting and the excellent playing of the LPO caught in admirably clear sound. It is an indication of how quickly fashions – and indeed expectations – change that, in these days of Mackerras, Östman and Norrington, some of Haitink's tempos do strike one as a little on the gentle side; two-in-a-bar andante markings, nowadays a red rag inspiring Brands Hatch-style spurts, elicit a more traditional amble here. This is a matter of overall impression, though, and only once or twice – a largo-inclined *larghetto* for the canon in the second finale, or too deliberate a pace for the opening of the first finale – does a tempo actually seem arguable.

There is some really thrilling singing from Carol Vaness as Fiordiligi: such sumptuousness of tone allied to such ease of coloratura is rare indeed. One slight drawback is the similarity of her mezzo-like sound to that of Delores Ziegler's lively Dorabella: without a score it would be hard to tell who was singing in the recitatives. The same is true of Claudio Desderi's bright-toned Alfonso and Dale Duesing's Guglielmo, though as both baritones are highly individual in their pointing of the words, the problem is less worrying . . . John Aler's Ferrando is freshly and easily sung, with the unruffled fluency of his *Ah! lo veggio* making one resent the internal cut in the aria even more. Lillian Watson makes a tough, alert Despina, and her disguised voices are mercifully free of undue exaggeration. Whereas at Glyndebourne Guglielmo as often as not sings *Rivolgete*, on this recording the more familiar *Non siate ritrosi* is used.

1987

LE NOZZE DI FIGARO

Music by Wolfgang Amadeus Mozart

Libretto by Lorenzo da Ponte

Sung in Italian

Figaro	Claudio Desderi (baritone, Italian)
Susanna	Gianna Rolandi (soprano, American)
Don Basilio	Ugo Benelli (tenor, Italian)
Marcellina	Anne Mason (soprano, English)
Cherubino	Faith Esham (mezzo-soprano, American)
Count Almaviva	Richard Stilwell (baritone, American)
Countess Almaviva	Felicity Lott (soprano, English)
Bartolo	Artur Korn (bass, Austrian)
Antonio	Federico Davià (baritone, Italian)
Barbarina	Anne Dawson (soprano, English)
Don Curzio	Alexander Oliver (tenor, Scottish)
Two bridesmaids	Anne Dawson/Janice Close (sopranos, English)

Glyndebourne Chorus	Chorus Master Ivor Bolton
London Philharmonic Orchestra	Leader David Nolan
Harpsichord continuo	Martin Isepp
Conductor	Bernard Haitink
Recorded	Studio No 1, Abbey Road
	17–21 and 24–26.2.1987
Recording Producer	John Fraser
Balance Engineer	Stuart Eltham

This recording was made possible with sponsorship from Vincent Meyer.

Original issue

EMI EX 749753–1	(3 LPs)	6.1988
EMI EX 749753–4	(3 cassettes)	6.1988
CDS7 49753–2	(3 CDs – 71'36"/64'06"/42'19")	6.1988

The accompanying booklet includes an essay *Mozart's Figaro in performance – from Vienna to Glyndebourne* by William Mann: a synopsis and biographies in English, French and German: and the libretto in English, French, German and Italian.

CDCC 49753	(USA) (3 CDs)

The recording of *Le nozze di Figaro* was undertaken at Studio No. 1, Abbey Road exactly a year after that of *Così fan tutte*. The sponsorship given by Vincent Meyer ensured that Sir Peter Hall's production, conducted by Bernard Haitink, was recorded almost exactly as it had been seen on stage, with only three changes to the 1984 cast.

Sixteen performances of *Figaro* were given at Glyndebourne that year, some of which were conducted by Bernard Haitink and others by Gustav Kuhn. The roles of Figaro, Susanna, Cherubino, the Count, the Countess, Antonio and Don Curzio were double-cast and, with three exceptions, it was the members of the first cast who participated in the recording. Both Isobel Buchanan and Gabriele Fontana sang the Countess on stage, but Felicity Lott, who had appeared in the role in 1981, was selected to sing it for EMI. Alexander Oliver and Anne Mason took on Don Curzio and Marcellina. Don Basilio was sung both on stage and on the recording by Ugo Benelli, whose first appearance at Glyndebourne in 1967 was as Nemorino in *L'elisir d'amore*. Dickie and Haitink cast the role of Basilio from strength in just the same way as Christie and Busch had done over fifty years earlier, allocating it to one of the world's foremost lyric tenors. Benelli was a worthy successor to Heddle Nash and, unlike him, had the opportunity to record his solo *In quegli anni*.

The recording of *Le nozze di Figaro* took place at two sets of sessions in February 1987, following which a concert performance of the opera was given at the Royal Festival Hall as part of the London Philharmonic Orchestra's subscription series. More than five years had elapsed since a new Glyndebourne recording of the opera was first mooted by Brian Dickie and Mike Allen; but it was the last of the three sets that was issued in celebration of the Festival's fiftieth anniversary.

Thus Glyndebourne's second recorded cycle of the Mozart/da Ponte operas was completed, a little more than fifty years after the first. In the intervening period more than just performance styles had changed (and Bernard Haitink's approach to Mozart differed very considerably from that of Fritz Busch); recording systems had also developed. The earlier version of *Le nozze di Figaro* took three mornings to record on wax discs on location in the theatre at Glyndebourne; the later one was taped using modern digital techniques over a period of eight days at Abbey Road.

Stuart Eltham was the balance engineer on all three of the Haitink series. His first experience of recording a Glyndebourne production was in 1950 when, as a junior engineer, he assisted Lawrance Collingwood and Douglas Larter at the sessions for *Così fan tutte*, the only post-war commercial recording to be made in the theatre itself. 'It was a simple recording compared to the present day, being in mono only. There was a fourway mixer on the van so only four microphones could be used. The recording was not a success as the acoustics of the theatre were very dead, making a very flat sound.' It is not surprising that subsequent EMI sessions took place at Abbey Road.

But modern techniques bring their own difficulties; for examples, the silent surfaces of compact discs and the sensitivity of digital recording. Stuart Eltham continues:

Because tape hiss and groove scratch are things of the past, a problem arises as the ambient sound of the studio becomes obvious. There is a noticeable difference in the sound of the 'silent' studio when a full orchestra and many singers are present from when there are, perhaps, just a harpsichordist and a couple of soloists recording recitatives. Yet on the final recording the two have to match. In cold weather even the warm air from the heating system can be heard as a low rumble as it rises to the top of the studio!

Is there a secret for obtaining the best vocal and dramatic performances from singers in a recording studio?

Long takes get the best results. They allow the performers to become involved in the drama of the opera, even in the 'untheatrical' atmosphere of a studio. Personally, I think that dramatically it's still better to record at live performances, but that's not often possible. Certainly with these Glyndebourne recordings the long takes we used helped the artists to give the best possible performances.

How very different from the constraints under which Busch and his musicians had to record. The maximum playing time of a 78 was four and a half minutes, and arias frequently had to be divided between two sides, sometimes even recorded on different days.

Which of the two systems engenders a more honest musical performance and a truer sense of theatre? Thanks to Stuart Eltham and his colleagues, past and present, we can hear both and make a decision for ourselves.

Alan Blyth in *Gramophone*, July 1988:

... Under Haitink's relaxed but vigilant beat, the singers seem to blossom into their most persuasive form, none more so than Claudio Desderi's Figaro. Here is a baritone very much in the mould of Stabile and Bruscantini, that is not possessing the most attractive voice but able to make the very best of it by dint of perfect Italian diction and intelligent use of tone and words, evident throughout this vivid interpretation of his role ... Rolandi's Susanna is an apt partner for this Figaro. Her slightly vibrant, forward voice produces a real character, at once warm and sharp-minded ... Rolandi may not sing *Deh vieni* (where she happily includes *appoggiaturas*) with quite the affecting delicacy of Cotrubas for Karajan, but she isn't far behind, and she gives real 'face' to the part. Similarly, Stilwell is a real personality, a Count to be reckoned with, singing with a fire ... while never resorting to rant.

Felicity Lott, as his Countess, gives a peach of a performance, both arias moulded in exemplary fashion and sung with strong yet yielding tones

. . . I love the way she leads into the reprise of *Dove sono*, then sings it with the most sensuous and melting tone . . . Esham is a lively but not particularly vivid Cherubino . . . Artur Korn, as at Glyndebourne, is a formidable Bartolo, and, as on stage, Benelli's Basilio is as characterful as any of his rivals and sweeter of voice than most. Anne Mason is no more successful than her mezzo predecessors in encompassing Marcellina's Fourth Act aria which definitely calls for a soprano, but she actually sings the rest of her role eagerly. A special mention for the veteran Davià, who delivers Antonio's imprecations with delightful relish . . .

[12]   Glyndebourne Commissions

Where the Wild Things Are, 1984 and *The Wind Serenades*, 1991

WHERE THE WILD THINGS ARE

Music by Oliver Knussen

Libretto by Maurice Sendak

Sung in English

Max	Rosemary Hardy (soprano, English)
Mama	Mary King (mezzo-soprano, English)
Tzippy, a Wild Thing	Mary King
Moishe, a Wild Thing	Hugh Hetherington (tenor, English)
Goat	Hugh Hetherington
Bruno, a Wild Thing	Stephen Richardson (baritone, English)
Emile, a Wild Thing	Stephen Rhys-Williams (bass-baritone, English)
Bernard, a Wild Thing	Andrew Gallacher (bass, English)

London Sinfonietta	Leader Nona Liddell
Conductor	Oliver Knussen
Recorded	St Peter's Church, Morden, Surrey 26–27.11.1984
Recording Producers	Ward Botsford and Oliver Knussen
Balance Engineer	Bob Auger

Original issue

Unicorn Kanchana DKP	9044	(1 LP)	6.1985
Unicorn Kanchana DKPC	9044	(1 cassette)	6.1985
Unicorn Kanchana DKPCD	9044	(1 CD – 37'48")	9.1985

These issues include notes with background information by Oliver Knussen and Maurice Sendak, performance history of the work and the English libretto.

This recording was made possible with financial support from Faber Music Ltd and Walker Books Ltd.

1. Audrey Mildmay (Christie) in front of the HMV recording van at Glyndebourne, June 1935

2. Aulikki Rautawaara, Audrey Mildmay, Willi Domgraf-Fassbaender,
   Roy Henderson and Fergus Dunlop in *Le nozze di Figaro*, 1934

3. Fritz Busch, Ina Souez and Salvatore Baccaloni at Glyndebourne, 1936

4.   Michael Redgrave as Macheath and Audrey Mildmay as Polly Peachum
in *The Beggar's Opera*, 1940

5. Peter Pears, Joan Cross and Flora Nielsen at Glyndebourne during rehearsals
for *The Rape of Lucretia*, 1946

6. Kathleen Ferrier as Orfeo, 1947

7   John Christie being interviewed by Rooney Pelletier for the first tv
    transmission from Glyndebourne, 23 July 1951

8. Sena Jurinac (Fiordiligi) and Alice Howland (Dorabella)
    in *Così fan tutte*, 23 July 1951

9. Marina de Gabarain (Cenerentola) and Juan Oncina (Don Ramiro)
   in *La Cenerentola*, 1952

10.   The opening scene from Act II of *Le Comte Ory*, 1954 with
Sari Barabas as Adèle and Monica Sinclair as Ragonde

11. Geraint Evans, Fritz Ollendorf, Murray Dickie and Elaine Malbin in *Arlecchino*, 1954

12. Sena Jurinac as the Countess and Franco Calabrese as Count Almaviva
    in Act IV of *Le nozze di Figaro*, 1955

13. Richard Lewis (Idomeneo) and James Milligan (Arbace) in *Idomeneo*, 1956

14. Richard Lewis and Magda Laszlo with the Glyndebourne Festival Chorus
    in the final scene of *L'incoronazione di Poppea*, 1962

15. Ileana Cotrubas (Calisto) and Ugo Trama (Jove) ascend to the stars
    in *La Calisto*, 1970

16.   Recording *La Calisto* in the Organ Room at Glyndebourne, August 1971

17. Sir Malcolm Sargent with Richard Lewis and the Glyndebourne Festival Chorus rehearsing the recording of *Trial by Jury*, 1960

18. John Pritchard with the artists at a playback of the recording of *Die Entführung aus dem Serail*, 1972

21. Raymond Leppard

22. Simon Rattle

19. Vittorio Gui

20. Bernard Haitink

23. Oliver Knussen

24.   Janet Baker as Orfeo, her last operatic role, 1982

25. Recording *Così fan tutte*, at Studio No 1, Abbey Road, London, February 1986

26. The Crap Game: Gregg Baker, Bruce Hubbard and Willard White in *Porgy and Bess*, 1986

27. Felicity Lott, Thomas Hampson and Franz Welser-Möst with the London Philharmonic after *Die lustige Witwe*, Royal Festival Hall, July 1993

Maurice Sendak's 1962 picture-story book *Where the Wild Things Are* became an immediate success in the United States. Since its initial publication it has been translated into fourteen languages and is now regarded as a modern classic of children's literature the world over.

In 1978 the Opéra National in Brussels commissioned the composition of a *fantasy-opera*, based on Sendak's story, from the English composer Oliver Knussen to celebrate the International Year of the Child, and by 1979 the author-illustrator's own adaptation of his original book was ready as a libretto. Knussen composed the first version of the score for the première at the Théâtre de la Monnaie in Brussels in November 1980. The following year he prepared a song-cycle suite from music in the opera and substantially revised the original work itself for a London production. The revision was still unfinished at its first concert performance at the Queen Elizabeth Hall in 1982, but after further re-working for a commission from Glyndebourne, it was completed four weeks before being produced at the National Theatre in January 1984 where it received seventeen performances – two on 9 January and three a day for five days thereafter. Later in the year *Where the Wild Things Are* toured as a double bill with Sendak and Knussen's second collaboration *Higglety Pigglety Pop!*: it was also brought into the 1985 Festival and broadcast on BBC television.

Where the Wild Things Are consists of nine brief scenes (the whole work lasts less than forty minutes) which relate the adventures of Max, a small boy, and his encounters with his mother, his dream like experiences on the sea and in the forest, and his confrontation with the Wild Things – frightening, shouting creatures that threaten, without success, to eat him up! It is scored for an orchestra of forty-eight musicians, with a large percussion section which includes, among other instruments, an anvil, cowbells, spring coil, two pairs of clogs, temple blocks, vibraslap, whip and wind machine. Nothing seems to have been forgotten that will make an exciting effect both on stage and on record. So much of the impact of *Where the Wild Things Are* is created by the sets and costumes (designed for the Glyndebourne production by Sendak himself) that a certain feeling of loss is inevitable on listening to a sound-only recording, but a real sense of the drama of the piece is conveyed on Unicorn-Kanchana's well produced issue, released in 1985.

Rosemary Hardy, a specialist in contemporary music, sang Max, the role she shared with Karen Beardsley in the Glyndebourne production; Mary King sang his Mama. The parts of the six Wild Things were performed by five young singers, Mary King, Hugh Hetherington, Stephen Richardson, Stephen Rhys-Williams and Andrew Gallacher, all of whom appeared in a number of Glyndebourne productions in the 1980s. The orchestra, The London Sinfonietta, was led by Nona Liddell.

Brian Dickie, Glyndebourne's General Administrator, first suggested a recording of *Wild Things* to Mike Allen of EMI in August 1982; Allen considered the possibility, and replied that he felt it was unlikely – it seemed simply not to be commercially viable. Fifteen months later Peter Andry, Director of the International Classical Division of EMI, raised the matter with his colleagues, but again the same decision was reached – it was not a recording in which the company was prepared to invest. To their credit, Unicorn-Kanchana undertook the project the following year, with generous support from Faber Books Ltd and Walker Books Ltd, two of Britain's leading publishing houses. It was an imaginative act of sponsorship, without which the work would not have been recorded.

Where the Wild Things Are was taped over two days in November 1984, in St Peter's Church, Morden in Surrey, and was conducted by the composer; Knussen, together with Ward Botsford, also produced the recording.

This extraordinary *fantasy-opera* may never achieve great fame, but Unicorn-Kanchana's issue provides a worthy reminder of Glyndebourne's first recorded commission.

Michael Oliver in *Gramophone*, June 1985:

On record one notices the imaginativeness of Knussen's sounds more [than on television]. In a way they can provide more evocative scenery than even Sendak can: the beautiful arching horn lines over harp and string shimmers (it is becoming recognizable as a characteristic Knussen sound) in the first Interlude for example, or the lovely violin melody that floats Max back from the island of the Wild Things to his own bedroom . . . I would have preferred a concert suite, in short, but in such a vivid performance this recording makes an agreeable souvenir of the stage production . . . If you've not seen it you may enjoy listening, as I did, with a copy of Sendak's picture-book to hand; it will not reinforce the effectiveness of the really imaginative pages, but it will give you something to look at in between them.

GLYNDEBOURNE WIND SERENADES
A tribute for the bi-centenary of Mozart's death

Figures in the Garden

by Jonathan Dove

1. Dancing in the Dark
2. Susanna in the Rain
3. A Conversation
4. Barbarina Alone
5. The Countess interrupts a Quarrel
6. Voices in the Garden
7. Nocturne: Figaro and Susanna

Members of the Orchestra of the Age of Enlightenment

Directed by   Jonathan Dove

Albanian Nights

by Nigel Osborne

Members of the Orchestra of the Age of Enlightenment

Directed by   Anthony Pay

Recorded   The Henry Wood Hall, London
                                     22.11.1991

Recording Producer   Mike Purton
Balance Engineer   Mike Clements

Serenade in Homage to Mozart

by Jonathan Harvey

First Movement   Second Movement

Members of the London Philharmonic

Directed by   Andrew Parrott

**Character Pieces for Wind Octet
derived from Metastasio's** *La Clemenza di Tito*

by Stephen Oliver

1. Rome   5. Rome
2. Vitellia and Sesto   6. Tito
3. Rome   7. Presto
4. Servilia and Annio

Members of the London Philharmonic

Directed by   Andrew Parrott

Paraphase on Mozart's *Idomeneo*

by Robert Saxton

1. Vivo   9. Electra
2. Ilia   10. A Storm Arises
3. Idamante   11. Idomeneo
4. Electra   12. The Sea Monster appears
5. Idomeneo   13. Ilia
6. Ciaconna   14. The Voice
7. Ilia   15. Ilia and Idamante
8. Ilia and Idamante   16. Vivo (Tempo Primo)

Members of the London Philharmonic

Directed by	Andrew Parrott
Recorded	The Henry Wood Hall, London 8–9.11.1991
Recording Producer	Mike Purton
Balance Engineer	Mike Clements

Original issue

EMI CDC7 54424–2	(1 CD – 59'44")	5.1992

This recording was funded by the Arts Council.
Part of the British Composers series from EMI Classics
The enclosed seven page booklet contains a revised version of a background article by Mark Pappenheim, originally published in the 1991 Glyndebourne Festival Programme Book.

At the instigation of Anthony Whitworth-Jones, six British composers were commissioned by Glyndebourne to write a series of Wind Serenades for Mozart's bi-centenary celebrations in 1991. Six Mozart operas were produced at Glyndebourne that year and each of the composers was invited to interpret one of them in modern musical terms, with scoring for small wind ensemble. Oliver Knussen's Serenade based on *Don Giovanni* was never completed, but the remaining five were first performed on the terrace or in the Organ Room at Glyndebourne as curtain-raisers to their respective operas – *Le nozze di Figaro, Così fan tutte, Idomeneo, La clemenza di Tito* and *Die Zauberflöte*.

The composers approached their tasks in very different ways, two of them – Jonathan Dove and Nigel Osborne – actually scoring their works for eighteenth century wind ensemble forces. Again in two instances there are passing musical references to the relevant Mozart opera – Harvey's *Die Zauberflöte* and Dove's *Le nozze di Figaro*; in others, the composers – notably Stephen Oliver in his violent tribute to *La clemenza di Tito* – use totally modern musical idioms in their re-interpretations. Oliver had a closer involvement with the opera than just the composition of a Serenade; he was also commissioned to provide new recitatives for the 1991 Glyndebourne production, to replace those unsatisfactorily composed by Süssmayer, Mozart's pupil, and generally used ever since.

In the article in *Gramophone* in June 1992, Robert Saxton described his approach to the composition of his *Paraphrase on Idomeneo*:

> I attempted to capture the dramatic energy of this marvellous score and re-create that drama in my own way. As a result, my Paraphrase is a ten minute long composition for eight wind players which follows the outline of the opera plot. It begins with a reminiscence of Mozart's overture (not stylistically) and proceeds to introduce instruments as characters in the drama, while being fairly faithful to the opera's tonal centres and character pieces.

All five Serenades were recorded in the Henry Wood Hall, a converted church in South London. On 8 and 9 November 1991 the pieces by Harvey, Oliver and Saxton were taped by members of the London Philharmonic (which played for the three relevant operas at Glyndebourne in 1991), directed by Andrew Parrott, the English conductor whose worldwide reputation has been largely based on his authentic performances of early and baroque music. Two weeks later members of the Orchestra of the Age of Enlightenment (which played for *Figaro* and *Così*) were conducted by Jonathan Dove, for the recording of his own Serenade, and by Anthony Pay for Osborne's. The CD of *Glyndebourne Wind Serenades* was issued in May 1992 as part of EMI Classics' *British Composers* series and the entire recording project was funded by the Arts Council.

Stephen Johnson in *Gramophone*, June 1992:

I can't say that each of these five composers convinced me that he was a natural for the medium, and the Mozartian connections struck me as sometimes effective, occasionally arch and in one case strained beyond breaking point. But the results are strongly contrasted, and perhaps the best way for the critic – as for the listener – is not to stretch comparisons, but to take each on its own, very different merits . . . The anonymity of the studio rather than a Glyndebourne ambience – I realise there would have been huge problems with taking the performances live, but I'm not sure the Henry Wood Hall was the ideal solution. The sound is clear though, and the balance is good, even if that means that the horns have had to be placed well back.

[13]   *Porgy and Bess*, 1988

PORGY AND BESS

Music by George Gershwin

Libretto by DuBose Heyward
Lyrics by DuBose Heyward and Ira Gershwin

Sung in English

Porgy	Willard White (bass-baritone, Jamaican)
Bess	Cynthia Haymon (soprano, American)
Clara	Harolyn Blackwell (soprano, American)
Sportin' Life	Damon Evans (tenor, American)
Jake	Bruce Hubbard (baritone, American)
Serena	Cynthia Clarey (mezzo-soprano, American)
Maria	Marietta Simpson (contralto, American)
Crown	Gregg Baker (baritone, American)
Mingo	Barrington Coleman (tenor, American)
Robbins	Johnny Worthy (tenor, English)
Jim	Curtis Watson (baritone, Jamaican)
Peter	Mervin Wallace (tenor, American)
Lily	Maureen Brathwaite (mezzo-soprano, English)
Undertaker	Autris Paige (baritone, American)
Annie	Paula Ingram (soprano, American)
Frazier	William Johnson (baritone, American)
Scipio	Linda Thompson (contralto, American)
Nelson/Crab Man	Colenton Freeman (tenor, American)
Strawberry Woman	Camellia Johnson (mezzo-soprano, American)
Detective	Alan Tilvern (spoken role, English)
Coroner	Billy J Mitchell (spoken role, Canadian)
Mr Archdale	Ted Maynard (spoken role, American)
Policeman	Ron Travis (spoken role, American)
Jasbo Brown	Wayne Marshall (piano player, English)

Glyndebourne Chorus	Chorus Master Craig Rutenberg
The London Philharmonic	Leader David Nolan
Conductor	Simon Rattle
Recorded	Studio No 1, Abbey Road
	8, 10, 11, 13, 14 and 16–19.2.1988
Recording Producer	David Murray
Balance Engineer	Mark Vigars

Original issue

EMI EX 749568–1	(3 LPs)	6.1989
EMI EX 749568–4	(3 cassettes)	6.1989
EMI CDS7 49568–2	(3 CDs – 57'58"/72'26"/59'08")	6.1989

The accompanying booklet includes an essay *The Roots of 'Porgy and Bess'* by Robert Kimball: a synposis and biographies in English, French and German: and complete libretto in English.

Angel CDCC 49568   (USA) (3 CDs)

Excerpts

1. Introduction
2. Summertime
3. Give him to me .. a woman is
4. My man's gone now
5. How de saucer stan' now?
6. Oh! the train
7. Oh, I'm agoin' out
8. Mus' be ... Oh I got plenty of nuttin'
9. Lissen there: I hates ..
10. Buzzard, keep on flyin'
11. Honey, we sure goin' ... Bess you is
12. Oh, I can't sit down
13. It ain't necessarily so
14. Oh what do you want wid Bess?
15. A red headed woman
16. Listen! There's a boat
17. Dem white folks
18. Here Mingo
19. Where's Bess?
20. Bess is gone
21. Oh Lawd, I'm on my way

EMI EL 754325–4	(1 cassette)	12.1991
EMI CDC7 54325–2	(1 CD – 74'21")	12.1991

This issue includes an essay *The Roots of 'Porgy and Bess'* by Robert Kimball an d a synopsis in English, French and German, by Avril Bardoni.

Angel CDC 54325   (USA) (1 CD)

'Glyndebourne will never be the same again, and it shouldn't,' said Trevor Nunn about *Porgy and Bess:* Glyndebourne's first production of an American opera, an opera with an all-black singing cast facing the challenge of the first British performances of the composer's original version.

For years many people had not regarded *Porgy* and *Bess* as an opera at all, but rather as one of the popular musicals for which George Gershwin is best remembered. But he and his collaborators – his brother Ira and the writer Dubose Heyward, author of the novel *Porgy* which originally inspired the composer – certainly considered it to be an opera, and almost sixty years after its first performance it remains the most famous of the genre composed in the United States. It has had a chequered history.

Porgy and Bess was first performed at the Colonial Theatre in Boston in September 1935 and a few days later it began a fifteen week run at the Alvin Theatre, New York. In spite of the fact that when it closed it proved to have been a financial disaster, Gershwin was not disheartened and shortly after-wards included orchestral and sung excerpts in two concerts in California. In 1937 he suggested a further operatic collaboration with Heyward, but before that could take place the composer died suddenly, at the age of only thirty-eight. Within five years of Gershwin's death two new productions of *Porgy and Bess* were mounted in the USA which, ironically, proved considerably more successful than the original. In Europe it was first performed (strange as it may seem) in German-occupied Denmark in 1943. In 1952 the US Department of State sponsored a touring production which played for three months at the Stoll Theatre in London, and also visited Berlin, Vienna, Milan and the USSR. But these productions did not present the opera as Gershwin composed it. In some cases the recitative was replaced by spoken dialogue, and musical numbers were cut, making a travesty out of a masterpiece.

The original version of *Porgy and Bess* was revived in 1976 by Houston Grand Opera – a production that was recorded – and in 1985 it was first performed at the Metropolitan Opera, New York; but not until Glyndebourne mounted Trevor Nunn's revelatory production the following year was it seen in Britain as the Gershwins and Heyward intended. The first performance at Glyndebourne took place on 5 July 1986, with Willard White as Porgy and Cynthia Haymon as Bess; it was conducted by Simon Rattle. There were fifteen performances that year and eight the following year, with largely the same cast.

As rehearsals progressed in 1986, Simon Rattle suggested recording *Porgy and Bess* 'live' during the first series of performances at Glyndebourne, and discussed the possibility with Peter Alward, Vice President of Artists and Repertoire at EMI. Rattle's recording producer David Murray was cautious, believing that the acoustics of the theatre were insufficiently expansive to record such a large piece there satisfactorily, and finally the decision was taken not to do so during the initial run as Rattle had hoped. After the production's great success, EMI regretted the missed opportunity, and arranged recording sessions, stipulating, however, that they take place under studio, rather than live performance, conditions. On twelve days in mid-February 1988 virtually the entire cast, the orchestra and conductor of the 1986 production re-assembled and recorded the opera at Abbey Road. Rattle wished to link the recording sessions with public performances and so conducted two concert presentations of *Porgy and Bess* at the Royal Festival Hall in London a few days before recording began.

Rattle and Murray adopted the principle of first making an uninterrupted take of all the music scheduled to be recorded at a given session; the cast then had the opportunity to hear a complete playback and to comment on every aspect of the performance. After a free and constructive discussion the conductor and producer would give notes to the singers and orchestral players, with suggestions about possible improvements in interpretation. A second complete take was then made incorporating these modifications after which, if necessary, further re-recording could take place for patching purposes. As a result of this procedure most of the issued material was from the second takes, and required comparatively little further editing.

David Murray remembers that the playbacks were frequently a revelation to the artists. They were, for many of the singers, the first opportunity to hear the production objectively, and their enthusiasm was sometimes mingled with considerable surprise at its impressive dramatic and musical effect. Twin-track and multi-track recording equipment was used in tandem at all the sessions, but, thanks to the skill of the producer and engineer, the final master tape was created almost entirely from the twin-track material without the need for further mixing and balancing. The sound effects employed were those used at Glyndebourne, and were transported to the studio from Sussex as they were required.

Murray's abiding memory of the fifteen sessions is the enthusiasm of the chorus. 'They gave,' he says 'three hundred per cent to this recording, and it can certainly be heard on the finished product.' But in one way this itself led to problems. 'At certain points in the opera, members of the chorus were encouraged to ad lib spontaneously within the context of a scene. It was sometimes difficult to match one take to another and be acceptably consistent if an edit had to made during this 'free expression'.'

One further difficulty that Murray encountered was the number of singers involved in the crap game in the first scene of the opera. 'Ten principals had to share five microphones at the front of the stage and the large chorus was placed further back. It was one of the most lively and crowded operatic scenes that I've ever recorded.'

No recording of a large scale work is entirely free from incident. In *Porgy and Bess* one member of the cast failed to turn up at all. Whilst he appears from time to time during the opera, the boy Scipio has no solo lines to sing and only two to speak, in Act 2 Scene 1. Nana Antwi-Nyanin played the role at Glyndebourne, but in his absence from Abbey Road Linda Thompson spoke his lines, in a way that is reminiscent of Elisabeth Schumann's substitution for Lotte Lehmann in their classic recording of *Der Rosenkavalier*! 'Linda, a member of the chorus, was a great mimic and surely without being told, no-one would ever know it wasn't the real Scipio,' David Murray comments.

One visitor of particular note who attended some of the sessions was Mrs Ira Gershwin, widow of the lyricist and sister-in-law of the composer. Her authoritative presence forged a direct link between this, the first British recording of the opera, and the first performance in Boston more than fifty-two years previously.

The recording of *Porgy and Bess* was issued on 3 LPs, cassettes and CDs in June 1989. Five months later it was awarded the Opera Recording of the Year by *Gramophone*. Writing of the award, Edward Seckerson commented in the magazine: '. . . from the very first bar, where Simon Rattle and his strings tear with Paganinian brilliance into their scorching tempo for the introduction, it's clear just how instinctively attuned this conductor and orchestra are to every aspect of a multi-faceted score. Rattle's reading is generous in every sense of the word, his expansive treatment of the great lyric ballads offset by an impulsive energy where Gershwin asks him to drive and swing. And the cast are so *right*, so much a part of their roles, so well integrated into the whole that one almost takes the excellence of their contributions for granted. Sample for yourself the final moments of the piece – *Oh Lawd, I'm on my way*. If that doesn't stir you, nothing will.'

Trevor Nunn's production of *Porgy and Bess* had a profound effect on all who were involved with it, and some interesting recollections were recorded by Willard White, who sang Porgy, and the music critic John Amis, as part of Glyndebourne's Oral History Project. [The Project was established in collaboration with the National Sound Archive in 1990; it aims to build up a collection of interviews with many of the people who have been connected with the Glyndebourne Festival over the last sixty years, including singers, players, producers and administrators.]

The following conversation is adapted from the Oral History interview.

John Amis: 'I was lucky enough to be there one day when the orchestra and the chorus came together for the first time. That was just like a wild scene from *Porgy* – a scene of great happiness and jubilation and everybody was thrilled with everybody else. The orchestra was knocked sideways by the guts and spirit of the chorus, and the chorus by the expertise of the orchestra.'

White: 'Many people in the chorus at the time had worked with other groups, which had treated the music as very ordinary and simple. They were very impressed by the care that Simon had taken to bring out all the nuances in the piece . . . it was a thrill to hear it – the full orchestra giving vent to their feelings and so loving the music.'

Amis: 'It was more of a discovery for the orchestra than it was for most of the singers! . . . I believe that many people in the cast who had done it before were amazed that it was being done 'properly'.'

White: 'Yes, people *were* amazed and there were a few moments of challenging what was being done. Some people said. 'Well, in one production, we did it like this', and Trevor always had a wonderful way of saying 'Yes, that's alright, but in a similar situation back home . . . such as the funeral of Robbins, when you have a wake – what do you do?' And people would say 'We do this and we do that', and Trevor said 'Well let's do it like that. Let's feel how it should be.' And that's how it came to be so powerful, because in everything Trevor sought to bring out our real feelings about the situations. That's how Trevor usually works anyway – with people and their feelings and responding to a situation . . . You do what is real for you and the general public usually loves it! I've heard Trevor say that the piece has a life of its own; you give vent to your feelings within the framework of the piece and it actually takes off. You serve the piece, and every night it will be different.'

In October and November 1992 Glyndebourne's production was transferred to the Royal Opera House, Covent Garden. Trevor Nunn again directed, the American Leonard Slatkin conducted the orchestra, and most of the principals from the Glyndebourne cast were engaged to play their original roles.

Immediately after these performances, the cast began rehearsing for a video version being recorded at Shepperton studios during November and December. The video, a Primetime/BBC production, was adapted for the screen by Nunn and Yves Baigneres. EMI's 1988 recording was used as the soundtrack, but was re-mixed from the original twenty-four track tapes in order to match more closely Nunn's new production. For example, a character originally recorded stage right by EMI might, on the video, be placed centre stage and the newly prepared sound track would have to reflect that change; or a soloist might need to be highlighted in close-up in a way that was not originally intended in the recording studio. With only four exceptions (from a cast of twenty-four), the same singers and actors took part in both the audio and video recordings – despite the four and a half years that elapsed between the two versions. The video runs approximately four minutes shorter than the audio version – the orchestral introduction and *Good mornin'* chorus at the opening of Act Three Scene Three are omitted from the former, and instead the scene begins with Mingo's line *It's Porgy comin' home.*

With the benefit of a full studio production, based on the Glyndebourne sets and using many of the original costumes, this performance of *Porgy and Bess* is extraordinarily vivid. The claustrophobic atmosphere of Catfish Row is well caught and the singers successfully achieve the notoriously difficult synchronisation of sound with vision. It is the first video based on Glyndebourne performances not to be made in the theatre itself, and it is by far the most ambitious in terms of scale and production effects.

By the time that the next Glyndebourne recording came to be made – *Die lustige Witwe* in July 1993 – the old theatre had been demolished and the building of its replacement was well on the way to completion.

Hugh Canning in *Opera*, July 1989:

. . . Simon Rattle treats *Porgy* as one of the great opera scores of the 20th century. Just listen to the sparkle and brilliance of the orchestral playing in the Introduction, the jabbing violence of the interlude where Porgy murders Crown, the sultry clarinet and trumpet solos, whose players sound as if they have been 'jamming' all their lives rather than sitting on the platforms of symphony halls. For the orchestral contribution alone this release must be counted one of the most important opera recordings of recent years, but the entire performance bristles with theatrical immediacy . . . If there are drawbacks to the present issue, they are fairly minor, but Rattle does tend to indulge in some inordinately slow tempos: the first singing of *Summertime* by Harolyn Blackwell's gleaming, bright Clara – none of Leontyne Price's smoky naughty-girl sensuality . . . – almost grinds to a halt and the song loses its shapeliness, and some of the fast numbers also lack the 'zip' of a Broadway-style performance . . .

. . . But the cast is a great one, led by White, a dark-voiced dignified, ultimately noble Porgy – unutterably moving in the love duet – and Cynthia Haymon's lustrous Bess, a kind of plantation Mimi, fatally submissive to Gregg Baker's sexually dominating Crown . . . I must express slight disappointment with Damon Evans's Sportin' Life: his singing is marvellous, a real operatic tenor, but I miss the husky sleaziness of John W Bubbles, the vaudevillier whom Gershwin chose for the role in 1935 . . . still, this is a great souvenir of a great Glyndebourne event. I do wonder how it will go down in America – is it just a bit too operatic? – but I shall listen to this set again and again.

[14] *Die lustige Witwe*, 1993

Glyndebourne on the South Bank

DIE LUSTIGE WITWE

Music by Franz Lehár

Libretto by Victor Léon and Leo Stein

Sung in German

Viscomte Cascada	Kurt Azesberger (tenor, Austrian)
Baron Mirko Zeta	Robert Poulton (baritone, English)
Valencienne	Elzbieta Szmytka (soprano, Polish)
Camille de Rosillon	John Aler (tenor, American)
Raoul de St Brioche	Rudolf Schasching (tenor, Austrian)
Kromow	Stuart MacIntyre (baritone, Scottish)
Hanna Glawari	Felicity Lott (soprano, English)
Graf Danilo Danilowitsch	Thomas Hampson (baritone, American)
Bogdanowitsch	Christopher Parke (baritone, English)
Pritschitsch	Howard Quilla Croft (baritone, English)
Grisettes	Anne O'Byrne (soprano, Irish)
	Paula O'Sullivan (soprano, Scottish)
	Philippa Daly (soprano, English)
	Michelle Walton (mezzo-soprano, English)
	Alison Duguid (mezzo-soprano, English)
	Joanna Campion (mezzo-soprano, English)

Glyndebourne Chorus	Chorus Master David Angus
The London Philharmonic	Leader Joakim Svenheden
Conductor	Franz Welser-Möst
Recorded	The Royal Festival Hall, London during public performances on 18, 20 and 22.7.1993
Recording Producer	Simon Woods
Balance Engineer	John Kurlander

Original issue
EMI CDC 555141–2   (1 CD 74'19")   6.1994
The accompanying booklet includes an essay *Lehar's Immortal Merry Widow* by Andrew Lamb, a
synopsis, and the text as sung in English, German and French.

In 1993, for the first time in forty-four years, opera was not performed at Glyndebourne. On 24 July 1992 the final performance in the old theatre took place. It was a special Gala Concert which reunited many notable singers who had appeared at Glyndebourne and taken part in Glyndebourne recordings over the years. Immediately afterwards demolition began and throughout 1993 building work on the new theatre proceeded apace.

Glyndebourne determined to make the most of this 'dark year'. They planned to give three concert performances of each of three operas at the Royal Festival Hall in London. The works chosen were Berlioz's *Béatrice et Bénédict*, Beethoven's *Fidelio*, which had been produced five times at the Glyndebourne Festival between 1959 and 1981, and Lehár's *Die lustige Witwe*. Internationally known conductors and singers were contracted to appear and the London Philharmonic, which has taken part in every Glyndebourne season since 1964, played on all nine evenings. On 21 June the season opened with *Béatrice et Bénédict* which alternated with *Fidelio*. The first of the three performances of *Die lustige Witwe* was almost a month later on 18 July. In addition, both the Beethoven and Lehár operas were given a single performance each at Symphony Hall in Birmingham with largely the same casts.

Plans were made by EMI to record two of the operas at the Royal Festival Hall. They would be the first official Glyndebourne audio recordings since *Porgy and Bess* was taped at Abbey Road in 1988, and the first ever to be made 'live'.

All three London performances of *Fidelio* were due to be recorded under Klaus Tennstedt, the London Philharmonic's Conductor Laureate. Julia Varady, the Rumanian soprano, was to sing Leonore, Peter Seiffert, Florestan and Artur Korn, Rocco. Six weeks before the first night Varady was forced to withdraw on medical grounds and was replaced by Anne Evans, a singer particularly noted for her interpretations of Wagner. Evans had last sung Leonore in 1983, and after a few days realised that there was insufficient time for her to re-learn the role and prepare it adequately; at little more than a month's notice, the American soprano Deborah Polaski agreed to take over. But Polaski, too, withdrew from her engagement and Leonore was finally sung at all the performances by Carol Yahr, who had made her British début with Glyndebourne Touring Opera in 1989 as Leonore.

Unfortunately, as rehearsals started, the health of Klaus Tennstedt forced him to cancel his appearances and he was replaced by Roger Norrington. It was at this juncture that EMI decided that they could not continue with their plans to record *Fidelio*. Had it taken place, the recording would have been the successor to three celebrated earlier EMI versions of the opera, conducted by Furtwängler, Klemperer and Karajan. The plans to tape *Die lustige Witwe* continued unaltered.

Lehár's continuing popularity rests very largely on this most famous of twentieth-century Viennese operettas. It has occasionally been performed in recent years by British opera companies, notably English National Opera, but has never been staged at Glyndebourne. For the Royal Festival Hall concert performances it was decided to dispense with the dialogue and use in its place a narrative, specially commissioned from the playwright Tom Stoppard.

Stoppard's solution was to give the story-telling role to Njegus, Secretary at the Embassy, a minor character usually sung by a *buffo* bass. At the Royal Festival Hall his few musical lines were taken by another character and, in his new guise as narrator, his words were spoken by Sir Dirk Bogarde, the eminent English actor. In the programme notes Stoppard is quoted as saying: '. . . it'll be as if Dirk were giving a platform performance at the National reminiscing about the period when he was on the Pontevedrian ambassadorial staff in Paris. We'll see Njegus talking about past events in which he imagines he is the principal player and everyone else is secondary: he believes he is the centre of a drama called *The Confidential Secretary* in which the Merry Widow constantly got in the way . . . The conceit, if you like, is to pretend that it's a real event that happened to real people. But since the concert is to be recorded, it has to be a detachable narrative that services the marvellous music.'

The apparent inconsistency of having the words *sung* in German but *spoken* in English presented no problem. The plot is notoriously convoluted and even in translation the original dialogue could not have achieved anything like the same witty, incisive effect.

The American soprano Carol Vaness was originally to have sung the role of Hanna Glawari – the Merry Widow herself – at the Royal Festival Hall, but withdrew two months before the engagement. She was replaced by Felicity Lott, a singer well known to Glyndebourne audiences. Lott has sung in twelve Festival seasons since 1977, in roles as diverse as Anne Trulove in Stravinsky's *The Rake's Progress* and Pamina in Mozart's *Die Zauberflöte*, but she is best known for her roles in operas by Richard Strauss, such as Christine in *Intermezzo*, and the Countess in *Capriccio*. Count Danilo was sung by the American Thomas Hampson – his first Glyndebourne engagement – and Camille by the tenor John Aler. Elzbieta Szmytka sang Valencienne and Franz Welser-Möst, Music Director of the London Philharmonic, conducted.

Preparations for the recording began in March 1993 when, in consultation with Glyndebourne, Simon Woods, the recording producer, and John Kurlander, the balance engineer, decided on the platform arrangement, including the positioning of the soloists and chorus and the placement of microphones. On the morning of 18 July EMI's mobile recording unit, equipped with a Sony 48 track digital recorder, parked outside the Royal Festival Hall, and thirty-nine microphones were set in the pre-determined pattern on the platform and in the auditorium. Because other concerts were booked to take place in the Hall on other evenings, the 'mikes' had to be removed after each performance: their positions and angles were carefully measured so that they could be accurately replaced. It was likely that parts of all three performances would be included on the issued CD and was thus imperative that the recorded sound should be consistent throughout.

Some weeks later Woods and Kurlander scrutinised the three complete recordings at Abbey Road and decided that the master tape would be assembled almost entirely from the second and third performances – just two very short orchestral passages were required from the first. Of the thirty-nine tracks which were recorded on the original tapes, only fifteen were needed for the final mix, a considerable technical achievement for such a complex platform layout. Eight tracks were taken from the soloists' microphones, three from the chorus and four from the orchestra.

The mixing from fifteen tracks to two was undertaken on Abbey Road's new digital Neve Capricorn mixing desk from 27-29 September 1993. Where necessary, volume adjustments were made in order to achieve a satisfactory balance between the soloists and the orchestra, and a small amount of digital echo was added to augment the acoustic of the Royal Festival Hall. On completion of the mixing, the digital tape master was prepared on a Sonic Solutions hard disc editing system. At this stage the prinicipal singers and the conductor were able to hear the final edited tape, and any changes to the mix or editing that were required could be made. Once musical or technical difficulties had been resolved, the master tape was used to manufacture the CDs. This recording of Lehár's original 1905 score of *Die lustige Witwe* is musically almost complete as, indeed, were the Royal Festival Hall performances. No vocal music is cut, but some orchestral links are omitted, as is Sir Dirk Bogarde's narration; thus the musical numbers follow each other without interruption, save for the audience's appreciative applause. It is due for release, on one CD, in May 1994.

Technically, *Die lustige Witwe* marks a great step forward in sound recording skills. It is the first Glyndebourne issue to have been taped, mixed and edited using an all-digital system. EMI are justifiably proud that Abbey Road is one of the first studios in the world to have a Neve Capricorn mixing desk; the superb results speak for themselves.

The performances at the Royal Festival Hall were generously received by the critics, some of whom commented with pleasure at the prospect of a future CD issue.

John Higgins in *The Times*, 20 July 1993:

... Franz Welser-Möst is the man in charge of Lehár. He has schooled the LPO thoroughly in the Viennese sound. The waltzes glide silkily by and gentlemen in tails smack their lips at the prospect of more champagne and showgirls.

Glyndebourne had the wit to invite that expert on Central European affairs, Tom Stoppard, to provide a few words of explanation of what goes on between musical numbers . . . It would be difficult to imagine a more dashing pair than Thomas Hampson and Felicity Lott as Danilo and Hanna . . . German opera houses sometimes cast Danilo as a tenor, but Hampson puts paid to all thought of that. A full-blooded baritone is needed as hero and generations of Broadway composers learnt from Lehár's example. Thomas Hampson has not sung Danilo before: it must now go straight into his repertory. Felicity Lott, though, is a thoroughly experienced Hanna, her soprano succulently creamy and dreamy in the Vilja song. But she carries too in her voice – and eye – a sense of rueful superiority, used to marvellous effect as the Countess in *Capriccio* . . .

. . . John Aler sings sweetly, but a bit too stolidly in the high tenor role of Camille. Elzbieta Szmytka could sparkle more as Valencienne, especially when leading the grisettes in their last act chorus . . .

. . . Those without [tickets] may take consolation from EMI's presence to record this merriest and wittiest of *Widows*.

[15] Orchestral Recordings, 1953 and 1955

GLYNDEBOURNE FESTIVAL ORCHESTRA

	Leaders David McCallum and Arthur Leavins
Conductor	Vittorio Gui

MOZART
Symphony No 39 in E Flat K 543

Recorded	Kingsway Hall
	16.3.1953

Mono recording

Recording Producer	David Bicknell
Balance Engineer	Douglas Larter

Original issue
ALP 1155   (1 LP)   9.1954
With sleeve notes by Robert Ponsonby

Victor LHMV 11   (USA) (1 LP)

CORELLI
Concerto Grosso No 2 in F Major

Recorded	Studio No 1, Abbey Road
	20.3.1953

Mono recording

Recording Producer	David Bicknell
Balance Engineer	Douglas Larter

NEVER ISSUED

HAYDN
Symphony No 60 in C Major
'Il Distratto'

Solo violin	David McCallum

Recorded	Studio No 1, Abbey Road 20.3.1953	
Mono recording		
Recording Producer Balance Engineer	David Bicknell Douglas Larter	

Original issue

ALP 1114	(1 12" LP)	3.1954

Sleeve notes on the two symphonies were written by William Mann.

HTA 7	(1 'tape record')	2.1955
Victor LHMV 1064	(USA) (1 12" LP)	

ROSSINI
Overture 'Tancredi'

78 rpm matrices
Part 1 2EA 17741–*2A*
Part 2 2EA 17742–*2A*

Recorded	Studio No 1, Abbey Road 18.9.1953	
Mono recording		
Recording Producer Balance Engineer	Lawrance Collingwood Robert Beckett	

Original issue

DB 21607	(1 12" 78)	1.1954

Re-issues

7ER 5024	(1 7" 45)	9.1954
XLP 30042	(1 12" LP)	10.1965

MOZART
**Symphony No 38
'Prague' K 504**

Recorded	Studio No 1, Abbey Road 21–22.9.1953	
Mono recording		
Recording Producer Balance Engineer	Lawrance Collingwood Robert Beckett	

Original issue

ALP 1114	(1 12" LP)	3.1954
HTA 7	(1 'tape record')	2.1955
Victor LHMV 1064	(USA)(1 12" LP)	

HAYDN
Symphony No 95 in C Minor

Recorded	Studio No 1, Abbey Road
	22–23.9.1953
Mono recording	

Recording Producer	Lawrance Collingwood
Balance Engineer	Robert Beckett

Original issue

ALP 1155	(1 12" LP)	9.1954
Victor LHMV 11	(USA) (1 12" LP)	

BIZET
Jeux d'enfants
(March, Berceuse, Impromptu, Duo)

Recorded	Studio No 1, Abbey Road
	23.9.1953
Mono recording	

Recording Producer	Lawrance Collingwood
Balance Engineers	Douglas Larter and Robert Beckett

NEVER ISSUED

GLUCK
Overture 'Alceste'

78 rpm matrices:
Part 1 2EA 17866–*3A*
Part 2 2EA 17867–*3A*

Recorded	Studio No 1, Abbey Road
	23.9.1953
Mono recording	

Recording Producer	Lawrance Collingwood
Balance Engineer	Robert Beckett

Original issue

DB 21616	(1 12" 78)	4.1954

VIOTTI
Violin Concerto No 22 in A Minor

Solo violin	Gioconda de Vito
(Omitting cadenzas)	

Recorded	Studio No 1, Abbey Road
	23–24.9.1953
Mono recording	

Recording Producers	David Bicknell and Lawrance Collingwood
Balance Engineer	Douglas Larter

NEVER ISSUED

VIOTTI
Violin Concerto No 22 in A Minor
Cadenzas for the first and
second movements

Solo violin	Gioconda de Vito
Recorded	Studio No 1, Abbey Road
	10.12.1953
Mono recording	
Recording Producer	David Bicknell
Balance Engineer	Douglas Larter

NEVER ISSUED

BIZET
Jeux d'enfants
(March, Berceuse, Impromptu,
Duo and Galop)

Recorded	Studio No 1, Abbey Road
	12.7.1955
Stereo recording	
Recording Producer	Lawrance Collingwood
Balance Engineer	Harold Davidson

Original issue		
SAT 1002	(1 stereo 'tape record')	10.1955

Re- issues		
7 ER 5111	(1 mono 45)	12.1958
RES 4252	(1 stereo 45)	9.1959

From the surviving correspondence in the archives at Glyndebourne and EMI it is not clear who originally suggested that the Royal Philharmonic Orchestra might record orchestral music for HMV under its 'other' name – The Glyndebourne Festival Orchestra. Whoever the instigator was certainly had a potentially excellent artistic and commercial idea. It seems surprising that more records were not made under this arrangement: those that were have had little circulation beyond their initial mono (and in one case, stereo) issue. For the most part, they simply became obsolete too quickly, and were insufficiently interesting to hold a place in the newly emerging world of stereophonic sound.

The Royal Philharmonic Orchestra was founded in 1946 by Sir Thomas Beecham, who conducted it regularly until his death in 1961. In 1948 it became Glyndebourne's 'in-house' orchestra, both in Sussex and at the Edinburgh Festival, and continued as such until 1963. It features, therefore, on all of HMV's Glyndebourne recordings of the 1950s and 1960s. Even *The Soldier's Tale*, which requires simply a chamber ensemble of seven players, was accompanied by selected instrumentalists from the desks of the RPO.

In February 1953 Moran Caplat confirmed in a letter that he and David Bicknell had come to an agreement to record orchestral music, played by the Glyndebourne Festival Orchestra, under the directorship of Vittorio Gui. With one exception these recordings were made the same year, some of the sessions being fitted in with the taping of operas at Abbey Road studios.

The first orchestral sessions took place on 16 March 1953 at Kingsway Hall, where Mozart's *Symphony No 39* was recorded. Four days later, at Abbey Road, Corelli's *Concerto Grosso No 2* was taped. This was a favourite work of Gui's and he gave several performances of it both in the UK and in Europe. 1953 was the tercentenary of Corelli's birth and there was renewed public interest in his music, but the recording made on the morning of 20 March 1953 has never been issued. The remainder of that session and the whole of the afternoon was given to setting down Haydn's *Symphony No 60 – Il Distratto*, in which David McCallum, leader of the orchestra, played the important violin part. This symphony was released, together with Mozart's *Prague Symphony* (recorded on 21 and 22 September at the end of the sessions for *La Cenerentola*), in two formats. A standard LP version came out in March 1954, and in February 1955 the coupling appeared in a new 'tape record' version, manufactured specifically for owners of reel-to-reel tape recorders. Four other Glyndebourne recordings were published in this format – *Arlecchino*, the 1955 *Le nozze di Figaro*, Bizet's *Jeux d'enfants* and Gilbert and Sullivan's *The Gondoliers*, recorded with the Glyndebourne Chorus in 1957.

During the sessions for *La Cenerentola* in September 1953 time was found to record the overture to Rossini's *Tancredi*. In 1954 it was released on both sides of a 12" 78, and later the same year, coupled with the overture to *La Cenerentola* (from the complete recording), on a 45. Their last appearance was in 1965 on an LP of Rossini overtures.

When the September 1953 *Cenerentola* sessions were completed, Gui and the Glyndebourne Festival Orchestra continued recording at Abbey Road; over the next three days they taped five further works. In addition to Mozart's *Prague Symphony*, these included Haydn's *Symphony No 95*, issued in September 1954 together with Mozart's *Symphony No 39*, which was the very first of the series of orchestral recordings to be made the previous March.

Bizet's *Jeux d'enfants* was taped on 23 September. Either the *Galop* was left unfinished, or the takes were unsatisfactory, as a day in May 1954 had to be reserved for Gui to record that section. In the event, it was never completed, but a replacement stereo version of the whole work, made on 12 July 1955 at the close of the sessions for *Le nozze di Figaro*, was released several years later.

Gluck's *Alceste*, which received its first Glyndebourne performances during the 1953 season, was represented at these sessions by the recording of its overture: released on both sides of a 12" 78 in April 1954, it has never been re-issued.

The last two orchestral sessions in 1953 accommodated the most unusual work in the series. On two days in September, the violinist Gioconda de Vito (in private life, Mrs David Bicknell) recorded most of Viotti's *Violin Concerto No 22* in A Minor. She was a great advocate of the music of Viotti and had performed his work at the 1953 Edinburgh Festival, just a few weeks previously. Undoutedly this recording was made as a direct result of that performance. Not surprisingly, Bicknell was the producer in charge as he had been of the March orchestral sessions, but not the remainder of those held in September. The entire work was recorded except for the cadenzas in the first and second movements, an omission that was rectified on 10 December, again at Abbey Road. The work appeared now to be complete, but it was never issued. Writing to Caplat on 1 October 1953, Bicknell confirmed the orchestral works that had been recorded by Gui and the Glyndebourne Festival Orchestra. He specified two Haydn symphonies, two Mozart symphonies, two overtures, an incomplete Bizet suite and, as an afterthought in a subsequent letter, Corelli's *Concerto Grosso*. No mention was made anywhere of Viotti's *Violin Concerto*. It was only a week since the greater part of it had been recorded, but for some reason he decided not to refer to it.

As well as the stereo *Jeux d'enfants* of 1955, one further orchestral recording was made by Gui with the Glyndebourne Festival Orchestra. They taped Rossini's overture to *Semiramide* in 1959. The recording sheets confirm Glyndebourne Festival Orchestra as the name under which it was recorded, but when issued the name was changed, and on the labels it appeared in its more usual form – The Royal Philharmonic Orchestra.

There seems no likelihood now that any of these orchestral recordings will be re-issued. Despite being of some historic interest, Glyndebourne Festival Orchestra's excursions into orchestral music no longer stand comparison with more recent recordings.

The *Musical Times*, June 1954:

It is agreeable to pass to . . . early Haydn and Mozart, represented by the sixtieth symphony in C Major (*Il Distratto*) and the *Prague* in D respectively. These are beautifully played on ALP 1114 by the Glyndebourne Festival Orchestra under Vittorio Gui, who shares with

Toscanini his clarity of thought and power to communicate his wishes precisely to the players. Both symphonies are unusual, Mozart's in having three movements only, Haydn's in having six. *Il Distratto* is, indeed, not a symphony at all, but a suite arranged from incidental music to a French comedy. But that does not make it any less welcome as a companion to Mozart's more familiar masterpiece.

Dyneley Hussey in *Gramophone Record Review*, October 1954:

The great *E Major Symphony*, one of the group of three composed in 1788 and never performed in Mozart's life-time, is given a splendid performance by the Glyndebourne Orchestra under Gui. The resilient rhythms, finely shaped phrasing and careful balancing of tone make this a most desirable recording, especially as the engineers have done their job well . . . the Andante seems to me a shade on the slow side, but this is purely a matter of personal opinion. Coupled with it is one of the less familiar of Haydn's *London Symphonies*, whose key of C Minor does not portend the tragic drama we should expect were it by Mozart or Beethoven. It is a thoroughly cheerful, vigorous work and a welcome addition to the recordings of Haydn's works.

Peter Brown in *Records and Recording*, January 1966, Rossini Overtures, XLP 30042:

. . . the record would be worth buying for these [the overtures to *La Cenerentola* and *Tancredi*] alone. Vittorio Gui and these players worked for years together, and if they produced a superhuman standard for Beecham, it was surely at Glyndebourne that they gave of their ordinary mortal best . . . Time and time again the magic, the *joie-de-vivre* of these performances takes one's breath away and the reason is not far to seek – an orchestra playing with love for the great maestro.

Joan Chissell in *Gramophone Record Review*, January 1959:

It [*Jeux d'enfants*] fits nicely on to a little 45 disk, but I had anticipated a far better performance from artists such as these. The slowish tempo chosen for the opening *Marche* is typical of the conductor's surprisingly pedestrian, almost heavy-handed, approach and though everything is extremely conscientious, there are few moments of Beechamesque magic.

[16]   The Gilbert and Sullivan Operas, 1956–1962

1956

THE MIKADO or
THE TOWN OF TITIPU

By WS Gilbert and Arthur Sullivan

The Mikado	Owen Brannigan (bass, English)
Nanki-Poo	Richard Lewis (tenor, English)
Ko-Ko	Geraint Evans (baritone, Welsh)
Pooh-Bah	Ian Wallace (baritone, Scottish)
Pish-Tush	John Cameron (baritone, Australian)
Yum-Yum	Elsie Morison (soprano, Australian)
Pitti-Sing	Marjorie Thomas (contralto, English)
Peep-Bo	Jeannette Sinclair (soprano, English)
Katisha	Monica Sinclair (contralto, English)

Glyndebourne Festival Chorus   Chorus Master   Peter Gellhorn
The Pro Arte Orchestra

Conductor   Sir Malcolm Sargent

Recorded   Studio No 1, Abbey Road
                                      5 and 6.5, 15.6 and 3.8.1956

Recording Producers   Lawrance Collingwood, David Bicknell
                                      and Raymond Leppard
Balance Engineer   Harold Davidson

Original issue
ALP 1485–6	(2 mono LPs)	12.1957
ASD 256–7	(2 stereo LPs)	8.1958
Angel 3573 B/L	(USA) (2 mono LPs)	
Angel S–3573 B/L	(USA) (2 stereo LPs)	

Re-issues
SXDW 3019	(2 stereo LPs)	2.1976
EXE 1021	(1 stereo cassette)	2.1976

CDS7 47773–8	(2 CDs – 54'26"/36'22")	6.1987

With background notes and synopsis by Arthur Jacobs.

CDCB 47773	(USA) (2 CDs)	
CMS7 64403–2	(2 CDs –54'26"/36'22")	10.1992

With background notes and synopsis by Arthur Jacobs.

CDMB 64403	(USA) (2 CDs)	

Excerpts

7ER 5174	(1 mono 7" 45)	4.1960
RES 4273	(1 stereo 7" 45)	4.1960
7ER 5177	(1 mono 7" 45)	6.1960
RES 4276	(1 stereo 7" 45)	6.1960
ALP 1904*	(1 mono LP)	6.1962
ASD 472*	(1 stereo LP)	6.1962
ALP 1922+	(1 mono LP)	10.1962
ASD 487+	(1 stereo LP)	10.1962
CFP 40238**	(1 stereo LP)	2.1976
CFP 40260++	(1 stereo LP)	7.1977
CFP 40282<<	(1 stereo LP)	2.1978
TC2–MOM 106<	(1 cassette)	4.1980
TC2–MOM 114>	(1 cassette)	10.1980
TC2–MOM 124~	(1 cassette)	10.1981
EX 749696–1	(2 LPs)	12.1987
EX 749696–4	(2 cassettes)	12.1987
CD CFP 4238**	(1 CD – 53'00")	9.1991
CDZ7 62531–2+	(1 CD)	5.1989

* Includes items from **The Mikado, The Gondoliers and HMS Pinafore**

+ Includes items from **The Mikado, The Gondoliers, HMS Pinafore and The Pirates of Penzance**

** Includes items from **The Mikado, The Gondoliers, HMS Pinafore, The Yeomen of the Guard, Iolanthe and The Pirates of Penzance**

++ Includes items from **The Mikado, The Gondoliers, Iolanthe, Patience, Trial by Jury and The Pirates of Penzance**

<< Includes items from **The Mikado, HMS Pinafore, Patience, Ruddigore and The Yeomen of the Guard**

< Includes items from **The Mikado, The Gondoliers, HMS Pinafore, Iolanthe and The Pirates of Penzance**

> Includes items from **The Mikado, The Gondoliers, HMS Pinafore, Patience, Iolanthe, The Pirates of Penzance, Ruddigore, Trial by Jury and The Yeomen of the Guard**

~ Includes items from **The Mikado, The Gondoliers, Patience, The Pirates of Penzance, Trial by Jury and The Yeomen of the Guard**

Angel SCB–3724 (USA) (3 stereo LPs) **Includes highlights from The Mikado and HMS Pinafore and Patter Songs**

Seraphim S–60149 (USA) (1 stereo LP) **The Best of Gilbert and Sullivan**

1957

THE GONDOLIERS or
THE KING OF BARATARIA

By WS Gilbert and Arthur Sullivan

The Duke of Plaza-Toro	Geraint Evans (baritone, Welsh)
Luiz	Alexander Young (tenor, English)
Don Alhambra del Bolero	Owen Brannigan (bass, English)
Marco Palmieri	Richard Lewis (tenor, English)
Giuseppe Palmieri	John Cameron (baritone, Australian)
Antonio	James Milligan (bass, Canadian)
Francesco	Alexander Young
Giorgio	James Milligan
The Duchess of Plaza-Toro	Monica Sinclair (contralto, English)
Casilda	Edna Graham (soprano, English)
Gianetta	Elsie Morison (soprano, Australian)
Tessa	Marjorie Thomas (contralto, English)
Fiametta	Stella Hitchens (soprano, English)
Vittoria	Lavinia Renton (soprano, English)
Giulia	Helen Watts (contralto, Welsh)
Inez	Helen Watts

Glyndebourne Festival Chorus	Chorus Master Peter Gellhorn
The Pro Arte Orchestra	
Conductor	Sir Malcolm Sargent
Recorded	Studio No 1, Abbey Road
	11–15.3.1957
Recording Producer	Peter Andry
Balance Engineer	Harold Davidson

Original issue

ALP 1504–5	(2 mono LPs)	9.1957
ASD 265–6	(2 stereo LPs)	4.1959
SAT 1015–6	(2 stereo 'tape records')	9.1957
Angel 3570 B/L	(USA) (2 mono LPs)	
Angel S–3570 B/L	(USA) (2 stereo LPs)	

Re-issues

SXDW 3027	(2 stereo LPs)	9.1976
TC2 SXDW 3027	(1 stereo cassette)	9.1976

CDS7 47775–8	(2 CDs – 57'56"/38'41")	7.1987

With background notes and a synopsis by Arthur Jacobs.

CMS7 64394–2	(2 CDs –57'56"/38'41")	10.1992

With background notes and a synopsis by Arthur Jacobs.

Seraphim SIB–6103	(USA) (2 stereo LPs)
CDMB 64394	(USA) (2 CDs)

Excerpts

ALP 1904	(1 mono LP)	6.1962
ASD 472	(1 stereo LP)	6.1962
ALP 1922	(1 mono LP)	10.1962
ASD 487	(1 stereo LP)	10.1962
CFP 40238		
CFP 40260		
CFP 40282		
TC2–MOM 106		
TC2–MOM 114		
TC2–MOM 124		
EX 749696–1	(2 stereo LPs)	12.1987
EX 749696–4	(2 cassettes)	12.1987
CD CFP 4238		
CDZ7 62531–2		

See above for contents

1957

THE YEOMEN OF THE GUARD or THE MERRYMAN AND HIS MAID

By WS Gilbert and Arthur Sullivan

Sir Richard Cholmondeley	Dennis Dowling (baritone, New Zealand)
Colonel Fairfax	Richard Lewis (tenor, English)
Sergeant Meryll	John Cameron (baritone, Australian)
Leonard Meryll	Alexander Young (tenor, English)
Jack Point	Geraint Evans (baritone, Welsh)
Wilfred Shadbolt	Owen Brannigan (bass, English)
First Yeoman	Alexander Young
Second Yeoman	John Carol Case (baritone, English)
Elsie Maynard	Elsie Morison (soprano, Australian)
Phoebe Meryll	Marjorie Thomas (contralto, English)
Dame Carruthers	Monica Sinclair (contralto, English)
Kate	Doreen Hume (soprano, English)

Glyndebourne Festival Chorus	Chorus Master Peter Gellhorn
The Pro Arte Orchestra	
Conductor	Sir Malcolm Sargent
Recorded	Studio No 1, Abbey Road 10–14.12.1957
Recording Producer	Peter Andry
Balance Engineer	Harold Davidson

Original issue

ALP 1601–2	(2 mono LPs)	9.1958
ASD 364–5	(2 stereo LPs)	10.1960
Angel 3596 B/L	(USA) (2 mono LPs)	
Angel S–3596 B/L	(USA) (2 stereo LPs)	

Re-issues

SXLP 30120–1	(2 stereo LPs)	11.1969
SXDW 3033	(2 stereo LPs)	11.1977
TC2 SXDW 3033	(1 stereo cassette)	11.1977
EX 749594–1	(2 stereo LPs)	11.1987
EX 749594–4	(2 stereo cassettes)	11.1987

CDS7 47781–8   (2 CDs – 55'49"/37'39")   9.1987
With background notes and a synopsis by Arthur Jacobs.

CDCB 47781   (USA) (2 CDs)

CMS7 64415–2   (2 CDs –55'49"/37'39")   10.1992
With background notes and a synopsis by Arthur Jacobs.

CDMB 64415   (USA) (2 CDs)

Excerpts

ALP 1932*	(1 mono LP)	12.1962
ASD 495*	(1 stereo LP)	12.1962
CFP 40238		
CFP 40282		
TC2–MOM 114		
TC2–MOM 124		
CD CFP 4238		

* Includes items from **The Yeomen of the Guard, The Pirates of Penzance, Iolanthe and Trial by Jury**

1958

HMS PINAFORE or
THE LASS THAT LOVED A SAILOR

By WS Gilbert and Arthur Sullivan

Sir Joseph Porter KCB	George Baker (baritone, English)
Captain Corcoran	John Cameron (baritone, Australian)
Ralph Rackstraw	Richard Lewis (tenor, English)
Dick Deadeye	Owen Brannigan (bass, English)
Boatswain	James Milligan (bass, Canadian)
	John Cameron
Bill Bobstay	James Milligan
	Owen Brannigan
Bob Becket	John Cameron
Josephine	Elsie Morison (soprano, Australian)
Hebe	Majorie Thomas (contralto, English)
Mrs Cripps (Little Buttercup)	Monica Sinclair (contralto, English)

Glyndebourne Festival Chorus	Chorus Master Peter Gellhorn
The Pro Arte Orchestra	
Conductor	Sir Malcolm Sargent
Recorded	Studio No 1, Abbey Road
	15–18.4.1958

| Recording Producer | Peter Andry |
| Balance Engineer | Harold Davidson |

Original issue

ALP 1650–1	(2 mono LPs)	12.1958
ASD 415–6	(2 stereo LPs)	6.1961
Angel 3589 B/L	(USA) (2 mono LPs)	
Angel S–3589 B/L	(USA) (2 stereo LPs)	

Re-issues

SXLP 30088–9<	(2 stereo LPs)	10.1967
SXDW 3034<	(2 stereo LPs)	2.1978
TC2 SXDW 3034<	(1 stereo cassette)	2.1978
4X2X–3589	(USA) (stereo cassette)	
EX 749594–1	(2 stereo LPs)	11.1987
EX 749594–4	(2 stereo cassettes)	11.1987
CDS7 47779–8<	(2 CDs – 57'37"/53'20")	8.1987

With background notes and a synopsis by Arthur Jacobs.

| CMS7 64397–2< | (2 CDs –57'37"/53'20") | 10.1992 |

With background notes and a synopsis by Arthur Jacobs.

| CDMB 64397< | (USA) (2 CDs) | |

< These issues are coupled with **Trial by Jury**

Excerpts
ALP 1904
ASD 472
ALP 1922
ASD 487
CFP 40238
CFP 40282
TC2–MOM 106
TC2–MOM 114
CD CFP 4238
CDZ7 62531–2
See above for contents

1958

IOLANTHE or
THE PEER AND THE PERI

By WS Gilbert and Arthur Sullivan

The Lord Chancellor	George Baker (baritone, English)
The Earl of Mountararat	Ian Wallace (baritone, Scottish)
Earl Tolloller	Alexander Young (tenor, English)
Private Willis	Owen Brannigan (bass, English)
Strephon	James Cameron (baritone, Australian)
Queen of the Fairies	Monica Sinclair (contralto, English)
Iolanthe	Marjorie Thomas (contralto, English)
Celia	April Cantelo (soprano, English)

| **Leila** | Heather Harper (soprano, Irish) |
| **Phyllis** | Elsie Morison (soprano, Australian) |

| Glyndebourne Festival Chorus | Chorus Master   Peter Gellhorn |
| The Pro Arte Orchestra | |

| Conductor | Sir Malcolm Sargent |

| Recorded | Studio No 1, Abbey Road |
| | 18.4 and 21–24.10.1958 |

| Recording Producer | Ronald Kinloch Anderson |
| Balance Engineer | Harold Davidson |

Original issue

ALP 1757–8	(2 mono LPs)	12.1959
ASD 323–4	(2 stereo LPs)	12.1959
Angel 3597 B/L	(USA) (2 mono LPs)	
Angel S–3597 B/L	(USA) (2 stereo LPs)	

Re-issues

SXLP 30112–3	(2 stereo LPs)	12.1968
SXDW 3047	(2 stereo LPs)	10.1978
TC2 SXDW 3047	(1 stereo cassette)	10.1978
EX 749597–1	(2 stereo LPs)	11.1987
EX 749597–4	(2 stereo cassettes)	11.1987

| CDS7 47831–8+ | (2 CDs – 62'46"/43'04") | 7.1987 |

With background notes and a synopsis by Arthur Jacobs.

| CDCB 47831+ | (USA) (2 CDs) | |
| CMS7 64400–2+ | (2 CDs –62'46"/43'04") | 10.1992 |

With background notes and a synopsis by Arthur Jacobs.

| CDMB 64400+ | (USA) (2 CDs) | |

+ Issued together with the **Overture di Ballo**

Excerpts
ALP 1932
ASD 495
CFP 40238
CFP 40260
TC2–MOM 106
TC2–MOM 114
CD CFP 4238
CDZ7 62531–2
See above for contents.

1959–60

THE PIRATES OF PENZANCE or
THE SLAVE OF DUTY

By WS Gilbert and Arthur Sullivan

Major-General Stanley	George Baker (baritone, English)
The Pirate King	James Milligan (bass, Canadian)
Samuel	John Cameron (baritone, Australian)
Frederic	Richard Lewis (tenor, English)
Sergeant of Police	Owen Brannigan (bass, English)
Mabel	Elsie Morison (soprano, Australian)
Edith	Heather Harper (soprano, Irish)
Kate	Marjorie Thomas (contralto, English)
Ruth	Monica Sinclair (contralto, English)

Glyndebourne Festival Chorus	Chorus Master Peter Gellhorn
The Pro Arte Orchestra	
Conductor	Sir Malcolm Sargent
Recorded	Studio No 1, Abbey Road
	6.2, 30–31.12.1959 and 1–2.1.1960
Recording Producer	Ronald Kinloch Anderson
Balance Engineer	Francis Dillnutt

Original issue

ALP 1801–2	(2 mono LPs)	1.1961
ASD 381–2	(2 stereo LPs)	1.1961
Angel 3609 B/L	(USA) (2 mono LPs)	
Angel S–3609 B/L	(USA) (2 stereo LPs)	

Re-issues

SXLP 30131–2	(2 stereo LPs)	12.1971
Seraphim S–6102	(USA) (2 stereo LPs)	
SXDW 3041	(2 stereo LPs)	8.1978
TC2 SXDW 3041	(1 cassette)	8.1978
EX 749693–1	(2 stereo LPs)	12.1987
EX 749693–4	(2 stereo cassettes)	12.1987
CDS7 47785–8>	(2 CDs – 47'47"/64'43")	8.1987
CMS7 64409–2>	(2 CDs – 47'47"/64'43")	10.1992
CDMB 64409>	(USA) (2 CDs)	

> Also includes the Overtures **The Sorcerer, Cox and Box, Princess Ida** and **In Memoriam**. With background notes and synopsis by Percy Young, CB Rees and Arthur Jacobs.

Excerpts
ALP 1922
ASD 487
ALP 1932
ASD 495
CFP 40238
CFP 40260
TC2–MOM 106

TC2–MOM 114
TC2–MOM 124
CD CFP 4238

1960

TRIAL BY JURY

By WS Gilbert and Arthur Sullivan

The Learned Judge	George Baker (baritone, English)
The Plaintiff	Elsie Morison (soprano, Australian)
The Defendant	Richard Lewis (tenor, English)
Counsel for the Plaintiff	John Cameron (baritone, Australian)
Usher	Owen Brannigan (bass, English)
Foreman of the Jury	Bernard Turgeon (baritone, Canadian)

Glyndebourne Festival Chorus   Chorus Master   Peter Gellhorn
The Pro Arte Orchestra

Conductor   Sir Malcolm Sargent

Recorded   Studio No 1, Abbey Road
                                                        29–30.12.1960

Stereo Production   Colin Graham
Recording Producer   Ronald Kinloch Anderson
Balance Engineer   Edward Huntley

Original issue
ALP 1851	(1 mono LP)	9.1961
ASD 419	(1 stereo LP)	9.1961
Angel 35966	(USA) (1 mono LP)	
Angel S–35966	(USA) (1 stereo LP)	

Re-issues
SXLP 30089	(1 stereo LP)	10.1967
SXDW 3034<	(2 stereo LPs)	2.1978
TC2 SXDW 3034<	(1 cassette)	2.1978
EX 749696–1	(3 stereo LPs)	12.1987
EX 749696–4	(3 stereo cassettes)	12.1987
CDS7 47779–8<	(2 CDs)	8.1987
CMS7 64397–2<	(2 CDs)	10.1992
CDMB 64397<	(USA) (2 CDs)	

< These issues are coupled with **HMS Pinafore**

Excerpts
ALP 1932
ASD 495
CFP 40260
TC2–MOM 114
TC2–MOM 124
See above for contents.

1961

PATIENCE or
BUNTHORNE'S BRIDE

By WS Gilbert and Arthur Sullivan

Colonel Calverley	John Shaw (baritone, Australian)
Major Murgatroyd	Trevor Anthony (bass, Welsh)
Lieut The Duke of Dunstable	Alexander Young (tenor, English)
Reginald Bunthorne	George Baker (baritone, English)
Archibald Grosvenor	John Cameron (baritone, Australian)
The Lady Angela	Marjorie Thomas (contralto, English)
The Lady Jane	Monica Sinclair (contralto, English)
The Lady Saphir	Elizabeth Harwood (soprano, English)
The Lady Ella	Heather Harper (soprano, Irish)
Patience	Elsie Morison (soprano, Australian)

Glyndebourne Festival Chorus	Chorus Master Peter Gellhorn
The Pro Arte Orchestra	
Conductor	Sir Malcolm Sargent
Recorded	Studio No 1, Abbey Road
	6.2.1959 and 17–20.10.1961
Recording Producer	Peter Andry
Balance Engineer	Harold Davidson

Original issue

ALP 1918–9	(2 mono LPs)	9.1962
ASD 484–5	(2 stereo LPs)	9.1962
Angel 3635B	(USA) (2 mono LPs)	
Angel S–3635B	(USA) (2 stereo LPs)	

Re-issues

SXDW 3031	(2 stereo LPs)	7.1977
TC2 SXDW 3031	(1 stereo cassette)	7.1977
EX 749597–1	(2 stereo LPs)	11.1987
EX 749597–4	(2 stereo cassettes)	11.1987
CDS7 47783–8>>	(2 CDs – 52'31"/60'28")	9.1987

With background notes and synopsis by Arthur Jacobs and Percy Young.

CDCB 47783>>	(USA) (2 CDs)

CMS7 64406–2>>	(2 CDs – 52'31"/60'28")	10.1992

With background notes and a synopsis by Arthur Jacobs and Percy Young.

CDMB 64406>>	(USA) (2 CDs)

>> Issued together with the **Irish Symphony**

Excerpts
CFP 40260
CFP 40282

TC2–MOM 114
TC2–MOM 124
See above for contents.

1962

RUDDIGORE or
THE WITCH'S CURSE

By WS Gilbert and Arthur Sullivan

Sir Ruthven Murgatroyd	George Baker (baritone, English)
Richard Dauntless	Richard Lewis (tenor, English)
Sir Despard Murgatroyd	Owen Brannigan (bass, English)
Sir Roderick Murgatroyd	Joseph Rouleau (bass, Canadian)
Old Adam Goodheart	Harold Blackburn (bass, Scottish)
Rose Maybud	Elsie Morison (soprano, Australian)
Mad Margaret	Pamela Bowden (contralto, English)
Dame Hannah	Monica Sinclair (contralto, English)
Zorah	Elizabeth Harwood (soprano, English)

Glyndebourne Festival Chorus	Chorus Master Peter Gellhorn
The Pro Arte Orchestra	
Conductor	Sir Malcolm Sargent
Recorded	Studio No 1, Abbey Road
	3.11.1960 and 11–14.12.1962
Stereo Production	Colin Graham
Recording Producer	Ronald Kinloch Anderson
Balance Engineer	Christopher Parker

Original issue

ALP2013–4	(2 mono LPs)	11.1963
ASD 563–4	(2 stereo LPs)	11.1963

Re-issues

SXDW 3029	(2 stereo LPs)	12.1976
TC2 SXDW 3029	(1 cassette)	12.1976
EX 749693–1	(2 stereo LPs)	12.1987
EX 749693–4	(2 stereo cassettes)	12.1987

CDS7 47787–8~	(2 CDs – 55'42"/67'45")	8.1987

With background notes and a synopsis by Arthur Jacobs and Percy Young.

CMS7 64412–2~	(2 CDs – 55'42"/67'45")	10.1992

With background notes and a synopsis by Arthur Jacobs and Percy Young.

CDMB 64412~	(USA) (2 CDs)

~ Issued together with incidental music from **The Tempest** and the suite **The Merchant of
Venice**.

Excerpts
CFP 40282
TC2–MOM 114
See above for contents.

Other USA Issues of excerpts from the Gilbert and Sullivan operas:

4XG–60149	(stereo cassette)
4XSS–32820	(stereo cassette)

OVERTURES
From the above performances

The Pirates of Penzance*	HMS Pinafore*
The Yeomen of the Guard*	Iolanthe*
The Gondoliers*	The Mikado*

Original issue

XLP 20003	(1 mono LP)	11.1959
SXLP 20003	(1 stereo LP)	10.1961
Angel 35929	(USA) (1 mono LP)	
Angel S–35929	(USA) (1 stereo LP)	

Re-issue

SXLP 30172	(1 stereo LP)	8.1975
EXE 35	(1 cassette)	8.1975

OVERTURES AND DANCES
From the above performances(+) and individual recordings (>)

The Pro Arte Orchestra

Conductor   Sir Malcolm Sargent

(+) Ruddigore*	(>) Cox and Box*
(+) Patience*	(>) The Sorcerer*
(>) Princess Ida*	(>) Henry VIII Dances] Sir
	] Edward
	(>) Nell Gwynn Dances] German

Original issue

XLP 20032	(1 mono LP)	3.1961
SXLP 20032	(1 stereo LP)	1.1962

Re-issue
The eleven overtures marked (*) above were issued as follows:

CFP 4529	(1 LP)	9.1987
CFP TC 4529	(1 cassette)	9.1987

Between 1926 and 1932 HMV recorded ten Gilbert and Sullivan operettas with several of the principals of the D'Oyly Carte Opera Company, using the recently introduced electrical recording system; before the series was quite complete, new abridged versions of three of the operettas were made with slightly different casts, and one of them – *The Sorcerer* – was recorded for the first time, also in abridged form. Eleven of these fourteen sets shared one important common factor; they were directed by the dynamic young conductor, Malcolm Sargent.

Sargent's contribution to these 78s was highly acclaimed; for his part, he expressed great admiration for Sullivan's music and conducted the operettas at several D'Oyly Carte seasons in London. At the end of the second world war, he expressed to HMV his interest in re-recording the works. To some extent this hope was thwarted when, in 1949, the D'Oyly Carte Company changed its contractual allegiance and signed with Decca, with whom it re-made eleven of the operettas in mono, and later all thirteen of the surviving Gilbert and Sullivan canon in stereo, over a period of eighteen years.

Until 1961, fifty years after the death of W S Gilbert, the copyright of the operettas was owned by the D'Oyly Carte Company. In effect, this gave that Company control over both live and recorded performances of the works; but an exception made in the law of copyright, known as the compulsory licence system, ensured that, once the copyright owner of a musical work in which words and music are associated has authorised a recording, he cannot withhold permission for other records to be made, so long as they comply with various formalities. For instance, a payment must be made and the work must be musically complete and unaltered. It may have been this latter requirement that eventually prevented the recordings of 'highlights only' of some of the operettas before the expiration of the copyright.

During the early 1950s Sargent continued his discussions with HMV, and an agreement was reached in principle that he would record some of the operettas complete and, if possible, others in a 'highlights only' form. In March 1956, David Bicknell confirmed that the best known of the works, *The Mikado*, was to be recorded during May and June; the music would be complete, but the dialogue was to be omitted. He invited several of Britain's most celebrated opera singers to participate, including Geraint Evans, Richard Lewis, Ian Wallace, Owen Brannigan and Monica Sinclair, all familiar to Glyndebourne audiences, but singing roles that they had never sung, nor ever would sing, on that stage. The orchestra was the Pro Arte, and Glyndebourne Festival Chorus was prepared for this special recording project by Peter Gellhorn who had been Assistant Conductor and Chorus Master at Glyndebourne since 1955.

Once the taping of *The Mikado* had been successfully completed, planning began for the *The Gondoliers*, with sessions booked for March 1957. Thereafter came *The Yeomen of the Guard*, also in 1957, *HMS Pinafore* and *Iolanthe* in 1958, *The Pirates of Penzance* and *Trial by Jury* completed in 1960, *Patience* in 1961 and, finally, *Ruddigore* in 1962. The possibility that some of the operettas would be recorded only in 'highlights' form was periodically raised at EMI during this period, but the favourable reception that greeted each successive issue, particularly in the United States, seems to have encouraged the continuation of the 'complete version' format. The only two of the commonly performed G&S operettas that were not recorded by Sargent in this series were *The Sorcerer* and *Princess Ida*, but their overtures featured on a compilation first issued in 1961, ten years after the copyright of Sullivan's music had expired.

Following *The Mikado*, other classical singers were engaged to join or replace some of the original principals. Geraint Evans sang in the first three recordings but was then replaced by George Baker, doyen of interpreters of the baritone comedy roles, who had taken part in all fourteen of HMV's earlier 78 rpm series. Baker was aged over seventy when *HMS Pinafore* was recorded in 1958, but the quality of his musicianship and diction was undiminished. Among others who recorded were Alexander Young, Helen Watts, John Cameron, Elizabeth Harwood, Heather Harper and Marjorie Thomas, but the only soloist to sing in all nine recordings was the Australian soprano Elsie Morison, Glyndebourne's first Anne Trulove in *The Rake's Progress* in 1953. The chorus also included several notable young singers, among them, in *The Gondoliers*, Raimund Herincx, Patricia Kern and Janet Baker. Gilbert and Sullivan could have asked for no better advocates than these.

In May 1956 David Bicknell wrote to Moran Caplat concerning his initial doubts about using Glyndebourne's name on non-Glyndebourne recordings, such as these Gilbert and Sullivan releases:

> We are nearing completion of a new recording of *The Mikado*, done with better singers than have ever been employed before for Gilbert and Sullivan . . . conducted by Sir Malcolm Sargent and last, by no means least, your excellent Glyndebourne Chorus with Peter Gellhorn as Chorus Master. Originally I thought perhaps it would be better not to use the Glyndebourne name but the Chorus sang so well and the standard of performance of the soloists is so high that I think we ought to use it.

The chorus was duly credited in publicity material and on the records themselves, and this gave rise to the impression among some collectors that these issues were of Glyndebourne productions. Even in the 1990s they are quite often erroneously referred to as the 'Glyndebourne' versions of the operettas; no work by Gilbert and Sullivan has ever been seen on Glyndebourne's stage. In 1958 the use of Glyndebourne's name still presented Caplat with a problem. The chorus was contracted to sing on a recital record with Joan Hammond, but at Caplat's request it remained anonymous: 'It should not be named in case people think it was in some way a Glyndebourne operatic recording, and that would lead to complications which might be embarrassing for all concerned.'

The Mikado was the only set to be recorded during a Glyndebourne season and Caplat wrote to remind Bicknell that on the third day of recording, 15 June, the members of the Chorus should leave Abbey Road studios in time to catch the 2.45 pm train from Victoria. They had to be back in Sussex that evening to appear in the season's first performance of *Die Entführung aus dem Serail*. Subsequently, bookings at EMI's studios were arranged so that such pressing matters did not interfere with recording schedules. The sessions generally took place over four or five consecutive days at Abbey Road, but, as is still customary, the numbers were recorded out of sequence to suit the availability of the singers. In 1956 Raymond Leppard, who had been on Glyndebourne's Music Staff for the last two years, was working for EMI and was the Recording Producer for *The Mikado*. Its overture was recorded as the final item on 15 June 1956, but it had to be repeated at a special session called on 3 August. On four other occasions the overtures were not recorded at the main sessions for the relevant operetta; that to *Iolanthe* was taped at the end of *HMS Pinafore* in April 1958, and those to *The Pirates of Penzance* and *Patience* on 6 February 1959, well before the sessions for those works had even been booked. The overtures to *Ruddigore*, *Princess Ida*, *Cox and Box* and *The Sorceror* were recorded together with the Dances from Sir Edward German's incidental music to *Nell Gwynn* and *Henry VIII* at sessions on 3 and 4 November 1960. In due course, two LPs were issued which between them included all these overtures and dances.

In November 1963 *Ruddigore* was issued in Geoffrey Toye's revised version, prepared for the D'Oyly Carte Company in 1921. The recording uses both Toye's new overture and his short Second Act finale, (merely a reprise of part of the First Act finale) which replaced Sullivan's original. Some later recordings by other companies have re-instated the composer's own version.

All these recordings were, of course, made in stereo, still something of a novelty in May 1956, but the first four issues on LP (*The Mikado, The Gondoliers, The Yeomen of the Guard* and *HMS Pinafore*) were originally available only in mono. Their stereo versions did not appear for many months, even years, after initial release; thereafter, mono and stereo were issued simultaneously. However, in September 1957, eighteen months before appearing on two stereo LPs, *The Gondoliers* was issued on two reel-to-reel tape records, a format reserved for a few of HMV's demonstration quality recordings. Despite being equally excellent performances, both technically and artistically, none of the other G&S operettas were released in this format.

Since 1962, the year after the end of D'Oyly Carte's control, there has been a prodigious quantity of re-issues of both complete performances and highlights of these nine recordings on LP, CD and cassette. Almost every permutation of overture, song, duet and chorus seems to have been offered, and their success has been enormous. Special credit for this must go to Bicknell and Sargent for their faith in the project and for the enthusiasm with which they undertook it. Critics have consistently praised the contribution of the many members of Glyndebourne Festival Chorus who, under the supervision of Jani Strasser, played such an important part in these classic recordings of Britain's best loved operettas.

Harry Walker in *The Evening Telegraph*, 24 October 1958: Re: *The Yeomen of the Guard*:

This is an exceedingly refined performance, happily getting a highly polished recording. It is musically complete, even to the Act 2 duet *Rapture, Rapture* seldom heard in stage presentation but we still have to wait for the dialogue . . . Much of the success achieved is due to the first-rate chorus singing and a great deal to the superb orchestral work.

Edward Greenfield in *The Manchester Guardian*, 29 December 1959: Re *Iolanthe*:

With [George Baker's] commanding presence at the centre, the whole performance gains perspective, and instead of comparing things with D'Oyly Carte at every point, one simply sits back to enjoy Sargent's delicacy with the score, the glorious singing of Monica Sinclair as the Fairy Queen (a fine caricature too) and above all the exquisite singing of the Glyndebourne Festival Chorus.

Moore Orr in *Gramophone Record Review*, January 1959: Re: *HMS Pinafore*:

The Glyndebourne Festival Chorus is first class throughout – note, for example, the vocal characterisation in the glee *A British tar is a soaring soul* – and for the highly important contribution by the Pro Arte Orchestra, the name of the famous conductor is sufficient guarantee. Indeed, it should not be forgotten that Sir Malcolm Sargent is no stranger to the D'Oyly Carte operas which he has conducted hundreds of times and often on very special occasions.

[17]   Choral Recordings, 1950 and 1970

1950

Sirènes from 'NOCTURNES'

Music by Claude Debussy

Sixteen women's voices from
Glyndebourne Festival Chorus   Chorus Master John Pritchard

Philharmonia Orchestra

Conductor   Alceo Galliera

Recorded   Kingsway Hall, London
                                       11.10.1950
Mono recording

Recording Producer   Walter Legge
Balance Engineers   Arthur Clarke and Douglas Larter

78 MATRIX NOS for **Sirènes**:   Never issued in this format.

CAX 10928–1–2   Part 1
CAX 10929–1–2   Part 2
CAX 10930–1–2   Part 3

Original issue for complete **Nocturnes**
Columbia 33S 1002   (1 10" LP)   10.1952
With sleeves notes by Norman Demuth

The work of John Pritchard as Chorus Master at Glyndebourne from 1948 to
1951 was held in very high regard by his colleagues in the music profession.
The 1950 season was his fourth at the Festival and in addition to his responsibility for the chorus, he was appointed Assistant Conductor to Fritz Busch. It
was not surprising, then, that sixteen women members of the Chorus, trained
by Pritchard, were invited to participate in a concert and the recording of a
choral work, otherwise entirely unconnected with Glyndebourne. These
were the first occasions on which members of the chorus as a body had
appeared away from a Glyndebourne production.
    The work to be recorded, and later performed at the Royal Albert Hall in
London, was Debussy's *Nocturnes*, which contains one section – *Sirènes* –

scored for a chorus of female voices. It was given in the definitive version, re-orchestrated by the composer himself.

The recording sessions began at Kingsway Hall on 11 October 1950, with the Italian Alceo Galliera conducting the Philharmonia Orchestra. In the morning the first (non-choral) section, *Nuages*, was recorded on two 12" waxes. At the afternoon session *Sirènes* itself was recorded on three sides – two takes of each. The following day the second (non-choral) section *Fêtes*, was recorded on two sides and the session continued with Debussy's *La Mer*, a purely orchestral work.

No mention is made in EMI's archives about the use of tape at either of the sessions on 11 October. It is, however, noted that on the following two days tape and wax were used simultaneously. Similarly, the recording producer is not named on the first day of recording, but subsequently he is identified as Walter Legge. Whether these omissions were accidental is not clear, but it seems likely that the same technical equipment and the same producer would have been used throughout. Legge had founded the Philharmonia Orchestra in 1945, but the Philharmonia Chorus was not formed until 1957, which explains the necessity of bringing in an independent choir for this 1950 recording.

Over the next two years the different sections of *Nocturnes* were issued in a strangely inconsistent way. *Nuages* and *Fêtes* were published, one 12" 78 apiece, in June and October 1951; they also appeared on both sides of a 7" 45, one of the earliest British releases in that format. As *Sirènes* required three sides it was never issued in the 78 format, maybe because of difficulty in finding a suitable coupling to fill the fourth side. All three sections were brought together for the first time on a 10" LP, issued in October 1952; this must have caused disappointment to the customers who had already bought the first two 78s, as they had to duplicate that purchase in order to hear *Sirènes*. The recording has never been reissued.

This was the first and only occasion on which Glyndebourne forces appeared on Columbia, a sister label of HMV.

Judging by the review of LP 33S 1002 which appeared in *The Gramophone*, the recording was not a great success. Of *Sirènes*, Alec Robertson wrote in October 1952:

> I found Galliera's *Sirènes* dull and became weary of the most unbeguiling vocalising of the Glyndebourne Chorus, who are placed so near the microphone as to give an impression of gargling.

1970–1
MADRIGALS
Books III and IV

Music by Claudio Monteverdi

Sung in Italian

Sopranos
Sheila Armstrong
Wendy Eathorne
Lillian Watson

Contraltos
Anne Collins
Alfreda Hodgson
Helen Watts

Tenors
Bernard Dickerson
Gerald English
Ian Partridge
Robert Tear

Basses
Stafford Dean
Christopher Keyte

Members of the Glyndebourne Chorus   Chorus Master Henry Ward

Conductor   Raymond Leppard

Original issue
Philips 6703.035   (3 LPs)   1.1974

Re-issue
MADRIGALS
Book IV

Philips 9502.024   (1 LP)
This set includes a 24 page booklet with historical notes by Raymond Leppard and translations
of the original text into English, French and German.

MADRIGALS
BOOKS VIII, IX and other fragments.

Music by Claudio Monteverdi

Sung in Italian

Sopranos
Sheila Armstrong
Heather Harper
Angela Bostock
Yvonne Fuller
Anne Howells
Lillian Watson

Contraltos
Anne Collins
Alfreda Hodgson

Tenors
Luigi Alva
Ryland Davies
Alexander Oliver
Robert Tear
John Wakefield

Bass
Stafford Dean

Members of the Glyndebourne Chorus   Chorus Master Henry Ward
Members of the Ambrosian Chorus

English Chamber Orchestra

Robert Spencer	Lute	Osian Ellis	Harp
Raymond Leppard	Harpsichord	Joy Hall	Cello
Leslie Pearson	Harpsichord	Kenneth Heath	Cello
Henry Ward	Harpsichord	Adrian Beers	Double bass

Conductor   Raymond Leppard

Recorded   Brent Town Hall
                                          10, 12–16, 18.8.1970,
                                          12.1970 and 1.1971

Original issue
Philips 6799.006   (5 LPs)   10.1971

Re-issues
Philips 6768.175   (3 LPs)
Philips 6500.663   (1 LP)   1.1975
(Madrigals of War)

Philips 6500.864   (1 LP)   1.1975
(Madrigals of Love)

Philips 432503–2PM2   (2 CDs – 61'21"/63'15")   7.1992
(Madrigals of War and Love)
The accompanying booklet includes essays in English, French, Italian and German and the texts
in Italian and English.

Philips 432503–2FM2   (USA) (2 CDs)

Glyndebourne Chorus's second venture into the field of choral recording,
which took place twenty years later, was more warmly received.

Raymond Leppard's association with Glyndebourne began in 1954 when
he was first engaged as a member of the music staff, and he continued to play
and conduct there from time to time for thirty years; as a player of
harpsichord continuo he can be heard on Glyndebourne's recordings of *Le
nozze di Figaro* (1955) and *L'incoronazione di Poppea* (1963) – he realised the
score of the latter for modern performance.

Leppard first conducted at Glyndebourne in 1964, when Günther Rennert's production of *Poppea* was revived. Subsequently he was conductor of
several new productions and revivals including *L'Ormindo* in 1967, *La Calisto*
and Maw's *The Rising of the Moon* in 1970, Monteverdi's *Il ritorno d'Ulisse in
patria* in 1972 and Janacek's *The Cunning Little Vixen* in 1975.

In the summer of 1970 Glyndebourne was asked by Philips record company, surely at Leppard's instigation, if members of the chorus would partici-

pate in an ambitious early music venture. Leppard himself was contracted by Philips to record several of Monteverdi's Books of Madrigals. A fine array of soloists, some of whom had appeared in several Glyndebourne seasons, had been assembled for the project and a well-trained chorus was required to sing a number of the Madrigals. With their acting Chorus Master Henry Ward, the chorus had the opportunity to rehearse together regularly in Sussex for three weeks before the Festival ended on 9 August; recording began the following day at Brent Town Hall in north London and continued until 18 August. Further sessions were held in December 1970 and January 1971, but it is not clear from Philip's archives whether the members of Glyndebourne Chorus were also present at these.

The main work in which the Glyndebourne Chorus participated was *Madrigali Guerrieri et Amorosi* – Monteverdi's Book VIII (*Madrigals of War and Love*) which dates from the mid 1630s, but Leppard also allocated to it some of the Book IV Madrigals. The Madrigals from Books III and IV originally appeared together on a three LP set in January 1974, and Book IV was subsequently reissued on a single LP. Books VIII and IX were released together with *Scherzi Musicali* and other surviving fragments by Monteverdi in a five LP album in October 1971. Various permutations of the Books of Madrigals have since been re-issued by Philips, the most recent being a double CD set which contained parts of *Madrigali Guerrieri et Amorosi*.

Kenneth Long in *Records and Recording*, October 1971:

The most impressive thing about these discs [Philips 6799 006 – the 5 LP set] is the unusually high standard of performance throughout – a rare feat in view of the diversity of the music itself, the forces required and the large number of artists involved. Leppard has gathered round him a dedicated group who have either specialised or been carefully coached by Leppard himself in the early baroque style. Not only is their performance stylish and idiomatic, but they blend and balance so well . . . Indeed, one cannot imagine a better ensemble either of singers or instruments. Philips and Raymond Leppard have provided one of the most important and satisfying Monteverdi recordings for years.

Richard D C Noble in *Records and Recording*, July 1980: [Reviewing Philips 9502 024 – Book IV]:

As in Book III, Monteverdi turned to the Ferarese poet Guarini for much of his inspiration. Even more than its predecessor, this set of madrigals is starkly impassioned, with clashes of dissonance and advanced harmonies, and it represents the culminating point and the end of the pure madrigal form. Instrumental support would not be out of place here although

Raymond Leppard adheres to the purer form of unaccompanied voices using a chorus drawn from the Glyndebourne Opera in lieu of individual voices in some of these settings . . . The absence of a well integrated madrigal group in favour of some remarkable individual soloists does not create the most convincing rapport between singers . . . Nevertheless these are well thought out readings breathing passion and tension – perhaps too much so for this remarkable music – which cannot fail to impress.

Part Two

The Video Recordings

1972

MACBETH

Music by Giuseppe Verdi

Opera in four acts
Libretto by Francesco Maria Piave

Sung in the original Italian, with English subtitles by Spike Hughes

Macbeth	Kostas Paskalis (baritone, Greek)
Banquo	James Morris (bass, American)
Lady Macbeth	Josephine Barstow (soprano, English)
Gentlewoman, attending on Lady Macbeth	Rae Woodland (soprano, English)
Macduff, a nobleman of Scotland	Keith Erwen (tenor, Welsh)
Malcolm, Duncan's son	Ian Caley (tenor, English)
Doctor	Brian Donlan (baritone, English)
Servant	Ian Caddy (baritone, English)
Murderer and First Apparition	John Tomlinson (bass, English)
Bloody Child	Angela Whittingham (soprano, English)
Third Apparition	Linda Esther Gray (soprano, Scottish)
Duncan, King of Scotland	Geoffrey Gilbertson (mute, Welsh)
Fleance, Banquo's son	Tom Redman (mute, English)

The Glyndebourne Chorus	Chorus Master Christopher Fifield
The London Philharmonic Orchestra	Leader Gerald Jarvis

Conductor	John Pritchard
Producer	Michael Hadjimischev
Designer	Emanuele Luzzati
Lighting	Robert Bryan
Choreographer	Pauline Grant

For Southern Television	
Producer	Humphrey Burton
Director	Dave Heather
Sound	Cyril Vine
Lighting	Hedley Versey

Recorded with audience	Glyndebourne theatre	7.8.1972
First UK transmission	ITV	27.12.1972

LONGMAN   LGVH 7017 VHS   Mono Pal Colour 3.1984
LONGMAN   LGBE 7017 BETA Mono Pal Colour 3.1984
Running time approximately 146 minutes

PICKWICK   SLL 7017   VHS   Mono   Pal Colour   5.1987
Running time approximately 146 minutes

Accompanying 2 page leaflet includes synopsis of the opera by Jonathan Burton

Copyright Southern Television Ltd
Distributed worldwide by Primetime

1973

LE NOZZE DI FIGARO

Music by Wolfgang Amadeus Mozart

Opera in four acts
Libretto by Lorenzo da Ponte

Sung in the original Italian, with English subtitles by Spike Hughes

Figaro, servant to Count Almaviva	Knut Skram (baritone, Norwegian)
Susanna, maid to the Countess	Ileana Cotrubas (soprano, Rumanian)
Cherubino, page to Count Almaviva	Frederica von Stade (mezzo-soprano, American)
Count Almaviva	Benjamin Luxon (baritone, English)
The Countess	Kiri Te Kanawa (soprano, New Zealand)
Bartolo, a doctor	Marius Rintzler (bass, Rumanian)
Marcellina, his former housekeeper	Nucci Condò (mezzo-soprano, Italian)
Don Basilio, a music teacher	John Fryatt (tenor, English)
Antonio, gardener to the Count	Thomas Lawlor (bass baritone, Irish)
Don Curzio, a notary	Bernard Dickerson (tenor, English)
Bridesmaids	Angela Whittingham (soprano, English)
	Eiddwen Harrhy (soprano, Welsh)

The Glyndebourne Chorus	Chorus Master Peter Robinson
The London Philharmonic Orchestra	Leader Rodney Friend
Harpsichord continuo	John Pritchard

Conductor	John Pritchard
Producer	Peter Hall
Designer	John Bury
Lighting	Robert Bryan
Choreographer	Pauline Grant

For Southern Television
Producer	Humphrey Burton
Director	Dave Heather
Sound	Cyril Vine
Lighting	Hedley Versey

Recorded with audience	Glyndebourne theatre	19.8.1973
First UK transmission	ITV	21.5.1974
Repeated	Channel 4	24.6.1984

LONGMAN   LGVH 7013   VHS   Mono   Pal Colour   3.1984
LONGMAN   LGBE 7013   BETA   Mono   Pal Colour   3.1984

PICKWICK   SLL 7013   VHS   Mono   Pal Colour 5.1987
Running time approximately 168 minutes

Accompanying 4 page leaflet includes synopsis of the opera by Jonathan Burton

Original production at Glyndebourne sponsored by
The Peter Stuyvesant Foundation

Copyright Southern Television Ltd
Distributed worldwide by Primetime

1973

IL RITORNO D'ULISSE IN PATRIA

Music by Claudio Monteverdi

Libretto by Giacomo Badoaro Realised by Raymond Leppard
Published by Faber Music

Sung in the original Italian, with English subtitles by Spike Hughes

L'humana fragiltà	Annabel Hunt (mezzo-soprano, English)
Tempo	Ugo Trama (bass, Italian)
Fortuna	Patricia Greig (soprano, Scottish)
Amore	Laureen Livingstone (soprano, Scottish)
Penelope	Janet Baker (mezzo-soprano, English)
Ericlea	Virginia Popova (contralto, Bulgarian)
Melanto	Janet Hughes (mezzo-soprano, English)
Eurimaco	John Wakefield (tenor, English)
Nettuno	Robert Lloyd (bass, English)
Giove	Brian Burrows (tenor, English)
Ulisse	Benjamin Luxon (baritone, English)
Minerva	Anne Howells (soprano, English)
Eumete	Richard Lewis (tenor, English)
Iro	Alexander Oliver (tenor, Scottish)
Telemaco	Ian Caley (tenor, English)
Antinöo	Ugo Trama (bass, Italian)
Anfimono	Bernard Dickerson (tenor, English)
Pisandro	John Fryatt (tenor, English)
Giunone	Rae Woodland (soprano, English)

The Glyndebourne Chorus   Chorus Master Peter Robinson
The London Philharmonic Orchestra   Leader Rodney Friend

Conductor   Raymond Leppard
Producer   Peter Hall
Designer   John Bury
Lighting   Robert Bryan

For Southern Television
Producer   Humphrey Burton
Director   Dave Heather
Sound   Cyril Vine
Lighting   Hedley Versey

Recorded with audience   Glyndebourne theatre   24.8.1973
First UK transmission   ITV   24.8.1975

PICKWICK   SL 2005   VHS   Mono   Pal Colour   3.1988
Running time approximately 150 minutes

Six cuts were made on this video.
Act II scene ix is cut entirely and small cuts were made to
Act I scenes ii, v and viii and Act II scenes xi and xii

Accompanying 4 page leaflet includes synopsis of the opera by Raymond Leppard

Copyright Southern Television Ltd
Distributed worldwide by Primetime

1974

IDOMENEO

Rè di Creta, ossia Ilia ed Idamante

Music by Wolfgang Amadeus Mozart

Opera in three acts
Libretto by Abbate Varesco

Sung in the original Italian, with English subtitles by Spike Hughes

Ilia, a Trojan princess	Bozena Betley (soprano, Polish)
Idamante, son of Idomeneo	Leo Goeke (tenor, American)
Arbace, counsellor to Idomeneo	Alexander Oliver (tenor, Scottish)
Electra, daughter of Agamemnon	Josephine Barstow (soprano, English)
Idomeneo, King of Crete	Richard Lewis (tenor, English)
High Priest	John Fryatt (tenor, English)
Voice of Neptune	Dennis Wicks (bass, English)

The Glyndebourne Chorus	Chorus Master Peter Gellhorn
The London Philharmonic Orchestra	Leader Rodney Friend
Harpsichord continuo	John Pritchard
Violoncello continuo	Alexander Cameron

Conductor	John Pritchard
Producer	John Cox
Designer	Roger Butlin
Lighting	Robert Bryan

For Southern Television

Producer	Humphrey Burton
Director	Dave Heather
Sound	Cyril Vine
Lighting	Bill Burgess

Recorded with audience	Glyndebourne theatre	10.8.1974
First UK transmission	ITV	30.8.1976

PICKWICK   SL 2003   VHS   Mono   Pal Colour   11.1987
Running time approximately 125 minutes

Several cuts were made to reduce the overall running time
including the whole of the first half of Act I

Accompanying 4 page leaflet includes synopsis of the opera

See also page 204 for details of the 1983 production of **Idomeneo**

Original production at Glyndebourne sponsored by
The Peter Stuyvesant Foundation

Copyright Southern Television Ltd
Distributed worldwide by Primetime

1975

COSÌ FAN TUTTE

ossia La scuola degli amanti

Music by Wolfgang Amadeus Mozart

Opera in two acts
Libretto by Lorenzo da Ponte

Sung in the original Italian, with English subtitles by Spike Hughes

Ferrando, lover of Dorabella	Anson Austin (tenor, Australian)
Guglielmo, lover of Fiordiligi	Thomas Allen (baritone, English)
Don Alfonso, a philosopher	Frantz Petri (bass, French)
Fiordiligi, a lady of Ferrara	Helena Döse (soprano, Swedish)
Dorabella, her sister	Sylvia Lindenstrand (mezzo-soprano, Swedish)
Despina, maid to the ladies	Danièle Perriers (soprano, French)

The Glyndebourne Chorus	Chorus Master Julian Dawson
The London Philharmonic Orchestra	Leader Rodney Friend
Harpsichord continuo	John Pritchard

Conductor	John Pritchard
Producer	Adrian Slack
Designer	Emanuele Luzzati
Lighting	Robert Bryan

For Southern Television	
Producer and Director	Dave Heather
Sound	Cyril Vine
Lighting	Hedley Versey

Recorded with audience	Glyndebourne theatre	13.8.1975
First UK transmission	ITV	10.8.1977

PICKWICK   SL 2002   VHS   Mono   Pal Colour   11.1987
Running time approximately 149 minutes

Accompanying 4 page leaflet includes synopsis of the opera
based on one written for Glyndebourne by James Strachey in 1936

Original production at Glyndebourne made possible by the support of
The Peter Stuyvesant Foundation

Copyright Southern Television Ltd
Distributed worldwide by Primetime

1976

FALSTAFF

Music by Giuseppe Verdi

Opera in three acts
Libretto by Arrigo Boito

Sung in the original Italian, with English subtitles by Spike Hughes

Dr Caius, a French physician	John Fryatt (tenor, English)
Sir John Falstaff	Donald Gramm (bass baritone, American)
Bardolph, follower of Falstaff	Bernard Dickerson (tenor, English)
Pistol, follower of Falstaff	Ugo Trama (bass, Italian)
Mrs Page (Meg)	Reni Penkova (mezzo-soprano, Bulgarian)
Mrs Ford (Alice)	Kay Griffel (soprano, American)
Mistress Quickly	Nucci Condò (mezzo-soprano, Italian)
Anne Ford (Nannetta)	Elizabeth Gale (soprano, English)
Fenton, a young gentleman	Max-René Cosotti (tenor, Italian)
Ford, a wealthy townsman	Benjamin Luxon (baritone, English)

The Glyndebourne Chorus	Chorus Master Richard Bradshaw
The London Philharmonic Orchestra	Leader Rodney Friend

Conductor	John Pritchard
Producer	Jean-Pierre Ponnelle
Designer	Jean-Pierre Ponnelle
Lighting	Robert Bryan

For Southern Television

Producer and Director	Dave Heather
Sound	Cyril Vine
Lighting	Bill Burgess

Recorded with audience	Glyndebourne theatre	14.8.1976
First UK transmission	ITV	29.4.1978

LONGMAN	LGVH 7014	VHS	Mono	Pal Colour	8.1984
LONGMAN	LGBE 7014	BETA	Mono	Pal Colour	8.1984

PICKWICK   SLL 7014   VHS   Mono   Pal Colour   5.1987
Running time approximately 118 minutes

Accompanying 4 page leaflet includes synopsis of the opera by Jonathan Burton

Original production at Glyndebourne sponsored by
the Fred Kobler Trust and the Corbett Foundation of Cincinnati, Ohio

Copyright Southern Television Ltd
Distributed worldwide by Primetime

1977

DON GIOVANNI

ossia Il Dissoluto Punito

Music by Wolfgang Amadeus Mozart

Opera in two acts
Libretto by Lorenzo da Ponte

Sung in the original Italian, with English subtitles by Spike Hughes

Don Giovanni	Benjamin Luxon (baritone, English)
Leporello, his servant	Stafford Dean (bass, English)
Donna Elvira	Rachel Yakar (soprano, French)
Donna Anna	Horiana Branisteanu (soprano, Rumanian)
Don Ottavio	Leo Goeke (tenor, American)
Zerlina, a peasant	Elizabeth Gale (soprano, English)
Masetto, her lover	John Rawnsley (baritone, English)
Commendatore	Pierre Thau (bass, French)

The Glyndebourne Chorus	Chorus Director Nicholas Cleobury
The London Philharmonic Orchestra	Leader David Nolan
Harpsichord continuo	Martin Isepp

Conductor	Bernard Haitink
Producer	Peter Hall
Designer	John Bury
Lighting	Robert Bryan
Choreographer	Pauline Grant

For Southern Television	
Producer	Dave Heather
Sound	Cyril Vine
Lighting	Hedley Versey

Recorded with audience	Glyndebourne theatre	13.8.1977
First UK transmission	ITV	9.8.1978

PICKWICK   SL 2001   VHS   Mono   Pal Colour   11.1987
Running time approximately 172 minutes

Accompanying 4 page leaflet includes synopsis of the opera
based on one written for Glyndebourne in 1936 by James Strachey

Original production at Glyndebourne sponsored by Imperial Tobacco Ltd

Copyright Southern Television Ltd
Distributed worldwide by Primetime

1977

THE RAKE'S PROGRESS

Music by Igor Stravinsky

Opera in three acts
Libretto by WH Auden and Chester Kallman
Published by Boosey & Hawkes

Sung in the original English

Anne	Felicity Lott (soprano, English)
Tom Rakewell	Leo Goeke (tenor, American)
Trulove, Anne's father	Richard Van Allan (bass, English)
Nick Shadow	Samuel Ramey (bass-baritone, American)
Mother Goose	Nuala Willis (mezzo-soprano, Irish)
Baba the Turk	Rosalind Elias (mezzo-soprano, American)
Sellem, an auctioneer	John Fryatt (tenor, English)
Keeper of the Madhouse	Thomas Lawlor (bass, Irish)

The Glyndebourne Chorus	Chorus Director Nicholas Cleobury
The London Philharmonic Orchestra	Leader David Nolan
Harpsichord played by	Jonathan Hinden

Conductor	Bernard Haitink
Producer	John Cox
Designer	David Hockney
Lighting	Robert Bryan

For Southern Television	
Producer	Dave Heather
Sound	Cyril Vine
Lighting	Hedley Versey

Recorded with audience	Glyndebourne theatre	22.8.1977
First UK transmission	ITV	2.8.1980

PICKWICK   SL 2008   VHS   Mono   Pal Colour   7.1989
Running time approximately 140 minutes

Accompanying 4 page leaflet includes synopsis of the opera by John Cox

Copyright RPTA
Distributed worldwide by Primetime

1978

DIE ZAUBERFLÖTE

Music by Wolfgang Amadeus Mozart

Opera in two acts
Libretto by Emanuel Schikaneder

Sung in the original German, with English subtitles by Spike Hughes

Tamino, a Prince	Leo Goeke (tenor, American)
1st Lady	Teresa Cahill (soprano, English)
2nd Lady	Patricia Parker (mezzo-soprano, English)
3rd Lady	Fiona Kimm (mezzo-soprano, English)
Papageno, a bird-catcher	Benjamin Luxon (baritone, English)
The Queen of the Night	May Sandoz (soprano, American)
1st Spirit	Kate Flowers (soprano, English)
2nd Spirit	Lindsay John (mezzo-soprano, English)
3rd Spirit	Elizabeth Stokes (soprano, English)
Monostatos, in the service of Sarastro	John Fryatt (tenor, English)
Pamina, daughter of the Queen of the Night	Felicity Lott (soprano, English)
The Speaker, a priest	Willard White (bass, Jamaican)
Sarastro, the High Priest	Thomas Thomaschke (bass, German)
Priest	Richard Berkeley Steele (tenor, English)
Priest & Armed Man	John Rath (bass, English)
Armed Man	Neil McKinnon (tenor, Scottish)
Papagena	Elisabeth Conquet (soprano, French)

The Glyndebourne Chorus	Chorus Master Nicholas Cleobury
The London Philharmonic Orchestra	Leader David Nolan

Conductor	Bernard Haitink
Producer	John Cox
Designer	David Hockney
Lighting	Robert Bryan

For Southern Television	
Producer and Director	Dave Heather
Sound	Ron Payne
Lighting	Bill Burgess

Recorded with audience	Glyndebourne theatre	12.8.1978
First UK transmission	ITV	30.12.1978

LONGMAN	LGVH	7015	VHS	Mono	Pal Colour	3.1984
LONGMAN	LGBE	7015	BETA	Mono	Pal Colour	3.1984

PICKWICK	SLL 7015	VHS	Mono	Pal Colour	5.1987

Running time approximately 165 minutes

Accompanying 4 page leaflet includes synopsis of the opera by John Cox

Original production at Glyndebourne sponsored by Imperial Tobacco Ltd

Copyright Southern Television Ltd
Distributed worldwide by Primetime

1980

FIDELIO

Music by Ludwig van Beethoven

Opera in two acts
Libretto by JN Bouilly with JF Sonnleithner and F Treitschke

Sung in the original German, with English subtitles by Spike Hughes

Jaquino	Ian Caley (tenor, English)
Marzelline, Rocco's daughter	Elizabeth Gale (soprano, English)
Rocco, gaoler	Curt Appelgren (bass, Swedish)
Leonore, Florestan's wife disguised as Fidelio	Elisabeth Söderström (soprano, Swedish)
Don Pizarro, governor of the prison	Robert Allman (baritone, Australian)
Florestan	Anton de Ridder (tenor, Dutch)
Don Fernando, Minister of State	Michael Langdon (bass, English)
First Prisoner	David Johnston (tenor, English)
Second Prisoner	Roger Bryson (bass, English)

The Glyndebourne Chorus	Chorus Master Nicholas Cleobury
The London Philharmonic Orchestra	Leader David Nolan

Conductor	Bernard Haitink
Producer	Peter Hall
Design and Original Lighting	John Bury
Lighting for television	Robert Bryan

For Southern Television	
Producer	Dave Heather
Sound	Ron Payne
Lighting	Bill Burgess
Executive Producer	Lewis Rudd

Recorded with audience	Glyndebourne theatre	13.1.1980
First UK transmission	ITV	29.12.1980

PICKWICK	SL 2004	VHS	Mono	Pal Colour	11.1987

Running time approximately 120 minutes

Accompanying 4 page leaflet includes synopsis of the opera by BA Young

Original production at Glyndebourne sponsored by Imperial Tobacco Ltd

Copyright Southern Television Ltd
Distributed worldwide by Primetime

1980

DIE ENTFÜHRUNG AUS DEM SERAIL

Music by Wolfgang Amadeus Mozart

Opera in three acts
Libretto by Christoph Friedrich Bretzner

Sung in the original German, with English subtitles by Spike Hughes

Belmonte, a Spanish nobleman	Ryland Davies (tenor, Welsh)
Osmin, overseer to the Bassa	Willard White (bass, Jamaican)
Pedrillo, servant to Belmonte	James Hoback (tenor, American)
Bassa Selim	Joachim Bissmeier (spoken role, German)
Constanze, betrothed to Belmonte	Valerie Masterson (soprano, English)
Blonde, maid to Constanze	Lillian Watson (soprano, English)

The Glyndebourne Chorus	Chorus Director Jane Glover
The London Philharmonic Orchestra	Leader David Nolan

Conductor	Gustav Kuhn
Producer	Peter Wood
Designer	William Dudley
Lighting	Robert Bryan

For Southern Television	
Producer	Dave Heather
Sound	Ron Payne
Lighting	Bill Burgess
Executive Producer	Lewis Rudd

Recorded with audience	Glyndebourne theatre	17.8.1980
First UK transmission	ITV	30.8.1981

LONGMAN	LGVH 7016	VHS	Mono	Pal Colour	4.1984
LONGMAN	LGBE 7016	BETA	Mono	Pal Colour	4.1984

This video was intially released without subtitles,
however subsequent issues have been subtitled

PICKWICK	SLL 7016	VHS	Mono	Pal Colour	5.1987

Running time approximately 138 minutes

Accompanying 4 page leaflet includes synopsis of the opera by Peter Wood

Original production at Glyndebourne sponsored by
Dresdner Bank AG and Deutsche BP AG

Copyright Southern Television Ltd
Distributed worldwide by Primetime

1981

IL BARBIERE DI SIVIGLIA

Music by Gioachino Rossini

Opera in two acts
Libretto by Cesare Sterbini

Sung in the original Italian, with English subtitles by Spike Hughes

Fiorello, the Count's servant	Robert Dean (bass, English)
Count Almaviva	Max-René Cosotti (tenor, Italian)
Figaro, a barber	John Rawnsley (baritone, English)
Rosina	Maria Ewing (soprano, American)
Bartolo, a doctor	Claudio Desderi (baritone, Italian)
Berta, Bartolo's housekeeper	Catherine McCord (soprano, Scottish)
Basilio, music master to Rosina	Ferruccio Furlanetto (bass, Italian)
1st Officer	Hugh Davies (bass, English)
2nd Officer	Andrew Gallacher (bass, English)
Ambrogio	Adrian Scott (tenor, English)

The Glyndebourne Chorus	Chorus Master Jane Glover
The London Philharmonic Orchestra	Leader David Nolan
Harpsichord continuo	Stephen Wilder

Conductor	Sylvain Cambreling
Producer	John Cox
Designer	William Dudley
Lighting	Robert Bryan

For TVS

Director for tv and video	Dave Heather
Sound	Ron Payne
Lighting	John James
Executive Producer	Herbert Chappell

Recorded with audience	Glyndebourne theatre	17.8.1981
First UK transmission	ITV	29.8.1982

CASTLE   CV1 2016   VHS   Stereo   Colour   9.1988
Running time approximately 160 minutes

Accompanying 5 page booklet includes synopsis of the opera

This video was initially released without subtitles,
however subsequent issues have been subtitled

Original production at Glyndebourne sponsored by Imperial Tobacco Ltd

Copyright National Video Corporation Ltd and Glyndebourne Productions Ltd
Distributed worldwide by NVC Arts International

Extracted re-issue
'Largo al factotum della città!' and 'Una voce poco fà' included in
Highlights from Glyndebourne, 1990, q.v. page 222

1981

A MIDSUMMER NIGHT'S DREAM

Music by Benjamin Britten

Opera in three acts
Libretto adapted from Shakespeare by Benjamin Britten and Peter Pears
Published by Boosey & Hawkes

Sung in the original English

Cobweb, a Fairy	Martin Warr (treble, English)
Mustardseed, a Fairy	Jonathan Whiting (treble, English)
Peaseblossom, a Fairy	Stephen Jones (treble, English)
Moth, a Fairy	Stuart King (treble, English)
Puck, a Fairy	Damien Nash (spoken role, English)
Tytania, Queen of the Fairies	Ileana Cotrubas (soprano, Rumanian)
Oberon, King of the Fairies	James Bowman (counter-tenor, English)
Lysander, in love with Hermia	Ryland Davies (tenor, Welsh)
Demetrius, in love with Hermia	Dale Duesing (baritone, American)
Hermia, in love with Lysander	Cynthia Buchan (mezzo-soprano, Scottish)
Helena, in love with Demetrius	Felicity Lott (soprano, English)
Quince, a carpenter	Roger Bryson (bass, English)
Snug, a joiner	Andrew Gallacher (bass, English)
Starveling, a tailor	Donald Bell (baritone, Canadian)
Flute, a bellows-maker	Patrick Power (tenor, New Zealand)
Snout, a tinker	Adrian Thompson (tenor, English)
Bottom, a weaver	Curt Appelgren (bass, Swedish)
Theseus, Duke of Athens	Lieuwe Visser (baritone, Dutch)
Hippolyta, betrothed to Theseus	Claire Powell (mezzo-soprano, English)

The Glyndebourne Chorus	Chorus Director Jane Glover
The London Philharmonic Orchestra	Leader David Nolan

Conductor	Bernard Haitink
Producer	Peter Hall
Design and Original Lighting	John Bury
Choreographer	Pauline Grant
Lighting for television	Robert Bryan

For TVS	
Producer	Dave Heather
Sound	Ron Payne
Lighting	Bill Burgess
Executive Producer	Herbert Chappell

Recorded with audience	Glyndebourne theatre	24.8.1981
First UK transmission	Channel 4	3.8.1983
Repeated	Channel 4	26.5.1985

CASTLE CV1 2008 VHS Stereo Colour   8.1988
Running time approximately 156 minutes

Accompanying 4 page booklet includes synopsis of the opera

Original production at Glyndebourne sponsored by
Commercial Union Assurance Company Ltd

Copyright National Video Corporation Ltd and Glyndebourne Productions Ltd
Distributed worldwide by NVC Arts International

1982

L'AMOUR DES TROIS ORANGES

Music by Serge Prokofiev

Opera in ten scenes with a prologue
Libretto by the composer after Carlo Gozzi
Published by Boosey & Hawkes

Sung in the original French, with English subtitles

Le Héraut	Roger Bryson (bass, English)
Le Roi	Willard White (bass, Jamaican)
Pantalon	Peter-Christoph Runge (baritone, German)
Trouffaldino	Ugo Benelli (tenor, Italian)
Léandre, the Prime Minister	John Pringle (baritone, Australian)
Tchélio, a magician	Richard Van Allan (bass, English)
Fata Morgana, a sorceress	Nelly Morpurgo (soprano, Dutch)
La Princesse Clarice, the King's niece	Nucci Condò (mezzo-soprano, Italian)
Sméraldine	Fiona Kimm (mezzo-soprano, English)
Le Prince, the King's son	Ryland Davies (tenor, Welsh)
Farfarello	Derek Hammond-Stroud (baritone, English)
La Cuisinière	Roger Bryson (bass, English)
Linette	Yvonne Lea (mezzo-soprano, English)
Nicolette	Susan Moore (soprano, Australian)
Ninette	Colette Alliot-Lugaz (soprano, French)
Le Maître de Cérémonies	Hugh Hetherington (tenor, English)

The Glyndebourne Chorus	Chorus Director Jane Glover
The London Philharmonic Orchestra	Leader David Nolan

Conductor	Bernard Haitink
Producer	Frank Corsaro
Designer	Maurice Sendak
Lighting	Robert Bryan
Choreographer	Pauline Grant

For TVS	
Producer for tv and video	Rodney Greenberg
Sound	Ron Payne
Lighting	Robert Byde
Executive Producer	Herbert Chappell

Recorded with audience	Glyndebourne theatre	17.8.1982
First UK transmission	Channel 4	26.12.1982

CASTLE   CV1 2050   VHS   Stereo   Colour   4.1989
Running time approximately 135 minutes

Accompanying 6 page booklet includes synopsis of the opera

Original production at Glyndebourne sponsored by Cointreau S A

Copyright National Video Corporation Ltd and Glyndebourne Productions Ltd
Distributed worldwide by NVC Arts International

1982

ORFEO ED EURIDICE

Music by Christoph Willibald von Gluck

Opera in three acts
Libretto by Ranieri de Calzabigi

Sung in the original Italian, with English subtitles by Spike Hughes

Orfeo	Janet Baker (mezzo-soprano, English)
Amor	Elizabeth Gale (soprano, English)
Euridice	Elisabeth Speiser (soprano, Swiss)

The Glyndebourne Chorus	Chorus Director Jane Glover
The London Philharmonic Orchestra	Leader David Nolan
Harpsichord continuo	Jean Mallandaine

Conductor	Raymond Leppard
Producer	Peter Hall
Design and Original Lighting	John Bury
Lighting	Robert Bryan
Movement	Stuart Hopps

For TVS	
Director for tv and video	Rodney Greenberg
Sound	Ron Payne
Lighting	Bill Burgess
Executive Producer	Herbert Chappell

Recorded with audience	Glyndebourne theatre	22.8.1982
First UK transmission	Channel 4	6.7.1983
Repeated	Channel 4	27.4.1985

CASTLE   CV1 2035   VHS   Stereo   Colour   2.1989
Running time approximately 130 minutes

Opera introduced by Dame Janet Baker

Accompanying 4 page booklet includes brief background note and
synopsis of the opera

Original production at Glyndebourne sponsored by John Player & Sons

Copyright National Video Corporation Ltd and Glyndebourne Productions Ltd
Distributed worldwide by NVC Arts International

Extracted re-issue
'Che puro ciel!' and 'Che farò senza Euridice?' included on
Highlights from Glyndebourne, 1990, q.v. page 222

Extracts from Janet Baker's final operatic performance on 17.7.1982 as Orfeo at
Glyndebourne together with some backstage scenes are included on
Janet Baker Full Circle Her Last Year in Opera

CASTLE   CV1 2030   VHS   Stereo   Colour   4.1989
Running time approximately 75 minutes

1983

LA CENERENTOLA

Music by Gioachino Rossini

Opera in two acts
Libretto by Jacopo Ferretti   Critical edition by Alberto Zedda

Sung in the original Italian, with English subtitles by Gillian Widdicombe

Clorinda, daughter of Don Magnifico	Marta Taddei (soprano, Italian)
Tisbe, daughter of Don Magnifico	Laura Zannini (mezzo-soprano, Italian)
Angelina (Cenerentola), their stepsister	Kathleen Kuhlmann (mezzo-soprano, American)
Alidoro, tutor of Ramiro	Roderick Kennedy (bass, English)
Don Magnifico, Baron Monte Fiascone	Claudio Desderi (baritone, Italian)
Ramiro, Prince of Salerno	Laurence Dale (tenor, English)
Dandini, his valet	Alberto Rinaldi (baritone, Italian)

The Glyndebourne Chorus
The London Philharmonic Orchestra
Harpsichord continuo

Chorus Director Jane Glover
Leader David Nolan
Jean Mallandaine

Conductor
Producer
Designer
Lighting

Donato Renzetti
John Cox
Allen Charles Klein
Robert Bryan

For BBC
Director for tv and video
Sound
Lighting

John Vernon
Jeff Baker
John Elfes

Recorded with audience	Glyndebourne theatre	15.8.1983
First UK transmission	BBC2	25.12.1983

THORN EMI   TVH 9026952   VHS   Stereo   Colour   12.1984
THORN EMI   TXH 9026954   BETA   Stereo   Colour   12.1984

Accompanying 39 page booklet includes synopsis of the opera by John Cox and libretto in Italian and English

CASTLE   CV1 2053   VHS   Stereo   Colour 5.1989
Running time approximately 155 minutes

Accompanying 5 page booklet includes synopsis of the opera by John Cox

This video was initially released without subtitles,
however subsequent issues have been subtitled

Original production at Glyndebourne sponsored by National Westminster Bank

Copyright Glyndebourne Productions Ltd
Distributed worldwide by NVC Arts International

Extracted re-issue
'Del barone le figlie io chiedo' and 'Finale Act I' included on
Highlights from Glyndebourne, 1990, q.v. page 223

Laserdisc
PHILIPS LASERVISION 04 A1 014, 19.9.1984

1983

IDOMENEO

Rè di Creta, ossia Ilia ed Idamante

Music by Wolfgang Amadeus Mozart

Opera in three acts
Libretto by Abbate Varesco

Sung in the original Italian, with English subtitles by Gillian Widdicombe

Ilia, a Trojan princess	Yvonne Kenny (soprano, Australian)
Idamante, son of Idomeneo	Jerry Hadley (tenor, American)
Electra, daughter of Agamemnon	Carol Vaness (soprano, American)
Arbace, Counsellor to Idomeneo	Thomas Hemsley (baritone, English)
Idomeneo, King of Crete	Philip Langridge (tenor, English)
High Priest	Anthony Roden (tenor, Australian)
Voice of Neptune	Roderick Kennedy (bass, English)
The Glyndebourne Chorus	Chorus Director Jane Glover
The London Philharmonic Orchestra	Leader David Nolan
Harpsichord continuo	Martin Isepp
Cello continuo	Mark Jackson
Conductor	Bernard Haitink
Producer	Trevor Nunn
Designer	John Napier
Lighting designer	David Hersey
Movement	Malcolm Goddard

For the BBC
Producer and Director for tv and video   Christopher Swann
Sound   Jeff Baker
Lighting   John Elfes

Recorded without audience	Glyndebourne theatre	20.8.1983
First UK transmission	BBC2	25.12.1983 Simultaneous broadcast with BBC Radio 3

THORN EMI	TVH 9026942	VHS	Stereo	Colour	12.1984
THORN EMI	TXH 9026944	BETA	Stereo	Colour	12.1984

Accompanying 26 page booklet includes synopsis of the opera by
Trevor Nunn and libretto in Italian and English

CASTLE	CV1 2019	VHS	Stereo	Colour	9.1988

Running time approximately 180 minutes

Accompanying 5 page booklet includes synopsis of the opera by Trevor Nunn

See also page 191 for details of the 1974 production of **Idomeneo**

Original production at Glyndebourne sponsored by Autobar Group Ltd

Copyright National Video Corporation Ltd and Glyndebourne Productions Ltd
Distributed worldwide by NVC Arts International

Extracted re-issue
'Andrò ramingo e solo' included on
Highlights from Glyndebourne, 1990, q.v. page 222

Laserdisc
PHILIPS LASERVISION 04 A1 019, 19.9.1984

1983

INTERMEZZO

Music and Text by Richard Strauss

A domestic comedy with symphonic interludes,
in the English translation made for Glyndebourne by Andrew Porter
Published by Boosey & Hawkes

INTERMEZZO (continued)

Christine	Felicity Lott (soprano, English)
Robert Storch, her husband	John Pringle (baritone, Australian)
Anna, her chambermaid	Elizabeth Gale (soprano, English)
Franzl, her son	Rupert Ashford (mute, English)
Therese, the housemaid	Maria Jagusz (mezzo-soprano, English)
Fanny, the cook	Yvonne Howard (mezzo-soprano, English)
Marie, a maid	Delith Brook (soprano, English)
Baron Lummer	Ian Caley (tenor, English)
The Lawyer's Wife	Rae Woodland (soprano, English)
Resi, the Baron's friend	Catherine Pierard (soprano, New Zealand)
The Commercial Counsellor	Ian Caddy (bass, English)
The Opera Singer	Andrew Gallacher (bass, English)
Stroh, the Conductor	Glenn Winslade (tenor, Australian)
The Legal Counsellor	Brian Donlan (bass, English)
The Lawyer	Roger Bryson (bass, English)

The London Philharmonic Orchestra   Leader David Nolan

Conductor	Gustav Kuhn
Producer	John Cox
Designer	Martin Battersby
Lighting	Robert Bryan
Choregrapher	Monique Wagemakers

For BBC
Director for tv and video	David Buckton
Sound	Jeff Baker
Lighting	John Elfes

Recorded with audience	Glyndebourne theatre	26.8.1983
First UK transmission	BBC2	15.10.1983 Simultaneous broadcast with BBC Radio 3

THORN EMI	TVH 9026962	VHS	Stereo	Colour	12.1984
THORN EM	TXH 9026964	BETA	Stereo	Colour	12.1984

Accompanying 27 page booklet includes synopsis of
the opera and English libretto

CASTLE   CV1 2024   VHS   Stereo   Colour   10.1988
Running time approximately 155 minutes

Accompanying 5 page booklet includes synopsis of the opera

Original production at Glyndebourne sponsored by the Fred Kobler Trust

Copyright Glyndebourne Productions Ltd
Distributed worldwide by NVC Arts International

Laserdisc
PHILIPS LASERVISION 04 A1 013, 19.9.1984

1983 and 1984

GLYNDEBOURNE

A Celebration of Fifty Years

Anniversary documentary tracing the history of Glyndebourne
and its achievements made by BBC tv

Contents

Programme begins with the voice of John Christie

Interviews with Geoffrey Gilbertson, George Christie, Anthony Whitworth-Jones,
Brian Dickie, Maurice Sendak, Moran Caplat, Carl Ebert, John Pritchard,
Martin Isepp, Peter Hall, Bernard Haitink, Carol Vaness, John Cox,
David Hockney, Jane Glover

Extracts from   **Le nozze di Figaro**, 1973, q.v. page 188
Where the Wild Things Are, 1984, q.v. page 208
Don Giovanni, 1977 q.v. page 194
Capriccio, 1976 q.v. appendix B page 246
Die Zauberflöte, 1978, q.v. page 196
Idomeneo, 1983, q.v. page 204
Così fan tutte, 1978, q.v. appendix B page 246

Archival footage of theatricals at Glyndebourne in the early 1930s
Feature on the Kent and East Sussex Schools Festival
with Richard Stilgoe, 12 October 1983
Archival footage from the 1950s mostly with Carl Ebert
Rehearsal for the EMI recording of **Don Giovanni**, December 1983/January 1984
Recording of **Don Giovanni** at Studio No.1, Abbey Road, London, January 1984
(q.v. page 125)
Julia Trevelyan Oman presenting her designs for **Arabella**, 1 November 1983
Footage of discussions at a Glyndebourne Board meeting and at a staff meeting
George Christie and Brian Dickie at auditions
in Cami Hall, New York, 8 March 1984
Scenes throughout of the house and gardens, the opera house, foyers,
auditorium and backstage areas

Producer and Director	Christopher Swann
Cameraman	John Goodyer
Film editor	Dave King
Recorded	15.7.1983-28.5.1984
First UK transmission BBC2	30.6.1984

Running time approximately 60 minutes

Copyright BBC
Distributed worldwide by RM Associates Ltd

Video not available in the UK, January 1994

1984

WHERE THE WILD THINGS ARE

Music by Oliver Knussen

A fantasy opera
Libretto by Maurice Sendak
Published by Faber Music

Sung in the original English

Max	Karen Beardsley (soprano, American)
Mama	Mary King (mezzo-soprano, English)
Tzippy, a Wild Thing	Mary King (mezzo-soprano, English)
	Jenny Weston (movement)
Moishe, a Wild Thing	Hugh Hetherington (tenor, English)
	Perry Davey (movement)
Bruno, a Wild Thing	Jeremy Munro (baritone, Scottish)
	Cengiz Saner (movement)
Emile, a Wild Thing	Stephen Rhys-Williams (bass baritone, English)
	Brian Andro (movement)
Bernard, a Wild Thing	Andrew Gallacher (bass, English)
	Bernard Bennet (movement)
Goat	Hugh Hetherington (tenor, English)
	Mike Gallant (movement)
Shades/movement	Anthony Bailey
	Serge Julian
The London Sinfonietta	Leader Nona Liddell
Conductor	Oliver Knussen
Producer	Frank Corsaro
Choreographer	Jonathan Wolken
Designer	Maurice Sendak
Lighting designer	Robert Bryan
For BBC	
Director for tv and video	Christopher Swann
Sound	Jeff Baker
Lighting	John Wilson
Executive Producer	John Vernon

Recorded without audience	Glyndebourne theatre	26 & 27.1.1984
First UK transmission	BBC2	23.4.1984 Simultaneous broadcast with BBC Radio 3
Repeated	BBC	2.1.1986 Simultaneous broadcast with BBC Radio 3

THORN EMI	TVT 9034492	VHS	Stereo	Colour	12.1985
THORN EMI	TXT 9034494	BETA	Stereo	Colour	12.1985

Accompanying 23 page booklet includes synopsis and libretto of the opera

CASTLE	CV1 2048	VHS	Stereo	Colour	3.1989

Running time approximately 45 minutes

Double video with **Higglety Pigglety Pop**! q.v. page 214

Accompanying 9 page booklet includes synopsis of the opera

Original production sponsored by Pearson

Copyright National Video Corporation Ltd and Glyndebourne Productions Ltd
Distributed worldwide by NVC Arts International

1984

ARABELLA

Music by Richard Strauss

Opera in three acts
Libretto by Hugo von Hofmannsthal
Published by Boosey & Hawkes

Sung in the original German, with English subtitles by Gillian Widdicombe

A fortune-teller	Enid Hartle (mezzo-soprano, English)
Adelaide, wife of Graf Waldner	Regina Sarfaty (mezzo-soprano, American)
Graf Waldner, a retired army captain	Artur Korn (bass, Austrian)
Zdenka, their daughter	Gianna Rolandi (soprano, American)
Arabella, their daughter	Ashley Putnam (soprano, American)
Matteo, an officer	Keith Lewis (tenor, New Zealand)
Mandryka	John Bröcheler (bass baritone, Dutch)
Graf Elemer, admirer of Arabella	Glenn Winslade (tenor, Australian)
Graf Dominik, admirer of Arabella	Jeremy Munro (baritone, Scottish)
Graf Lamoral, admirer of Arabella	Geoffrey Moses (bass, Welsh)
Die Fiakermilli	Gwendolyn Bradley (soprano, American)
Waiter	John Oakman (tenor, English)
Welko	John Hall (bass, Welsh)
Djura	Timothy Evans-Jones (tenor, Welsh)
Jankel	Peter Coleman-Wright (baritone, Australian)

The Glyndebourne Chorus	Chorus Director Jane Glover
The London Philharmonic Orchestra	Leader David Nolan

Conductor	Bernard Haitink
Producer	John Cox
Designer	Julia Trevelyan Oman
Lighting	Robert Bryan
Choreographer	Monique Wagemakers

For BBC	
Director for tv and video	John Vernon
Sound	Graham Haines
Lighting	John Elfes

Recorded with audience	Glyndebourne theatre	22.8.1984
First UK transmission	BBC2	1.12.1984 Simultaneous broadcast with BBC Radio 3

THORN EMI   TVH 9031282   VHS   Stereo   Colour 1985
THORN EMI   TXH 9031284   BETA   Stereo   Colour 1985

Accompanying 44 page booklet includes synopsis of the opera by John Cox
and libretto in German and English

CASTLE   CV1 2036   VHS   Stereo   Colour   5.1989
Running time approximately 160 minutes

Accompanying 5 page booklet includes synopsis of the opera by John Cox

This video was initially released without subtitles,
however subsequent issues have been subtitled

Original production at Glyndebourne sponsored by John Player & Sons

Copyright Glyndebourne Productions Ltd
Distributed worldwide by NVC Arts International

1984

L'INCORONAZIONE DI POPPEA

Music by Claudio Monteverdi

Opera in two acts
Libretto by GF Busenello in the revised version of the edition
realised for Glyndebourne in 1962 by Raymond Leppard
Published by Faber Music

Sung in the original Italian, with English subtitles by Gillian Widdicombe

Fortuna, Goddess of Fortune	Patricia Kern (mezzo-soprano, Welsh)
Virtù, Goddess of Virtue	Helen Walker (soprano, English)
Amor, God of Love	Linda Kitchen (soprano, English)
Ottone, Poppea's former lover	Dale Duesing (baritone, American)
First Soldier	Keith Lewis (tenor, New Zealand)
Second Soldier	Donald Stephenson (tenor, English)
Poppea	Maria Ewing (soprano, American)
Nerone, Emperor of Rome	Dennis Bailey (tenor, American)
Arnalta, Poppea's old nurse	Anne-Marie Owens (mezzo-soprano, American)
Ottavia, the Empress	Cynthia Clarey (mezzo-soprano, American)
Drusilla, a Court lady	Elizabeth Gale (soprano, English)
Seneca, elder statesman	Robert Lloyd (bass, English)
Liberto, Captain of the Guard	Roderick Kennedy (bass, English)
Pallade, Goddess of Wisdom	Jenny Miller (mezzo-soprano, American)
Damigella, in Ottavia's service	Lesley Garrett (soprano, English)
Valetto, in Ottavia's service	Petros Evangelides (tenor, Cypriot)
Lucano, a friend of Nerone	Keith Lewis (tenor, New Zealand)
A Lictor	Roger Bryson (bass, English)

The Glyndebourne Chorus	Chorus Director Jane Glover
The London Philharmonic Orchestra	Leader David Nolan
Harpsichord continuo	Jean Mallandaine and Aniko Peter-Szabo

Organ continuo	Ivor Bolton and Christopher Fifield	

Conductor	Raymond Leppard
Producer	Peter Hall
Design and Lighting	John Bury

For BBC

Producer	Robin Lough
Director	Peter Hall
Sound	Graham Haines
Lighting	John Elfes

Recorded without audience	Glyndebourne theatre	27 & 29.8.1984
First UK transmission	BBC2	15.12.1984 Simultaneous broadcast with BBC Radio 3

THORN EMI	TVH 9031292	VHS	Stereo	Colour	1985
THORN EMI	TXH 9031294	BETA	Stereo	Colour	1985

Accompanying 27 page booklet includes synopsis of the opera by Raymond Leppard and libretto in Italian and English

CASTLE	CV1 2040	VHS	Stereo	Colour	3.1989

Running time approximately 155 minutes

Opera introduced by Sir Peter Hall

Accompanying leaflet includes synopsis of the opera by Raymond Leppard

Original production at Glyndebourne sponsored by IBM (UK) Ltd

Copyright Glyndebourne Productions Ltd
Distributed worldwide by NVC Arts International

Extracted re-issue
'The Coronation' ('Pur ti miro') included on
Highlights from Glyndebourne, 1990, q.v. page 223

1985

ALBERT HERRING

Music by Benjamin Britten

A comic opera in three acts
Libretto by Eric Crozier adapted from Maupassant's *Le Rosier de Madame Husson*.
Published by Boosey & Hawkes

Sung in the original English

ALBERT HERRING (continued)

Lady Billows, an elderly autocrat   Patricia Johnson (mezzo-soprano, English)
Florence Pike, her housekeeper   Felicity Palmer (mezzo-soprano, English)
Miss Wordsworth, Head Teacher   Elizabeth Gale (soprano, English)
Mr Gedge, the Vicar   Derek Hammond-Stroud (baritone, English)
Mr Upfold, the Mayor   Alexander Oliver (tenor, Scottish)
Superintendent Budd   Richard Van Allan (bass, English)
Sid, a butcher's assistant   Alan Opie (baritone, English)
Albert Herring, from the greengrocer's   John Graham-Hall (tenor, English)
Nancy, from the bakery   Jean Rigby (mezzo-soprano, English)
Mrs Herring, Albert's mother   Patricia Kern (mezzo-soprano, English)
Emmie, village child   Maria Bovino (soprano, Italian)
Cis, village child   Bernadette Lord (soprano, English)
Harry, village child   Richard Peachey (treble, English)

The Glyndebourne Chorus   Chorus Master Ivor Bolton
The London Philharmonic Orchestra   Leader David Nolan

Conductor   Bernard Haitink
Producer   Peter Hall
Designer   John Gunter
Lighting   David Hersey

For BBC
Producer for tv and video   Robin Lough
Director for tv and video   Peter Hall
Sound   Graham Haines
Lighting   Alan Woolford
Executive Producer   John Vernon

Recorded without audience   Glyndebourne theatre   19-20.8.1985
First UK transmission   BBC2   9.11.1985 Simultaneous
                                                        broadcast with BBC Radio 3

THORN EMI TVT 9034472 VHS   Stereo Colour   1986
THORN EMI TXT 9034474 BETA Stereo Colour   1986

Accompanying 36 page booklet includes synopsis of the opera
by Eric Crozier and English libretto

CASTLE CV1 2051 VHS Stereo Colour   4.1989
Running time approximately 150 minutes

Accompanying 5 page booklet includes synopsis of the opera
written by Eric Crozier for the world première at Glyndebourne in 1947

Original production at Glyndebourne sponsored by Autobar Group Ltd and Hays Group Ltd

Copyright Glyndebourne Productions Ltd
Distributed worldwide by NVC Arts International

1985

CARMEN

Music by Georges Bizet

Opera in four acts
Text by Henri Meilhac and Ludovic Halévy after Prosper Mérimée's novel

Sung in the original French, with English subtitles by Gillian Widdicombe

Moralès, an officer	Malcolm Walker (baritone, American)
Micaëla, a peasant girl	Marie McLaughlin (soprano, Scottish)
Don José, a corporal of dragoons	Barry McCauley (tenor, American)
Zuniga, a captain	Xavier Depraz (bass, French)
Carmen, a gypsy	Maria Ewing (soprano, American)
Frasquita, a gypsy, friend of Carmen	Elizabeth Collier (soprano, English)
Mercédès, a gypsy, friend of Carmen	Jean Rigby (mezzo-soprano, English)
Lillas Pastia	Federico Davià (bass baritone, Italian)
Escamillo, a toreador	David Holloway (baritone, American)
Le Dancaïre, a smuggler	Gordon Sandison (baritone, Scottish)
Le Remendado, a smuggler	Petros Evangelides (tenor, Cypriot)
Guide	Robert Neil Kingham (spoken role, English)

The Glyndebourne Chorus	Chorus Master Ivor Bolton
The London Philharmonic Orchestra	Leader David Nolan

Conductor	Bernard Haitink
Producer	Peter Hall
Design and Lighting	John Bury
Choreographer	Elizabeth Keen

For BBC	
Producer for tv and video	Robin Lough
Director for tv and video	Peter Hall
Sound	Graham Haines
Lighting	John Elfes
Executive Producer	John Vernon

Recorded without audience	Glyndebourne theatre	24-25.8.1985
First UK transmission	BBC2	24.5.1986

THORN EMI TVT 9034482	VHS	Stereo	Colour	12.1985
THORN EMI TXT 9034484	BETA	Stereo	Colour	12.1985

Accompanying 59 page booklet includes synopsis of the opera by
Rodney Milnes and libretto in French and English

CASTLE CV1 2018 VHS	Stereo	Colour	9.1988

Running time approximately 175 minutes

Accompanying 6 page booklet includes synopsis of the opera by Rodney Milnes

Original production at Glyndebourne sponsored by Citicorp International Bank Ltd

Distributed worldwide by NVC Arts International

Extracted re-issue
'Habañera' and 'La fleur que tu m'avais jetée' included on
Highlights from Glyndebourne, 1990, q.v. page 222

1985

HIGGLETY PIGGLETY POP!

Music by Oliver Knussen

A fantasy opera
Libretto by Maurice Sendak Published by Faber Music

Sung in the original English

Jennie, a Sealyham terrier	Cynthia Buchan (mezzo-soprano, Scottish)
The Potted Plant/Baby/Mother Goose	Deborah Rees (soprano, Welsh)
Pig-in-Sandwich Board/	
Low voice of Ash Tree	Andrew Gallacher (bass, English)
Cat-Milkman/high voice of Ash Tree	Neil Jenkins (tenor, English)
Rhoda, a parlourmaid/	
Voice of Baby's Mother	Rosemary Hardy (soprano, English)
Lion	Stephen Richardson (bass, English)
Movement	Clive Duncan
	George Reid

The London Sinfonietta   Leader Nona Liddell

Conductor	Oliver Knussen
Producer and Choreographer	Frank Corsaro
Designer	Maurice Sendak
Lighting designer	Robert Bryan
Assistant choreographer	Cengiz Saner

For BBC
Director for tv and video	Christopher Swann
Sound	Graham Haines
Lighting	Alan Woolford
Executive Producer	John Vernon

Recorded without audience	Glyndebourne theatre	28 & 29.8.1985
First UK transmission	BBC2	3.1.1986 Simultaneous broadcast with BBC Radio 3

THORN EMI	TVT 9034492	VHS	Stereo	Colour	12.1985
THORN EMI	TXT 9034494	BETA	Stereo	Colour	12.1985

Accompanying 23 page booklet includes synopsis of the
opera and libretto in English

CASTLE   CV1 2048   VHS   Stereo   Colour   3.1989

Running time approximately 50 minutes
Double video with **Where the Wild Things Are**, q.v. page 208

Accompanying 9 page booklet includes synopsis of the opera

Original production sponsored by Pearson

Copyright National Video Corporation Ltd and Glyndebourne Productions Ltd
Distributed worldwide by NVC Arts International

1987

LA TRAVIATA

Music by Giuseppe Verdi

Opera in three acts
Libretto by Francesco Maria Piave

Sung in the original Italian, with English subtitles by Gillian Widdicombe

Violetta, a courtesan	Marie McLaughlin (soprano, Scottish)
Flora, a friend	Jane Turner (mezzo-soprano, English)
Marchese d'Obigny	Christopher Thornton-Holmes (baritone, English)
Baron Douphol, a rival of Alfredo	Gordon Sandison (baritone, Scottish)
Doctor Grenvil	John Hall (bass, Welsh)
Gastone, Viscount de Letorières	David Hillman (tenor, English)
Alfredo Germont, Violetta's lover	Walter MacNeil (tenor, American)
Annina, Violetta's maid	Enid Hartle (mezzo-soprano, English)
Giuseppe, Violetta's servant	Martyn Harrison (tenor, English)
Giorgio Germont, Alfredo's father	Brent Ellis (baritone, American)
Messenger	Charles Kerry (bass, English)

The Glyndebourne Chorus	Chorus Master Ivor Bolton
The London Philharmonic Orchestra	Leader David Nolan

Conductor	Bernard Haitink
Producer	Peter Hall
Designer	John Gunter
Lighting	David Hersey
Choreographer	Elizabeth Keen

For TVS	
Producer	Derek Bailey
Director	Peter Hall
Sound	Chris Harnett
Lighting	Brian Turner
Executive Producer	Graham Benson

Recorded without audience	Glyndebourne theatre	27 & 28.8.1987
First UK transmission	Channel 4	17.4.1988

PICKWICK SL 2006 VHS Stereo Colour   4.1988
Running time approximately 133 minutes

Accompanying 4 page leaflet includes synopsis of the opera by Rodney Milnes

Original production at Glyndebourne sponsored by BAT Industries

Copyright Glyndebourne Productions Ltd
Distributed worldwide by RM Associates Ltd

Laserdisc
PIONEER PLMCC 00291, 1993

1987

L'HEURE ESPAGNOLE

Music by Maurice Ravel

Musical comedy in one act
Libretto by Franc-Nohain

Sung in the original French, with English subtitles by Gillian Widdicombe

Ramiro, a muleteer	François Le Roux (baritone, French)
Torquemada, a clockmaker	Rémy Corazza (tenor, French)
Concepcion, wife of Torquemada	Anna Steiger (soprano, English)
Gonzalve, a poet	Thierry Dran (tenor, French)
Don Inigo Gomez, a banker	François Loup (bass, French)

The London Philharmonic Orchestra	Leader David Nolan
Conductor	Sian Edwards
Producer	Frank Corsaro
Designer	Maurice Sendak
Lighting designer	Robert Ornbo
Choreographer	Jenny Weston
For BBC	
Director for tv	Dave Heather
Producer	Dennis Marks
Sound	Graham Haines
Lighting	Alan Woolford

Recorded with audience	Glyndebourne theatre	3.9.1987
First UK transmission	BBC 2	29.12.1987

Double video with **L'enfant et les sortilèges**

Original production at Glyndebourne sponsored by IBM United Kingdom Trust

Copyright National Video Corporation Ltd and Glyndebourne Productions Ltd
Distributed worldwide by NVC Arts International

Video not available in the UK, January 1994

1987

L'ENFANT ET LES SORTILÈGES

Music by Maurice Ravel

Lyric fantasy in two parts
Libretto by Colette

Sung in the original French, with English subtitles by Gillian Widdicombe

The Child	Cynthia Buchan (mezzo-soprano, Scottish)
His Mother	Fiona Kimm (mezzo-soprano, English)
The Tom Cat	Malcolm Walker (baritone, American)
The Armchair	François Loup (bass, French)
The Louis XIV Chair	Hyacinth Nicholls (mezzo-soprano, Trinidadian)
The Grandfather Clock	Malcolm Walker
The Tea Pot	Thierry Dran (tenor, French)
The Chinese Cup	Louise Winter (mezzo-soprano, English)
The Fire	Lillian Watson (soprano, English)
A Shepherd	Jady Pearl (mezzo-soprano, English)
A Shepherdess	Carol Smith (soprano, English)
The Princess	Harolyn Blackwell (soprano, American)
The Little Old Man (Arithmetic)	Thierry Dran
The Cat	Fiona Kimm
A Tree	François Loup
The Dragonfly	Louise Winter
The Nightingale	Lillian Watson
The Bat	Hyacinth Nicholls
The Squirrel	Anna Steiger (soprano, English)
The Frog	Thierry Dran
The Little Owl	Alison Hagley (soprano, English)

The Glyndebourne Chorus	Chorus Master Ivor Bolton
The London Philharmonic	Leader David Nolan

Conductor	Simon Rattle
Producer	Frank Corsaro
Designer	Maurice Sendak
Lighting	Robert Ornbo
Film Animator & slide designer	Ronald Chase
Choreographer	Jenny Weston

For BBC	
Director for tv	Tom Gutteridge
Producer	Dennis Marks
Sound	Graham Haines
Lighting	Alan Woolford

Recorded with audience	Glyndebourne theatre	3.9.1987
First UK transmission	BBC2	30.12.1987

Double video with **L'heure espagnole**

Original production at Glyndebourne sponsored by IBM United Kingdom Trust

Copyright National Video Corporation Ltd and Glyndebourne Productions Ltd
Distributed worldwide by NVC Arts International

Video not available in the UK, January 1994

1988

KÁT'A KABANOVÁ

Music by Leoš Janáček

Opera in three acts
Text after A.N. Ostrovky's *The Storm* translated by Vincenč Cervinka
By arrangement with Alfred A Kalmus Ltd (Universal Edition)

Sung in the original Czech, with English subtitles by Jonathan Burton

Kát'a	Nancy Gustafson (soprano, American)
Kabanicha, her mother-in-law	Felicity Palmer (mezzo-soprano, English)
Tichon, her husband	Ryland Davies (tenor, Welsh)
Boris, Dikoj's nephew	Barry McCauley (tenor, American)
Váňa Kudrjaš, clerk to Dikoj	John Graham-Hall (tenor, English)
Varvara, the Kabanov's foster-daughter	Louise Winter (mezzo-soprano, English)
Dikoj, a rich merchant	Donald Adams (bass, English)
Gláša, a servant	Christine Bunning (soprano, English)
Fekluša, a servant	Linda Ormiston (mezzo-soprano, Scottish)
Kuligin, friend of Vana	Robert Poulton (baritone, English)
Woman	Rachael Hallawell (mezzo-soprano, English)
Bystander	Christopher Ventris (tenor, English)

The Glyndebourne Chorus	Chorus Director Ivor Bolton
The London Philharmonic	Leader David Nolan

Conductor	Andrew Davis
Producer	Nikolaus Lehnhoff
Designer	Tobias Hoheisel
Lighting designer	Wolfgang Göbbel

For TVS
Producer	John Miller
Director	Derek Bailey
Sound Director	Robert Edwards
Lighting Director	Brian Turner
Executive Producer	Graham Benson

Recorded without audience	Glyndebourne theatre	24.8.1988
First UK transmission	Channel 4	27.3.1989
Repeated	Channel 4	11.2.1990

RM ASSOCIATES VHS Stereo Colour   6.1990
Running time approximately 100 minutes

MCEG/VIRGIN VISION   VVD 929   VHS   Stereo   Colour   1991

Running time approximately 99 minutes

Accompanying 16 page booklet includes synopsis of the opera
and background article *Kát'a Kabanová: a conventional tragedy?*

VISION VIDEO   0700183   VHS   Stereo   Colour 1994

Original production at Glyndebourne sponsored by
the Philip and Pauline Harris Charitable Trust

Copyright Glyndebourne Productions Ltd
Distributed worldwide by RM Associates Ltd

1989

JENŮFA

Její Pastorkyña (Her Foster-daughter)

Music by Leoš Janáček

Opera in three acts
Text by the composer based on a story by Gabriela Preissová
By arrangement with Alfred A. Kalmus Ltd (Universal Edition)
The Brno version, edited by Charles Mackerras and John Tyrrell

Sung in the original Czech, with English subtitles by Jonathan Burton

Jenůfa, Kostelnička's foster-daughter	Roberta Alexander (soprano, American)
Kostelnika, Grandmother Buryja's daughter-in-law	Anja Silja (soprano, German)
Laca Klemeň) grandsons of	Philip Langridge (tenor, English)
Števa Buryja) Grandmother Buryja	Mark Baker (tenor, American)
Grandmother Buryja, owner of the mill	Menai Davies (contralto, Welsh)
Foreman at the mill	Robert Poulton (baritone, English)
The Mayor	Gordon Sandison (baritone, Scottish)
His wife	Linda Ormiston (mezzo-soprano, Scottish)
Karolka, their daughter	Alison Hagley (soprano, English)
A maid	Helen Cannell (mezzo-soprano, English)
Barena, servant at the mill	Sarah Pring (soprano, English)
Jano, a shepherd boy	Lynne Davies (soprano, Welsh)
Aunt	Deirdre Crowley (soprano, Irish)

The Glyndebourne Chorus	Chorus Master David Angus
The London Philharmonic	Leader David Nolan

Conductor	Andrew Davis
Producer	Nikolaus Lehnhoff
Designer	Tobias Hoheisel
Lighting designer	Wolfgang Göbbel

For TVS
Producer   John Miller
Director   Derek Bailey
Sound   Robert Edwards
Lighting   Brian Turner
Executive Producer   Graham Benson

Recorded with audience   Glyndebourne theatre   3.9.1989
First UK transmission   Channel 4   4.2.1990

RM ASSOCIATES   VHS   Stereo   Colour   6.1990
Running time approximately 118 minutes

MCEG/VIRGIN VISION   VVD 928   VHS   Stereo   Colour 1994
Running time approximately 118 minutes

VISION VIDEO   0700173   VHS   Stereo   Colour   1994

Original production at Glyndebourne sponsored by Allied Lyons
Copyright Glyndebourne Productions Ltd
Distributed worldwide by RM Associates Ltd

1990

DEATH IN VENICE

Music by Benjamin Britten

Opera in two acts
Libretto by Myfanwy Piper, based on the short story by Thomas Mann
By arrangement with Faber Music

Sung in the original English

Gustav von Aschenbach, a novelist   Robert Tear (tenor, Welsh)
Traveller/Elderly Fop/
Old Gondolier/Hotel Manager/
Hotel Barber/Leader of the Players/
Voice of Dionysus   Alan Opie (baritone, English)
Apollo   Michael Chance (counter tenor, English)
English Clerk   Gerald Finley (baritone, Canadian)
Hotel Porter/Youth/
Third Gondolier   Christopher Ventris (tenor, English)
Youth/First Gondolier/Strolling Player Gordon Wilson (tenor, Scottish)
Youth/Glass Maker   Iain Paton (tenor, Scottish)
Youth/Second Gondolier/Priest   Aneirin Huws (baritone, Welsh)
Youth/German Father   Peter Snipp (baritone, English)
Youth/Jaschiu's Father/Guide   Jozik Koc (bass baritone, English)
Girl/Danish Lady   Heather Lorimer (soprano, English)

Girl/Strawberry Seller	Linda Clemens (soprano, English)
Girl/Beggar Woman	Alison Hudson (mezzo-soprano, English)
Ship's Steward/Restaurant Waiter	Graham Stone (baritone, English)
Lido Boatman/Hotel Waiter	Jonathan Veira (baritone, English)
French Girl	Karen Hoyle (soprano, English)
French Mother	Rebecca de Pont Davies (mezzo-soprano, English)
First American	Robert Gibbs (tenor, English)
Second American	Duncan Mackenzie (tenor, English)
German Mother	Helen Cannell (mezzo-soprano, English)
English Lady	Sally Driscoll (soprano, English)
Russian Nanny	Deirdre Crowley (soprano, Irish)
Russian Mother	Penelope Randall-Davis (soprano, English)
Russian Father	Charles Kerry (bass, English)
Governess	Jennifer Rose (actress, English)
Tadzio	Paul Zeplichal (dancer, Austrian)
Tadzio's Mother	Caroline Pope (dancer, English)
Lace Seller	Elizabeth Rodger (soprano, English)
Jaschiu	Tristan Maguire (dancer, English)
Newspaper Seller	Susan Arnold (soprano, English)
Strolling Player	Deborah Hawksley (mezzo-soprano, English)
Strolling Player	Rusty Goffe (dancer, English)
Older Boys	Julian Essex Spurrier
	Anthony Payne
	David Ruffin
Younger Boys	Alex Walkinshaw
	Daniel Hughes
Younger Girls	Natalie Casey
	Heather Jones
	Katie Jordan
	Zoë Kuppermann
	Yvonne Perdiou
The Glyndebourne Chorus	Chorus Master David Angus
The London Sinfonietta	Leader Nona Liddell
Conductor	Graeme Jenkins
Producers	Stephen Lawless
	Martha Clarke
Designer	Tobias Hoheisel
Lighting designer	Paul Pyant
For BBC	
Producer	Dennis Marks
Director for video	Robin Lough
Sound	James Hamilton
	Graham Haines
Lighting	Alan Woolford

Recorded without audience	Glyndebourne theatre	8-10.1.1990
First UK transmission	BBC2	16.9.1990 Simultaneous
		broadcast with BBC Radio 3

MCEG/VIRGIN VISION   VVD 847   VHS   Stereo   Colour   1991
Running time approximately 137 minutes

Accompanying 19 page booklet contains synopsis of opera by Myfanwy Piper
and article *Death in Venice – an introduction* by Christopher Palmer

Original production sponsored by Hays plc
with additional support from The Britten Estate Ltd

Copyright RM Arts/Glyndebourne Productions Ltd/BBC
Distributed worldwide by RM Associates Ltd

1990

HIGHLIGHTS FROM GLYNDEBOURNE

Excerpts from **Il barbiere di Siviglia, Orfeo ed Euridice, Carmen, Idomeneo,
La Cenerentola and L'incoronazione di Poppea**

Il barbiere di Siviglia 1981 q.v. page 199

Figaro	John Rawnsley
Rosina	Maria Ewing

Conductor   Sylvain Cambreling

'Largo al factotum della città!' and 'Una voce poco fà'

Orfeo ed Euridice 1982 q.v. page 202

Orfeo   Janet Baker

Conductor   Raymond Leppard

'Che puro ciel!' and 'Che farò senza Euridice?'

Carmen 1985 q.v. page 213

Carmen	Maria Ewing
Don José	Barry McCauley

Conductor   Bernard Haitink

'Habañera' and 'La fleur que tu m'avais jetée'

Idomeneo 1983 q.v. page 204

Idomeneo	Philip Langridge
Ilia	Yvonne Kenny
Idamante	Jerry Hadley
Electra	Carol Vaness

Conductor   Bernard Haitink

'Andrò ramingo e solo'

La Cenerentola 1983 q.v. page 203

Cenerentola	Kathleen Kuhlmann
Ramiro	Laurence Dale

Conductor	Donato Renzetti

'Del barone le figlie io chiedo' and
'Finale Act I' with Cenerentola, Ramiro and ensemble

L'incoronazione di Poppea 1984 q.v. page 210

Poppea	Maria Ewing
Nerone	Dennis Bailey

Conductor	Raymond Leppard

'The Coronation' - 'Pur ti miro'

CASTLE CV1 3071 VHS Stereo Colour 5.1990
Running time approximately 60 minutes

Copyright National Video Corporation Ltd and Glyndebourne Productions Ltd
Distributed worldwide by NVC Arts International

1991

LA CLEMENZA DI TITO

Music by Wolfgang Amadeus Mozart

Opera in two acts
Libretto by Caterino Mazzolà after the text by Pietro Metastasio
Newly composed secco recitatives by Stephen Oliver commissioned by Glyndebourne

Sung in the original Italian, with English subtitles by David Stevens

Sesto, a young patrician	Diana Montague (mezzo-soprano, English)
Vitellia, daughter of the deposed Emperor	Ashley Putnam (soprano, American)
Annio, a young patrician	Martine Mahé (mezzo-soprano, French)
Tito, Emperor of Rome	Philip Langridge (tenor, English)
Servilia, sister of Sesto	Elzbieta Szmytka (soprano, Polish)
Publio, captain of the Patrician Guard	Peter Rose (bass, English)

The Glyndebourne Chorus	Chorus Master David Angus
The London Philharmonic	Leader Stephen Bryant
Harpsichord continuo	Joyce Fieldsend

Conductor	Andrew Davis
Producer	Nicholas Hytner
Designer	David Fielding
Lighting designer	Jean Kalman
Movement director	Jane Gibson

For BBC
Director   Robin Lough
Sound   Graham Haines
Lighting   Clive Potter
Executive Producer   Dennis Marks

Recorded without audience   Glyndebourne theatre   2-3.9.1991
First UK transmission   BBC2   25.12.1991

Original production at Glyndebourne sponsored by IBM United Kingdom Trust

Copyright Poorhouse Productions/Glyndebourne Productions Ltd/BBC
Distributed worldwide by RM Associates Ltd

Video not available in the UK, January 1994

1992

THE GLYNDEBOURNE GALA

Glyndebourne's first gala concert in the presence of HRH The Prince of Wales
was staged as the final event in the old opera house on 24 July 1992

Introduction by Sir George Christie

'Voi che sapete' from **Le nozze di Figaro**
Frederica von Stade   Conductor Andrew Davis

'Patria oppressa!' and 'Ah, la paterna mano' from **Macbeth**
Kim Begley   The Glyndebourne Chorus   Conductor Andrew Davis

'Salce, salce' and 'Ave Maria' from **Otello**
Montserrat Caballé   Conductor Andrew Davis

'Una voce poco fà' from **Il barbiere di Siviglia**
Frederica von Stade   Conductor Andrew Davis

'La calunnia' from **Il barbiere di Siviglia**
Ruggero Raimondi   Conductor Andrew Davis

'Pleurez, pleurez mes yeux' from **Le Cid**
Montserrat Caballé   Conductor Andrew Davis

'Ruin, disaster, shame' from **The Rake's Progress**
Felicity Lott   The Glyndebourne Chorus   Conductor Andrew Davis

Introduction by Dame Janet Baker

'Illustratevi o cieli' from **Il ritorno d'Ulisse in patria**
Frederica von Stade and Benjamin Luxon   Conductor Andrew Davis

'Summertime' from **Porgy and Bess**
Cynthia Haymon   Conductor Andrew Davis

Storm interlude from **Peter Grimes**
The London Philharmonic   Conductor Andrew Davis

Introduction by Elisabeth Söderström

Closing scene from **Capriccio**
Felicity Lott   Conductor Bernard Haitink

Introduction by Sir Geraint Evans

'Là ci darem la mano' from **Don Giovanni**
Cynthia Haymon and Ruggero Raimondi   Conductor Bernard Haitink

'Nettuno s'onori' from **Idomeneo**
The Glyndebourne Chorus   Conductor Bernard Haitink

Closing sentences by Sir George Christie

Overture to **Le nozze di Figaro**
The London Philharmonic   Conductor Andrew Davis

Concert ends with a firework display in the gardens during the closing music

The Glyndebourne Chorus	Chorus Master David Angus
The London Philharmonic	Leader Tina Gruenberg
Harpsichord continuo	Martin Isepp
Producer	Stephen Lawless
Lighting designers	Paul Pyant
	Keith Benson

For BBC

Director	Christopher Swann
Sound	Graham Haines
Lighting	Dennis Butcher
Executive Producer	Dennis Marks

Recording and live transmission	Glyndebourne theatre and garden	24.7.1992
First UK transmission	BBC 2	24.7.1992

Running time approximately 112 minutes

Gala concert supported by NM Rothschild and Sons Ltd and
Rothschild et Cie Banque

Copyright Glyndebourne Productions Ltd/BBC
Distributed worldwide by RM Associates Ltd

Video not available in the UK, January 1994

1992

THE QUEEN OF SPADES

Pikovaya Dama/Pique Dame

Music by Pyotr Ilyich Tchaikovsky

Opera in three acts and seven scenes
Libretto by Modest Tchaikovsky with contributions by the composer,
based on the novel by Alexander Pushkin

Sung in the original Russian, with English subtitles by Gillian Widdicombe

Herman, an officer	Yuri Marusin (tenor, Russian)
Count Tomsky	Sergei Leiferkus (baritone, Russian)
Prince Yeletsky	Dimitri Kharitonov (baritone, Russian)
Tchekalinsky, an officer	Graeme Matheson-Bruce (tenor, Scottish)
Surin, an officer	Andrew Slater (bass, English)
Tchaplitsky, friend of Herman	Robert Burt (tenor, English)
Narumov, friend of Herman	Christopher Thornton-Holmes (baritone, English)
The Countess	Felicity Palmer (mezzo-soprano, English)
Lisa, her granddaughter	Nancy Gustafson (soprano, American)
Pauline, Lisa's friend	Marie-Ange Todorovitch (mezzo-soprano, French)
Governess	Enid Hartle (mezzo-soprano, English)
Chloë	Anne Dawson (soprano, English)
Master of Ceremonies	Geoffrey Pogson (tenor, English)
Masha, Lisa's maid	Rachael Tovey (soprano, English)

The Glyndebourne Chorus	Chorus Master David Angus
The London Philharmonic	Leader Tina Gruenberg
Conductor	Andrew Davis
Producer	Graham Vick
Designer	Richard Hudson
Lighting designer	Thomas Webster
Choreographer	Ron Howell
For BBC	
Producer	Stephany Marks
Director	Peter Maniura
Sound	Paul Cunliffe
Lighting	Dennis Butcher
Executive Producer	Dennis Marks

Recorded without audience	Glyndebourne theatre	29-30.7.1992
First UK transmission	BBC2	27.12.1993

Original production at Glyndebourne sponsored by Johnson Matthey

Copyright Poorhouse Productions/Glyndebourne Productions Ltd/BBC
Distributed worldwide by RM Associates Ltd

Video not available in the UK, January 1994

Laserdisc
PIONEER PLMCC 00841 1993

1992

PORGY AND BESS

Music by George Gershwin

Lyrics by DuBose Heyward and Ira Gershwin
Libretto by DuBose Heyward,
based on the play **Porgy** by Dorothy and DuBose Heyward

Sung in the original English using the EMI soundtrack

Jasbo Brown	Wayne Marshall (pianist, English)
Clara, Jake's wife	Paula Ingram
	sung by Harolyn Blackwell (soprano, American)
Mingo	Barrington Coleman (tenor, American)
Sportin' Life	Damon Evans (tenor, American)
Jake	Gordon Hawkins
	sung by Bruce Hubbard (baritone, American)
Serena, Robbins' wife	Cynthia Clarey (soprano, American)
Robbins	D Alonzo Washington
	sung by Johnny Worthy (tenor, English)
Jim	Curtis Watson (baritone, Jamaican)
Peter, the honeyman	Mervin Wallace (tenor, American)
Lily, Peter's wife	Maureen Brathwaite (mezzo-soprano, English)
Maria	Marietta Simpson (contralto, American)
Porgy	Willard White (bass, Jamaican)
Crown	Gregg Baker (baritone, American)
Bess	Cynthia Haymon (soprano, American)
Undertaker	Autris Paige (baritone, American)
Annie	Yolanda Grant
	sung by Paula Ingram (soprano, American)
Frazier	William Johnson (baritone, American)
Neighbour	Linda Thompson (mezzo-soprano, American)
Scipio	Andrez Harriott
	spoken by Linda Thompson
Nelson/Crab Man	Colenton Freeman (tenor, American)
Strawberry Woman	Camellia Johnson (mezzo-soprano, American)
Detective	Alan Tilvern (spoken role, English)
Coroner	Billy J Mitchell (spoken role, Canadian)
Mr Archdale	Ted Maynard (spoken role, American)
Policeman	Ron Travis (spoken role, American)
Dancer	Steve Agyei
Dancer	Bruce Leader
The Glyndebourne Chorus	Chorus Master Craig Rutenberg
The London Philharmonic	Leader David Nolan
Conductor	Simon Rattle
Director	Trevor Nunn
Original set designer	John Gunter
Original costume designer	Sue Blane
Original lighting designer	David Hersey
Choreographer	Charles Augins

For BBC
Producers   Greg Smith
                           Stephany Marks
Designer for tv   Eric Walmsley
Sound   Paul Cunliffe
Lighting director   Chris Townsend
Executive Producers   Richard Price
                           Dennis Marks

Recorded   Shepperton Studios, London   21.11 – 18.12.1992
First UK transmission   BBC2   26.12.1993

EMI   MVB 4911313   VHS   Stereo   Colour   4.10.1993
Running time approximately 183 minutes

LASERDISC   EMI   LDD 4911311   Stereo   Colour   4.10.1993

Accompanying 10 page booklet includes synopsis of the opera in English,
German, French and Italian based on one written by Charles Strickland
for the 1986 Glyndebourne Festival Programme

Orchestral introduction and Good mornin' chorus at the beginning of
Act III Scene 3 have been cut

A television adaptation by Trevor Nunn with Yves Baigneres
based on the original Glyndebourne Festival Opera stage production

Soundtrack EMI recording of **Porgy and Bess**, 1988, q.v. pages 142

Original production at Glyndebourne sponsored by
Citicorp Investment Bank Ltd

Copyright Primetime/BBC (film) EMI (soundtrack)
Distributed in the UK by EMI
Distributed worldwide by RPTA

[19] Glyndebourne on Television 1951–1993

'We are all here tonight as guests of the BBC because for tonight Glyndebourne has been turned into a television studio.' Thus Moran Caplat introduced the specially invited audience to the first transmission of a complete opera on British television – *Così fan tutte*[1] from Glyndebourne on 23 July 1951.

Since the 1930s Glyndebourne had enjoyed a good relationship with the BBC and the first radio broadcast from the theatre – Act I of *Don Giovanni* – was made in May 1936. The idea of a television transmission first seems to have been discussed in 1950 by David Harris, Opera Manager at Broadcasting House, and Moran Caplat, General Manager of Glyndebourne. An approach was then made to Cecil McGivern, Head of Television Programmes, and a year later the concept of opera on television became a reality. In the technologically advanced 1990s it is difficult for us to appreciate what a bold decision this was on the part of the BBC. They had never undertaken a live relay over a distance as far as the 60 miles from Glyndebourne to their principal transmitting station at Alexandra Palace and the logistics were highly complicated. Firstly, the performance had to be transmitted out of the valley in which Glyndebourne lies to a receiver positioned on the Downs; from there it was passed to another high point, Turner's Hill, near Haywards Heath, thirdly to Colley Hill, near Reigate, fourthly to the tallest part of the University of London, Senate House, and finally to Alexandra Palace.

Each site had to be manned by two engineers who worked for six days before the broadcast, testing their units and establishing picture links. During the dress rehearsal both the engineers and their equipment were soaked by thundery rain and there were fears that the pictures would never reach London. On the day they did, and the BBC were much praised for allowing a wider audience to enjoy something of the magic of an evening at Glyndebourne. The novelty of such coverage was emphasised by the amount of press comment, headlines appeared such as '60-Mile TV Relay is successful' (*Morning Advertiser*) and 'Television in Tails' (*Daily Mirror*) referring to the camera crews appearance in white tie and tails. There were also the now familiar complaints about the monopolisation of television by a boring opera in a lan-

---

1. Full details of Glyndebourne television transmissions not released on video may be found in Appendix B on page 243.

guage that could not be understood – *plus ça change*. Nevertheless the experiment was judged sufficiently successful to be repeated the following year.

The opera selected in 1952 was a much larger scale work – Verdi's *Macbeth*. One of the reasons for choosing *Così fan tutte* as the first transmission was that it had a small cast and chorus. *Macbeth* had eleven principal singers, forty-eight choristers, seven dancers and a number of supers (extras) who took the parts of soldiers and pages. Glyndebourne had trodden a new path in 1938 when it gave the first professional production in England of this opera. It was still little known in 1952 and again the BBC showed a pioneering spirit in taking *Macbeth* rather than a perhaps more accessible piece such as *La Cenerentola*. On this occasion the cameras were situated in the auditorium rather than in the wings as they had been for *Così fan tutte*. The singers could therefore perform to the front, rather than the sides, of the stage which must have made the performance appear more natural as well as being more enjoyable for the audience. Sadly, because the operas were transmitted live, the only footage of *Macbeth* that survives in the BBC Archive is the introductory and interval material in which Carl Ebert tells the audience about the workings of the different departments backstage at Glyndebourne. There is no record of the opera itself.

From 1951 until 1965 an opera from Glyndebourne's repertoire was seen on television each year. In 1956 to celebrate the Mozart bi-centenary excerpts from five Mozart operas were shown, a considerable task for the scene shifters who, as the programme was being transmitted live, had to change over from one opera to another whilst Dennis Arundell narrated a short link piece. These excerpts set a pattern for the transmissions over the next two years. In 1957 only Act II of Rossini's *Le Comte Ory* was shown and in 1958 the last five (out of eight) scenes of Stravinsky's *The Rake's Progress*. The transmission time was thus reduced to one or one and a half hours rather than the two and a half hours duration of *Macbeth*. This policy becomes understandable when we recall that BBC 2 did not come into existence until 20 April 1964; so a full-length opera transmission monopolised their only channel for the greater part of the evening.

From the beginning the BBC had tried to overcome the problem of transmitting opera in a foreign language by having a well-known personality or someone closely connected with the Glyndebourne production to introduce the programme and explain the story. This was felt to be increasingly insufficient and in 1964 John Vernon (the producer for BBC/Glyndebourne productions for over twenty years) and his team suggested that subtitles should be used. The opera transmission that year, *Die Zauberflöte*, was felt to be particularly appropriate because of 'its considerable recitative (sic) and complicated plot'.[1] Subtitling was at that time in a very primitive state, the translations were mounted on separate cards and literally held in front of a tv camera at

---

1.   John Vernon in a letter to Moran Caplat, 29 June 1964

the appropriate moment. On this occasion the person responsible for changing the cards was Brian Dickie, later to become Glyndebourne's General Administrator. It was an experiment which worked. Considering its success it is interesting to note that subtitles were not generally used at live opera performances until twenty years later.

In 1965 three one-act operas were recorded especially for BBC 2, now one year old. They were Busoni's *Arlecchino*, Purcell's *Dido and Aeneas* and Ravel's *L'heure espagnole*. The first was an adaptation of an existing production which had been recorded by EMI in 1954. *Dido and Aeneas*, with Janet Baker as Dido, her first principal role at Glyndebourne, and *L'heure espagnole* were new productions mounted especially for television which were then performed as a double bill during the 1966 Festival.

During the late 1960s the number of productions given at Glyndebourne each season was reduced to four. This was a decision reluctantly taken for financial reasons. It also meant that the selection of operas from which the BBC could choose was more limited. With increasing opportunities to take operas from other venues that would attract higher viewing figures (Glyndebourne's more adventurous repertoire such as *Jephtha* could not be classed as peak viewing) the relationship faltered. The BBC did record *La Calisto* in 1971 which was the first Glyndebourne opera to be transmitted in colour. However, for the next five years Southern Television with their talented team of Humphrey Burton as Producer and Dave Heather as Director stepped into the BBC's shoes.

Moran Caplat, has described Southern's approach as more 'populist', ie, they were attuned to the need to make opera accessible to the public. They forged close links with the Glyndebourne production team working on an opera, gained a good understanding of the way in which the producer wanted to portray the piece and therefore what they in turn had to do to convey that feeling and atmosphere on the small screen. The result was a series of sensitive and imaginative operas on television. In an article for the 1977 Glyndebourne programme book Spike Hughes wrote: 'David Heather has found a way of televising opera which critics have come to regard as the most satisfying yet: by combining the clarity of studio production and the feel and excitement of a real theatrical performance. But most of all it succeeds because, like Glyndebourne itself, it has unmistakeable style.'

Macbeth was the first opera Southern recorded and, twelve years later, it was also one of the first to be released on video. The plan was to show Verdi's masterpiece on ITV on Christmas Day 1972. This caused an anti-opera furore which hit the headlines and angry viewers eventually won the battle when it was rescheduled for 27 December. If *Macbeth* was scheduled for 25 December today there would be some complaints, but nothing like the public outcry of twenty-one years ago. Pavarotti, Domingo and Carreras have undoubtedly transformed public opinion about opera, but the solid groundwork already done for them by the television companies should not be underestimated.

The following year ITV felt Southern had overstepped the mark in recording a baroque opera, Monteverdi's *Il ritorno d'Ulisse in patria*, and refused to transmit it nationally. Southern had an ace up their sleeve in the form of a Covent Garden production of *La bohème* with Placido Domingo as Rodolfo which they refused to release until agreement had been reached about *Ulisse*. An impasse followed with the result that *Ulisse* was not shown until 24 August 1975, two years to the day after it had been recorded. About 2,500,000 viewers watched it, at that time the equivalent of the entire audience for forty-seven seasons at Glyndebourne.

The cost of recording opera for television was, and is, very high. In 1951 the BBC recording of *Così fan tutte* cost over £4,000 which was then their most expensive relay ever. (Nowadays a recording might cost anywhere between £200-£300,000 depending on the size of the cast and chorus, length of recording time etc.) There were those within the BBC, and later ITV, who complained vociferously that the expense was disproportionate to the audience size and claimed that the money could be better spent on other outside broadcasts such as sporting events. However, if 2,500,000 people watch a baroque opera the importance of so called 'minority viewing' programmes, not only for the arts but also for other disciplines, is put into perspective.

When Southern Television came to Glyndebourne in 1972 one of their original aims had been to record the five Mozart operas with which the Festival had established its reputation before the war – *Le nozze di Figaro, Così fan tutte, Don Giovanni, Die Zauberflöte,* and *Die Entführung aus dem Serail.* By 1978 they had achieved their aim and added one for luck – *Idomeneo.* In between, the BBC returned to Glyndebourne to record the acclaimed production of *Capriccio* with Elisabeth Söderström as the Countess. It was the first simultaneous broadcast with BBC Radio 3, enabling viewers to watch the performance on television and at the same time to listen in stereo. Further steps along the path of trying to obtain a 'perfect' recording were taken in 1983 when the BBC recorded *Idomeneo* without an audience. Since then a large number of Glyndebourne operas have been recorded using the theatre as a studio rather than a public auditorium. It allows the television production team more freedom to use a greater number of cameras in a highly creative way, but it does not give the viewer, who may never have attended an opera, any sense of the excitement or expectation of waiting for the curtain to rise on an evening at the theatre.

More recently the BBC has played an important role in helping to put on contemporary operas at Glyndebourne. As part of their policy to support new work in British opera houses they commissioned Nigel Osborne's *The Electrification of the Soviet Union* based on Boris Pasternak's novella *The Last Summer.* Nigel Osborne has described the close collaboration on this project between himself, the director, Peter Sellars and the librettist Craig Raine as 'very combative ... which was good because I found that what was coming out in the middle was what I wanted'.[1] *The Electrification* was premièred on 5 October 1987 by Glyndebourne Touring Opera. Later that year it was recorded by the BBC who had also been drawn into the collaborative process by attending production meetings, orchestral run-throughs and stage rehearsals.

Michael Tippett's space-age opera *New Year*, premièred at Houston in 1989, was jointly commissioned by the BBC, Glyndebourne and Houston Grand Opera. In composing the opera Tippett had been strongly influenced by television, in particular the programmes *Fame* and *The Flip Side of Dominic Hyde*. For this reason the BBC felt they could come closer to Tippett's original conception of the piece by making a special studio production for the small screen rather than adapting the original staging at Houston and Glyndebourne. This studio version was shown on BBC 2 in September 1991.

The newest release on video, *Porgy and Bess*, is the first film based on a Glyndebourne production. During the winter of 1992 almost the entire cast of the original Glyndebourne production were reassembled at Shepperton Studios and the film was shot using the EMI/Glyndebourne recording (see page 142) as the soundtrack. The outcome is a gripping evening of opera which it would be hard to surpass – in this instance a definite argument *for* the studio.

And what of the videos themselves? There are now 33 different Glyndebourne productions, one highlights video and two special events (*Glyndebourne A Celebration of Fifty Years* and *The Glyndebourne Gala*) available on VHS either in Britain, the United States or both and many are distributed worldwide. As well as the Mozart operas with which Glyndebourne is most associated they include a wide range of other works from Stravinsky's *The Rake's Progress* 'The most visually exact and satisfying opera transmission I have seen'[2] to Strauss's *Intermezzo* 'I find every minute pure delight'[3] to Britten's *Death in Venice* 'Where so much is dependent on the feeling and motion and proximity of the Venetian lagoon it is perverse to be denied some image of it'.[4] Longman released the first four Glyndebourne videos in this country in time for the Festival's fiftieth anniversary in 1984. In just ten years we have come from a world where videos were uncommon to one where they are taken for granted, from a world where videos cost around £45 each to one where they cost £12 – £15 each and from a world of demure grey packaging to one of maximum-impact colour and vibrancy. Will the new format laserdisc capture the market as completely in the next ten years?

1. Nigel Osborne in an interview with Noël Goodwin for the Glyndebourne Oral History Project, July 1991
2. Sylvia Clayton in *The Daily Telegraph*, 4 August 1980
3. Rodney Milnes in *The Gramophone*, July 1986
4. Noël Goodwin in *Opera*, August 1991

APPENDIX A – GLYNDEBOURNE RADIO BROADCASTS IN PUBLIC ARCHIVES

The tapes and discs listed in this appendix may be heard on application to the following repositories:

1) BBC and National Sound Archive (NSA),
   29 Exhibition Road, London SW7 2AS. Telephone: 071-412 7418
2) Music Performance Research Centre (MPRC),
   Barbican Music Library, Barbican Centre, London EC2Y 8DS.
   Telephone: 071-638 0672

The following programmes were live broadcasts from the theatre at Glyndebourne unless otherwise indicated.

Opera	Broadcast date	Programme	Cast & Archive Reference Number
Le nozze di Figaro Overture & Act I	18.6.1936 (M)*	Regional	Brownlee, Rautawaara, Mildmay, Stabile, Helletsgruber, Baccaloni, Willis, Nash, Dunlop, Radford, Morgan Jones Busch/Glyndebourne Festival Orchestra **BBC Sound Archives Tape 28000 [F36/3]**
The Rape of Lucretia Excerpts Studio broadcast from Camden Hippodrome	11.10.1946 (M)	Third	Pears, Cross, Brannigan, Sharp, Kraus, Ferrier, Pollak, Ritchie Goodall/Glyndebourne Orchestra **BBC Sound Archives Tape 39584** **NSA Tape T9202WR**
Arlecchino	16.7.1954 (M)	Third	Wallace, Gester, Evans, Ollendorf, Malbin, Dickie Pritchard/RPO **BBC Sound Archives Tape 30701**
Ariadne auf Naxos	16.7.1954 (M)	Third	Franklin, Evans, Jurinac, Lewis, Carolan, Dickie, Griffiths, Atkins, Dobbs, Amara, Gester, Oncina, Ollendorf, Springer, Berry, Malbin Pritchard/RPO **BBC Sound Archives Tape 30700**

Opera	Broadcast date	Programme	Cast & Archive Reference Number
Alceste 1st 45 minutes of each act only	1.6.1958 (M)	Third	Griffiths, Holman, Rubio, Massard, Lewis, Wicks, Blankenburg Gui/RPO **NSA Tape T10981W**
Falstaff Last 15 minutes of Act III missing	8.6.1958 (M)	Third	Cuenod, Evans, Carlin, Stefanoni, Cadoni, Ligabue, Dominguez, Sciutti, Oncina, Borriello Gui/RPO **NSA Tape T10980WR**
Le Comte Ory	16.7.1958 (M)	Home	Blankenburg, Illing, Oncina, Sinclair, Depraz, Cadoni, Barabas, Holman Pritchard/RPO **NSA Tape T10917WR**
Der Rosenkavalier Excerpt from Act I and all of Act III	7.6.1959 (M)	Third	Söderström, Crespin, Czerwenka, Kentish, Evans, McAlpine, Ferenz, Rothenberger, Crook, Robertson, Alan Ludwig/RPO **MPRC ACQ 74**
Così fan tutte Special broadcast	6.7.1959 (M)	Home	Oncina, Bruscantini, Feller, Ligabue, Lane, Sciutti Pritchard/RPO **NSA Tapes T3556W&R, T3557W**
La Cenerentola Act II only	31.7.1960 (M)	Third	Zanolli, Pace, Rota, Alan, Wallace, Oncina, Bruscantini Pritchard/RPO **NSA Tape T10981R**
L'elisir d'amore	4.6.1961 (M)	Third	Ratti, Alva, Sordello, Badioli, Maire Cillario/RPO **NSA Tape T10916WR**
Elegy for Young Lovers	15.7.1961 (M)	Third	Dorow, Meyer, Hemsley, Turp, Alexander, Söderström, Kentish Pritchard/RPO **BBC Sound Archives Tape 29016**

Opera	Broadcast date	Programme	Cast & Archive Reference Number
Pelléas et Mélisande	27.5.1962 (M)	Third	Roux, Duval, Meyer, Hoekman, Gui, Brédy, Shirley-Quirk Gui/RPO **MPRC ACQ 29**
Idomeneo Act III only From the Royal Albert Hall, London	17.8.1964 (M)	Home	Janowitz, Pavarotti, Taylor, Tarrés, Lewis, Hughes, Wicks Pritchard/LPO **BBC Transcription Service Discs 114614,5,6**
L'Ormindo	30.7.1967 (M)	Third	Wakefield, Runge, Garcisanz, Stadler, Lehane, Cuenod, Howells, Berbié, Davià, Van Allan Leppard/LPO **BBC Sound Archives Tape 31657 NSA Tapes T149W, T150W, M878W**
La Calisto	30.5.1970 (M)	Radio 3	Hartle, Lensky, Lebrun, Trama, Gottlieb, Cotrubas, Bowman, Baker, Cuenod, Hughes, Davià, Brannigan, Stadler Leppard/LPO **NSA Tapes T258R, T259W**
The Rising of the Moon	2.8.1970 (M)	Radio 3	Oliver, Howells, Gibbs, Van Allan, Fryatt, Gottlieb, Woodland, Meyer, Lee Silver, Donlan, Wakefield, Peters, Wicks, Jones, Roden Leppard/LPO **NSA Tapes T258W, P542W, P543**
Eugene Onegin Excerpts only From the Royal Albert Hall, London	11.8.1970 (S)*	Radio 3	Bowden, Söderström, Milcheva, Popova, Vassilev, Ochman, Petkov, Williams, Van Allan, Cuenod, Jenkins Pritchard/LPO **BBC Transcription Service Discs 128077–82**

Opera	Broadcast date	Programme	Cast & Archive Reference Number
Il ritorno d'Ulisse in patria From the Royal Albert Hall, London	3.8.1972 (S)	Radio 3	Hunt, Trama, Greig, Livingstone, Baker, Popova, J Hughes, Wakefield, Grant, D Hughes, Luxon, Howells, Lewis, Oliver, Caley, Dickerson, Fryatt, Townley Leppard/LPO **NSA Tapes T511W, T512W, 2015W, 2016W**
Le nozze di Figaro From the Royal Albert Hall, London	6.8.1974 (S)	Radio 3	Skram, Mandac, Trama, Condò, Jungwirth-Ahnsjö, Devlin, Fryatt, Te Kanawa, Lawlor, Gale, Dickerson Pritchard/LPO **MPRC ACQ 51**
Intermezzo	31.3.1975 (S) R 13.7.1974*	Radio 3	Söderström, Bakker, Gale, Allfrey, Whittingham, Dix, Varley, Oliver, Woodland, Buchan, Bell, Wicks, Rolfe Johnson, Donlan, Lawlor Pritchard/LPO **BBC Sound Archives Tape 60865**
La bohème	8.7.1978 (S)	Radio 3	Ellis, Cupido, White, Charles, Lawlor, Zoghby, Putnam, Davià, McKinnon, Donlan, Nemeer Rescigno/LPO **BBC Sound Archives Tape 54794**
Die schweigsame Frau	8.7.1979 (S)	Radio 3	Rintzler, Peters, Gottlieb, Pruett, Laki, Flowers, Hartle, Watt, Rouleau, Trama Davis/LPO **NSA Tapes T2352BW, T2353BW, T2354BW**

Opera	Broadcast date	Programme	Cast & Archive Reference Number
Die Zauberflöte From the Royal Albert Hall, London	12.8.1980 (S)	Radio 3	Davies, McCord, Moll, Kimm, Luxon, Shane, Rees, Lea, Findlay, Egerton, Burrowes, White, Thomaschke, Hetherington, Johnston, Bryson, Drower Haitink/LPO **NSA Tapes T3379BW, 4071BW, T3380BW, T3381BW**
Il barbiere di Siviglia	20.6.1981 (S)	Radio 3	Dean, Cosotti, Rawnsley, Ewing, Desderi, McCord, Furlanetto, Davies Howarth/LPO **BBC Sound Archives Tape 054943**
A Midsummer Night's Dream	27.6.1981 (S)	Radio 3	Warr, Whiting, Jones, King, Nash, Cotrubas, Bowman, Davies, Duesing, Buchan, Lott, Bryson, Gallacher, Bell, Power, Thompson, Applegren, Visser, Powell Haitink/LPO **NSA Tapes T4173BW, T4174BW, T4175BW**
Ariadne auf Naxos From the Royal Albert Hall, London	13.8.1981 (S)	Radio 3	Fox, Bell, Ewing, Bailey, Hetherington, Oliver, Ebrahim, Hall, Rolandi, Döse, Duesing, White, Fryatt, Rees, Kimm, Ritchie Kuhn/LPO **NSA Tapes T4297-98BW, 5277BW**
L'Amour des Trois Oranges	8.6.1982 (S)	Radio 3	Bryson, White, Runge, Benelli, Pringle, Van Allan, Morpurgo, Condò, Kimm, Davies, Hammond-Stroud, Lea, Moore, Alliot-Lugaz, Hetherington Haitink/LPO **NSA Tapes T4989BW, T4990BW**

Opera	Broadcast date	Programme	Cast & Archive Reference Number
Orfeo ed Euridice From the Royal Albert Hall, London	11.8.1982 (S)	Radio 3	Baker, Gale, Speiser Leppard/LPO **BBC Sound Archives Tape 81134 BBC Transcription Service Tape MS 640.00; CN 4112.03 BBC Transcription Service Discs 151860,61,62 (Excerpts only)**
Intermezzo Simultaneous broadcast with BBC 2	15.10.1983 (S) R 26.08.1983	Radio 3	Lott, Pringle, Gale, Ashford, Jagusz, Howard, Brook, Caley, Woodland, Pierard, Caddy, Gallacher, Winslade, Donlan, Bryson Kuhn/LPO **NSA Tapes T5943BW, T5944BW**
Where the Wild Things Are Simultaneous broadcast with BBC 2	23.4.1984 (S)	Radio 3	Beardsley, King, Hetherington, Munro, Rhys-Williams, Gallacher Knussen/London Sinfonietta **NSA Tape T6740BW**
Arabella Simultaneous broadcast with BBC 2	1.12.1984 (S) R 22.8.1984	Radio 3	Hartle, Sarfaty, Korn, Rolandi, Putnam, Lewis, Bröcheler, Winslade, Munro, Moses, Bradley Haitink/LPO **NSA Tapes T7419BW, T7420BW, T7421BW**
L'incoronazione di Poppea Simultaneous broadcast with BBC 2	15.12.1984 (S) R 27 & 29.8.1984	Radio 3	Howard, Walker, Kitchen, Duesing, Lewis, Stephenson, Ewing, Bailey, Owens, Clarey, Gale, Lloyd, Kennedy, Miller, Garrett, Evangelides, Bryson Leppard/LPO **NSA Tapes T7522BW, T7523BW, T7524BW**
Albert Herring Simultaneous broadcast with BBC 2	9.11.1985 (S) R 19-20.8.1985	Radio 3	Johnson, Palmer, Gale, Hammond-Stroud, Oliver, Van Allan, Opie, Graham-Hall, Rigby, Kern, Bovino, Lord, Peachey Haitink/LPO **NSA Tape T8331BW**

Opera	Broadcast date	Programme	Cast & Archive Reference Number
Higglety Pigglety Pop! Simultaneous broadcast with BBC 2	3.1.1986 (S) R 28-29.8.1985	Radio 3	Buchan, Rees, Gallacher, Jenkins, Hardy, Richardson Knussen/London Sinfonietta **NSA Tape B704**
Simon Boccanegra From the Royal Albert Hall, London	17.8.1986 (S)	Radio 3	Sandison, Miles, Noble, Moses, Vaness, Malagnini, Close, Roden Haitink/LPO **NSA Tape B1146**
Porgy and Bess	25.8.1986 (S) R 1.8.1986	Radio 3	Marshall, Blackwell, Coleman, Evans, Hubbard, Clarey, Worthy, Watson, Wallace, Ross, Simpson, White, Baker, Haymon, Paige, Ingram, Johnson, Antwi-Nyanin, Freeman, Brathwaite Rattle/LPO **NSA Tapes B1157, B1158**
La traviata From the Royal Albert Hall, London	23.8.1987 (S)	Radio 3	Cotrubas, Powell, Thornton-Holmes, Sandison, Hall, Hillman, MacNeil, Hartle, Harrison, Ellis, Kerry Haitink/LPO **NSA Tape B2668**
The Electrification of the Soviet Union Simultaneous broadcast with BBC 2	26.3.1988 (S) R 30.11-2.12.1987	Radio 3	Herford, Ebrahim, Hirst, Veira, Oosterkamp, Laurence, O'Reilly, Davies, Steiger, Gates Howarth/London Sinfonietta Opera Orchestra **NSA Tape B9391**
Kát'a Kabanová	6.6.1988 (S)	Radio 3	Graham-Hall, Bunning, Adams, McCauley, Ormiston, Palmer, Davies, Gustafson, Winter, Poulton Davis/LP **NSA Tape B2848**

Opera	Broadcast date	Programme	Cast & Archive Reference Number
Falstaff From the Royal Albert Hall, London	27.8.1988 (S)	Radio 3	Corazza, Desderi, Evangelides, Davià, Howells, Gustafson, Palmer, Lind, Sorrentino, McFarland Haitink/LP **NSA Tape B3222**
Jenůfa	17.6.1989 (S)	Radio 3	Davies, Langridge, Baker, Silja, Alexander, Poulton, Sandison, Ormiston, Hagley, Pring, Davies, Crowley Davis/LP **NSA Tape B4393**
Le nozze di Figaro From the Royal Albert Hall, London	31.8.1989 (S)	Radio 3	Duesing, Rodgers, Loup, Palmer, Rorholm, Bolognesi, Shimell, Bohman, Hall, Hagley, Graham-Hall, Bennett Rattle/Orchestra of the Age of Enlightenment **NSA Tapes B4464, B4465**
New Year	14.7.1990 (S) R 13.7.1990	Radio 3	Robson, Field, St Hill, Shaulis, Maddalena, Langridge, Manager Davis/LP **NSA Tape H1874**
Kát'a Kabanová From the Royal Albert Hall, London	24.8.1990 (S)	Radio 3	Graham-Hall, Kerr, Adams, Begley, Hartle, Palmer, Davies, Gustafson, Winter, Finley, Cannell, Mackenzie-Wicks Davis/LP **NSA Tape B7201**
Death in Venice Simultaneous broadcast with BBC 2	16.9.1990 (S) R 8-10.1.1990	Radio 3	Tear, Opie, Chance, Finley, Ventris, Veira, Zeplichal, Pope Jenkins/London Sinfonietta **NSA Tape B7290**
Le nozze di Figaro Simultaneous broadcast with BBC 2	26.12.1990 (S) R 28-29.08.1989	Radio 3	Duesing, Rodgers, Loup, Palmer, Rorholm, Bolognesi, Shimell, Bohman, Adams, Hagley, Graham-Hall Rattle/Orchestra of the Age of Enlightenment **NSA Tape B7707**

Opera	Broadcast date	Programme	Cast & Archive Reference Number
Così fan tutte	8.6.1991 (S)	Radio 3	Streit, Gardner, Desderi, Roocroft, Johnston, Rolandi, Rattle/Orchestra of the Age of Enlightenment **NSA Tapes B8330, B8331**
La clemenza di Tito From the Royal Albert Hall, London	25.8.1991 (S)	Radio 3	Montague, Putnam, Mahé, Langridge, Szmytka, Rose Davis/LP **NSA Tape B8586**
New Year A BBC studio adaptation Simultaneous broadcast with BBC 2	21.9.1991 (S) R 12.1990	Radio 3	Henry, Field, St Hill, Shaulis, Maddalena, Begley, Manager Davis/LP **NSA Tape V553**
Peter Grimes	16.5.1992 (S)	Radio 3	Drakulich, Tierney, Opie, Davies, Waters, Pring, Graham-Hall, Adams, Bickley, Fryatt, Poulton, Moses, Haughey Davis/LP **NSA Tape B H 345/H 346**
The Queen of Spades From the Royal Albert Hall, London	26.7.1992 (S)	Radio 3	Marusin, Leiferkus, Kharitonov, Matheson-Bruce, Slater, Burt, Thornton-Holmes, Palmer, Gustafson, Todorovitch, Hartle, Dawson, Pogson, Tovey Davis/LP **NSA Tapes B H 463/H 518**
Béatrice et Bénédict From the Royal Albert Hall, London	17.7.1993 (S) R 25.6.1993	Radio 3	Upshaw, von Otter, Hadley, Cachemaille, Rose, Rigby, Van Allan Davis/LP **NSA Tape H 1624**
The Song of the Love and Death of Cornet Christoph Rilke	27.10.1993 (S) R 9.10.1993	Radio 3	Unwin, Mills, Pritchard, Davies, Thomas, Marrion André/GTO Orchestra **NSA Tape H 2049**

*(M) = Mono recording
*(S) = Stereo recording
*R 13.7.1974 A second date beneath the broadcast date beginning with the letter R indicates
that the performance was pre-recorded before transmission

APPENDIX B – GLYNDEBOURNE TELEVISION TRANSMISSIONS NOT ISSUED ON VIDEO

Opera	Transmitted # Live	Cast
Così fan tutte BBC	23.7.1951 #	Lewis, Rothmüller, Bruscantini, Jurinac, Howland, Quensel Royal Philharmonic Orchestra c.Busch p.Ebert d.Gérard
Macbeth BBC	25.7.1952 #	Rothmüller, Ernster, Dow, Bartlett, Johnston, Kentish, Wicks Royal Philharmonic Orchestra c.Gui p.Ebert d.Neher
Die Entführung aus dem Serail BBC	30.7.1953 #	Krebs, Ollendorf, Dickie, Ebert, Barabas, Loose Royal Philharmonic Orchestra c.Wallenstein p.Ebert d.Gérard
Don Giovanni BBC (3 arias & final sextet cut)	29.7.1954 #	Kusche, Harshaw, Pease, Alan, Simoneau, Jurinac, Schlemm, Hemsley Royal Philharmonic Orchestra c.Solti p.Ebert d.Piper
Il barbiere di Siviglia BBC	29.7.1955 #	Griffiths, Oncina, Bruscantini, D'Angelo, Wallace, Sinclair, Williams, Dalamangas, Kelly, McCoshan Royal Philharmonic Orchestra c.Balkwill p.Ebert d.Messel
Excerpts from **Don Giovanni, Così fan tutte, Die Zauberflöte, Die Entführung, Le nozze di Figaro** BBC	16.8.1956 #	Evans, Jurinac, Merriman, Rizzieri, Bruscantini, Oncina, Sardi, Dobbs, Bernardic, Miller, Lorengar, Haefliger, Roux, Cuenod, Bruscantini, Canne Meijer Royal Philharmonic Orchestra c.Pritchard
Le Comte Ory BBC (Act II only)	15.8.1957 #	Blankenburg, J Sinclair, Oncina, M Sinclair, Lagger, Cadoni, Barabas, Doucet Royal Philharmonic Orchestra c.Pritchard p.Ebert d.Messel

Opera	Recorded	Transmitted # Live	Cast
The Rake's Progress BBC (Last 5 scenes of the opera)		07.8.1958 #	Morison, Lewis, Ward, Kraus, Chumakova, Lane, Cuenod, Griffiths Royal Philharmonic Orchestra c.Balkwill p.Ebert d.Lancaster
La Cenerentola BBC also Eurovision to Italy, France, Belgium, Switzerland, Denmark, Holland		20.8.1959 #	Zanolli, Pace, Rota, Alan, Wallace, Oncina, Bruscantini Royal Philharmonic Orchestra c.Gui p.Ebert d.Messel
Falstaff BBC and Eurovision to Italy, Denmark, Switzerland, Belgium		15.9.1960 #	Cuenod, Evans, Carlin, Stefanoni, Rota, Ligabue, Dominguez, Adani, Oncina, Bruscantini, Williams Royal Philharmonic Orchestra c.Gui p.Ebert d.Lancaster
Il barbiere di Siviglia BBC and Eurovision to Belgium, Austria Switzerland, Italy, Denmark, Sweden		24.8.1961 #	Robertson, Oncina, Bruscantini, Valentini, Wallace, Sarti, Williams, Cava, J Evans Royal Philharmonic Orchestra c.Gui p.Ebert d.Messel
L'elisir d'amore BBC and Eurovision to Belgium, Denmark, Sweden, Norway, Holland Switzerland, Portugal		23.8.1962 #	Maire, Alva, Freni, Sordello, Bruscantini Royal Philharmonic Orchestra c.Cillario p.& d.Zeffirelli
Le nozze di Figaro BBC and Eurovision to Germany and Eire	22.8.63	29.8.1963	Blankenburg, Berton, Cava, Laghezza, Mathis, Roux, Cuenod, Gencer, Davies, Zeri, Kentish Royal Philharmonic Orchestra c.Varviso p.Ebert d.Messel
Die Zauberflöte BBC and Eurovision Denmark, Holland, Switzerland,Belgium, Eire (S)*	21.8.64	10.9.1964 BBC 1	Ulfung, Kalmus, Reynolds, Bainbridge, Blankenburg, Arnaud, Neville, Wilson, Darroll, Robertson, Raskin, Bryn Jones, Cava, Brandt, Wicks, Zeri London Philharmonic Orchestra c.Balkwill p.Enriquez d.Luzzati

Opera	Recorded	Transmitted	Cast
La pietra del paragone BBC (S)	19.8.65	9.9.1965 BBC 1	Hartley, Blankenburg, Reynolds, Valentini, Trama, Grilli, Veasey, Roux London Philharmonic Orchestra c.Pritchard p.Rennert d.Lancaster
Arlecchino BBC	21.9.65	30.11.1965 BBC 2	Blankenburg, Wallace, Modenos, Wicks, Dickie, Venora, S Ebert London Philharmonic Orchestra c.Pritchard p.P Ebert d.Rice
Dido & Aeneas BBC	28.9.65	12.10.1965 BBC 2 Repeated 5.8.1966 BBC 1	Baker, Hemsley, Robson, Minton, Davies, Elias, Walmesley, Bainbridge London Philharmonic Orchestra c.Pritchard p.Enriquez d.Ghiglia
L'heure espagnole BBC (S)	6.10.65	28.12.1965 BBC 2 Repeated 7.3.1966 BBC 2	Le Hémonet, Cuenod, Venora, Sénéchal, Autran London Philharmonic Orchestra c.Pritchard p.P Ebert d.Lancaster
Don Giovanni BBC (S) (overture cut)	6.8.67	3.9.1967 BBC 1	Montarsolo, Bridges, Paskalis, Rintzler, Lewis, Zylis-Gara, Armstrong, Monreale London Philharmonic Orchestra c.Pritchard p.Enriquez d.Luzzati
An Opera in the Country BBC	1967	10.12.1967 BBC 2	Documentary
'A Goodly Manor for a Song' Southern Television	1969	21.7.1970 ITV	Documentary
La Calisto BBC (S)	9.8.71	26.11.1971 BBC 2 Repeated 4.11.1972 BBC 2	Biggar, Hartle, Cahill, Trama, Gottlieb, Cotrubas, Bowman, Baker, Cuenod, Hughes, Davià, Brannigan, Kubiak, Brodie London Philharmonic Orchestra c.Leppard p.Hall d.Bury

Opera	Recorded	Transmitted	Cast
Die Entführung aus dem Serail Southern Television (S)	13.8.72	27.5.1973 ITV	Roden, Mangin, Lappalainen, Van Allan, Price, Perriers, Bremner, Sadler London Philharmonic Orchestra c.Pritchard p.Cox d.Luzzati
Capriccio BBC (S) 1st simultaneous broadcast with Radio 3	20.8.76	19.3.1977 BBC 2 Repeated 10.2.1979 BBC 2	Davies, Duesing, Rintzler, Söderström, Hagegård, Meyer, Cassinelli, Ratti, Lawlor, Cuenod London Philharmonic Orchestra c.Davis p.Cox d.Lennon/Battersby
'Do the Thing Properly' BBC	1978	13.4.1979 BBC 2	Documentary
Così fan tutte BBC (S)	18.8.78	14.4.1979 BBC 2	Cosotti, Hagegård, Dean, Betley, Ewing, Christie London Philharmonic Orchestra c.Haitink p.Hall d.Bury
Gardeners World BBC	1986	16.1.1987 BBC 2 Repeated 19.1.1987 BBC 1	Documentary
The Electrification of the Soviet Union BBC	30.11-2.12. 1987	26.3.1988 BBC 2	Herford, Ebrahim, Veira, O'Reilly, Oosterkamp, Laurence, Steiger, Davies, Hirst, Gates The London Sinfonietta c.Howarth p.Sellars d.Tsypin/Ramicova
Le nozze di Figaro BBC (S)	28-29.8. 1989	26.12.1990 BBC 2	Duesing, Rodgers, Loup, Palmer, Rorholm, Bolognesi, Shimell, Bohman, Adams, Hagley, Graham-Hall Orchestra of the Age of Enlightenment c.Rattle p.Hall d.Gunter
New Year BBC Simultaneous broadcast with Radio 3	12.1990	21.9.1991 BBC 2	Henry, Field, St Hill, Shaulis, Maddalena, Begley, Manager London Philharmonic c.Davis p.Marks d.Buruma A BBC studio version of the Houston/Glyndebourne production

* (S) = Production shown with subtitles

APPENDIX C – GLYNDEBOURNE FILMS

Only one Glyndebourne film has ever been commercially released to be shown at cinemas throughout Britain, details of which are given below. A number of television documentaries on Glyndebourne have been made by both the BBC and ITV and information about these may be found in Appendix B.

1955

'ON SUCH A NIGHT'

Cast

David Cornell	David Knight
Lady Falconbridge	Marie Lohr
Virginia Ridley	Josephine Griffin
First Gentleman	Alan Cuthbertson
Second Gentleman	Peter Jones

In the extract from Mozart's **Le nozze di Figaro**

Figaro	Sesto Bruscantini (baritone, Italian)
Susanna	Elena Rizzieri (soprano, Italian)
Bartolo	Ian Wallace (bass, Scottish)
Marcellina	Monica Sinclair (contralto, English)
Cherubino	Frances Bible (soprano, American)
Count Almaviva	Franco Calabrese (bass, Italian)
Don Basilio	Hugues Cuenod (tenor, Swiss)
The Countess	Sena Jurinac (soprano, Yugoslav)
Antonio	Gwyn Griffiths (baritone, Welsh)
Barbarina	Jeannette Sinclair (soprano, English)
Don Curzio	Daniel McCoshan (tenor, Scottish)

Royal Philharmonic Orchestra	Leader Arthur Leavins
Conductor	Vittorio Gui
Producer	Carl Ebert
Designer	Oliver Messel

For Rank Screen Services Limited

Director	Anthony Asquith
Associate Producer	Francis Edge
Script	Paul Dehn
Musical director	Benjamin Frankel
Photographer	Frank North
Editor	Anthony Harvey
Production Supervisor	Donald Wynne

Filmed	Victoria and Lewes Stations,	
	Glyndebourne theatre and gardens	6.1955
First showing	Gaumont Cinema, Haymarket, London	24.11.1955
Released to selected cinemas throughout the UK		2.1956

Colour print

Running time approximately 37 minutes

'On Such a Night' was made by The Rank Organisation as a gift to the Glyndebourne Arts Trust.

The film was originally called **Puzzle, Find the Countess**, but prior to release the title was changed to **'On Such a Night'**.

'On Such a Night' may be viewed, by appointment only, by contacting
The Viewing Service, National Film and Television Archive,
21 Stephen Street, London W1P 1PL.
Telephone: 071-255 1444

APPENDIX D – UNAUTHORISED RECORDINGS

This list of unauthorised recordings of productions which have been issued on LP, cassette and CD does not claim to be comprehensive, however it includes several performances by well-known singers dating from the 1940s to the 1980s. These recordings do not reflect the high technical quality of those authorised by Glyndebourne, but are listed for their musical and historical interest.

Opera	Date of Recording	Cast and Record/CD Number(s)
The Rape of Lucretia (Excerpts recorded at Stadsschouwburg Amsterdam)	4.10.1946 (M)*	Pears, Cross, Brannigan, Donlevy, Kraus, Ferrier, Pollak, Ritchie Oppenheim/Glyndebourne Opera Orchestra **Educ Media IGI 369**
Macbeth (Complete recording from Edinburgh Festival)	27.8.1947 (M)	Valentino, Grandi, Midgley, Tajo, Terry, Orkin, McKinley, Vivian, Thomas, Christie Goldschmidt/Scottish Orchestra **Golden Age of Opera EJS 383 A/D**
Un ballo in maschera (Complete recording from Edinburgh Festival)	29.8.1949 (M)	Picchi, Silveri, Welitsch, Watson, Noni, Wallace, Alan, Loring Gui/RPO **Golden Age of Opera EJS 553 A/E**
Macbeth (Excerpts recorded at Glyndebourne)	10 or 19.7.1952 (M)	Rothmüller, Dow, Johnston, Dalberg, Bartlett, Wicks Gui/RPO **Royale LP 1409**
Falstaff (Complete recording from Glyndebourne)	29.6.1957 (M)	Evans, Cuenod, Lewis, Alan, Cadoni, Moscucci, Dominguez, Pastori, Oncina, Boyer Gui/RPO **Replica RPL 2454/56**
Arlecchino (Complete recording from Edinburgh Festival)	1.9.1960 (M)	Wallace, Blankenburg, Griffiths, Feller, Pilarczyk, Troy Pritchard/RPO **Opera Society Suisa OSCD 225 and OSMC 225**

Opera	Date of Recording	Cast and Record/CD Number(s)
Idomeneo (Complete recording from Glyndebourne)	24.7.1964 (M)	Janowitz, Pavarotti, Taylor, Tarrès, Lewis, Hughes, Wicks Pritchard/LPO **Butterfly Music BMCD 010 and BMK 010 Opera CD 54039** (Excerpts only)
Idomeneo (Complete recording from Royal Albert Hall, London)	17.8.1964 (M)	Cast as above **HRE 364, Melodram 32 CD MEL 27003, Verona 27038/9**
Anna Bolena (Complete recording from Glyndebourne)	13.6.1965 (M)	Gencer, Johnson, Cava, Morelle, Oncina, Garrard, Strauss Smith Gavazzeni/LPO **Melodram 458 2 HUNT CD 554**
Orfeo ed Euridice (Complete recording from Royal Albert Hall, London)	11.8.1982 (S)*	Baker, Gale, Speiser Leppard/LPO **Music & Arts Programs of America CD 295**

*(M) = Mono recording
*(S) = Stereo recording

Index